Recent Advances in Digital Humanities

Anca Dinu / Madalina Chitez /
Liviu Dinu / Mihnea Dobre (eds.)

Recent Advances in Digital Humanities

Romance Language Applications

PETER LANG

Bibliographic Information published by the Deutsche Nationalbibliothek
The Deutsche Nationalbibliothek lists this publication in the Deutsche Nationalbibliografie; detailed bibliographic data is available online at http://dnb.d-nb.de.

Library of Congress Cataloging-in-Publication Data
A CIP catalog record for this book has been applied for at the Library of Congress.

Cover illustration:
© Cristina Onet, member of CODHUS Research Centre.

ISBN 978-3-631-81147-4 (Print)
E-ISBN 978-3-631-87773-9 (E-PDF)
E-ISBN 978-3-631-88384-6 (EPUB)
DOI 10.3726/b19920

Peter Lang – Berlin · Bruxelles · Lausanne · New York · Oxford

This publication has been peer reviewed.

www.peterlang.com

Table of Contents

Anca Dinu, Mădălina Chitez, Liviu Dinu and Mihnea Dobre
Introduction 7

Section 1: Resources and Digitalisation

Annamaria Goy, Cristina Re, Davide Colla and Marco Leontino
Chapter 1 Turning 1968 Memories into Usable Texts 17

Valentina Mureşan, Roxana Rogobete, Ana-Maria Bucur, Mădălina Chitez and Andreea Dincă
Chapter 2 Phraseology in Romanian Academic Writing: Corpus Based Explorations into Field-Specific Multiword Units 29

Tommaso Spinelli
Chapter 3 The Latin Diachronic Database: A New Digital Tool for the Study of Latin 49

Cecilia Mihaela Popescu and Oana-Adriana Duţă
Chapter 4 A Proposal for a Multilingual E-Glossary of Discourse Markers 65

Eugen Istodor
Chapter 5 The Meme That Brings About the Roar. Then, Discredit. The Tismăneanu Case in Pandemic Times 81

Section 2: Tools and Interfaces

Haifa Alharthi and Diana Inkpen
Chapter 6 Natural Language Processing for Book Recommender Systems 99

Claudius-Marian Teodorescu
Chapter 7 Syntactic Tree Editor 117

Mihnea Dobre, Ovidiu Babeş and Ioana Bujor
Chapter 8 Cartesian Visual Cosmology: Ways Towards a Digital Platform 131

Alexandra Liţu and Valentin Bottez
Chapter 9 An Evaluation of the *Ithaca* Tool Performance for Restoring Lost Texts (Ancient Greek) 149

Section 3: Computational Methods: Analysis, Classification, Clustering

Andrea Sgarro
Chapter 10 At the Boundaries of Syntactic Prehistory: Metric and Non-Metric Distances 173

Miguel Cavadas Docampo and Pablo Gamallo Otero
Chapter 11 Automatic Authorship Attribution in the Work of Tirso de Molina 185

Anca Dinu, Dan Ioan Dobre, Andreea-Codrina Moldovan and Elena-Daniela Nicolescu
Chapter 12 Computational Analysis and Author Detection for Political Discourses of Romanian Presidents 197

Arya Rahgozar, Mehran Rahgozar and Diana Inkpen
Chapter 13 Contemporary Chronological Classifications of Hafez Poetry and Influences on French Literature 215

Thierry Declerck
Chapter 14 On the Use of Knowledge Graphs for Representing Past Classification Schemes for Various Genres of Literature 231

Notes on Contributors 243

Anca Dinu, Mădălina Chitez, Liviu Dinu and Mihnea Dobre

Introduction

1. Background to this collection

This volume contains selected papers and invited talks from *The First Recent Advances in Digital Humanities Conference* (RADH), held on the 29th of October 2021, as an online conference, and organized by the Faculty of Foreign Languages and Literatures, Digital Humanities Research Centre, Faculty of History, University of Bucharest in collaboration with the CODHUS Research Centre (*Centre for Corpus Related Digital Approaches to Humanities*) of the Faculty of Letters, History and Theology at the West University of Timisoara.

The field of Digital Humanities grows in popularity at an unprecedented speed, while digital methods and tools in all domains of Humanities are exploding. Therefore, it becomes a necessity for scholars within the expanding community of Digital Humanities to gather, share ideas and learn from each other, and discuss the most recent trends, challenges, and solutions in the field. The wide range of Digital Humanities topics presented at the conference documents the diversity of current research problems and proves that the domain attracts researchers with different background, who can only benefit from such interactions.

Most of the papers presented in the RADH2021 conference were prepared during the COVID pandemic. This is not to complain about the lack of materials or access to some resources, but to acknowledge the creativity of the research presented in many of the chapters included in the volume. If there is a lesson to be learned from the pandemic, it is the enormous potential of the Digital Humanities as a field of research. It needs, however, to foster the growth of digital literacy of scholars in connected fields, and, at the same time, to embrace a broader variety of approaches, questions, and formats. Digital Humanities can play the role of a new cultural setting in which to base all sorts of scholarship, widening one's understanding of the modern world.

Since the central focus of the conference was digitalization, methods and tools for the Romance languages, this volume covers work on most of the Romance languages: Latin, Italian, Romanian, Spanish, French, but also branches out to include English, Arab and Greek.

The three sections of the conference are reflected in the topic organization of this volume: Resources and digitalization, Tools and interfaces, and Computational methods analysis, classification, and clustering. The section order reflects the natural lifespan of a digital object, from its creation and representation to its pre-processing and processing and, finally, to its analysis and interpretation.

2. Content: Sections and chapters overview

During the pandemic, many scholars have turned to digital resources and have expanded the use of digital tools to several areas of research and communication. At the time when mobility restrictions limited the physical space one could access, the virtual world was always available. Social media, conference platforms, eLearning systems, and digital repositories or libraries were quickly adopted by scholars.

The first section of the book, **Resources and Digitalisation** has an applicative character. It starts from the awareness that Digital Humanities has become the buzzword in academic circles and beyond (Burghardt and Wolff 2017). More and more research initiatives approach traditional or new emerging topics related to the field of Digital Humanities for higher visibility and faster contribution to scientific development. But such effervescence is challenging to grasp; that is why it is important to obtain latest information on existing resources and digitalization strategies. At the same time, it is essential to acknowledge emerging synergies between the disciplines that can support further advancements for the larger Digital Humanities domain. One such complementarity relationship has been shaped around the discipline of corpus linguistics. These two aspects represent the focus in Section 1 (five chapters). The topic is also adapted for the target languages of the volume, namely Romance languages. Contributions on this topic showcase the process of using corpus linguistics methods to teach and conduct teaching-oriented research in the humanities. Exemplifications of typical tools (for example, OCR techniques for Italian documents) for text digitalizations are also provided.

In Chapter 1, "Turning 1968 Memories into Usable Texts", the authors, Annamaria Goy, Cristina Re, Davide Colla and Marco Leontino, provide their readership with ways to use the Optical Character Recognition (OCR) system to read and recover intelligible texts in Italian and prepare them for further analyses. The main findings presented in this study are associated with the project PRiSMHA (Providing Rich Semantic Metadata for Historical Archives).

Chapter 2, "Phraseology in Romanian Academic Writing: Corpus Based Explorations into Field-Specific Multiword Units", by Valentina Mureșan, Roxana Rogobete, Ana-Maria Bucur, Mădălina Chitez and Andreea Dincă, draws on a comparative analysis of two self-complied corpora (ROGER *Corpus of Romanian Academic Genres* and EXPRES *Corpus of Expert Writing in Romanian and English*) which are used to test a computational method for extracting filed-specific multi-word units in Romanian academic writing. The findings of the study serve as a first stage in the development of a collocation or n-gram extraction method which results in the creation of academic word / collocation / phrase lists for the Romanian language.

Tommaso Spinelli's research (Chapter 3), "The Latin Diachronic Database: A New Digital Tool for the Study of Latin", highlights a new digital toolkit that helps scholars and students to identify and analyse the use of Latin in literary texts, both from the perspective of the words' frequency and development throughout time.

In Chapter 4, "A Proposal for a Multilingual E-Glossary of Discourse Markers", Cecilia Mihaela Popescu and Oana Adriana Duță aim to establish an e-glossary of discourse markers in English and four romance languages, with the help of digital tools; this process would help scholars in their linguistic research endeavours.

Section 1 is closed by Eugen Istodor's chapter (Chapter 5): "The Meme That Brings About the Roar. Then, Discredit. The Tismăneanu Case in Pandemic Times", which offers a critical analysis of how social codes and social media have been reshaped in the early pandemics. Istodor examines the case of Vladimir Tismăneanu, professor of political sciences in the United States, and an important public figure in the Romanian cultural space. The use of social media, and especially the culture of sharing encouraged by social media platforms, brings into question the relation between private and public space, but also the shifted boundaries between humour and discrimination in the case of a meme shared in the early pandemics.

The second section of the volume, **Tools and Interfaces**, puts forth four chapters that propose new tools or evaluate existing ones.

Because the electronic resources such as corpora, archives, repositories, etc. exploded in the last decade and the data quantity generated by humanity on a daily basis is overwhelming, managing this kind of data by hand or with only a few specialized professionals has become simply unfeasible. The sheer quantity and complexity of data nowadays require more and more user-friendly and intelligent tools and platforms to be processed with. Almost in every domain of the Humanities, the apparition of such new tools and interfaces is a reality. For instance, in disciplines such as the history of philosophy and science, which rely more on traditional library and archival research, the use of digital resources was, during the pandemic, the predominant way of doing research. The four chapters in this section are a fair sample of that research phenomenon.

The section begins with Chapter 6, "Natural Language Processing for Book Recommender Systems", by Haifa Alharthi and Diana Inkpen, who describe several approaches to a literary book recommender system, that takes the text of the books into consideration. One approach considers the writing style of the authors by transferring the information learned by an author-identification model into a book recommender system. Another approach represents books using more than one hundred linguistic features including lexical, syntactic, stylometric, and fiction-based features. The two proposed systems are evaluated in a top-k recommendation scenario, and both provide higher recommendation accuracy compared with state-of-the-art content and collaborative filtering methods.

Chapter 7, "Syntactic Tree Editor", authored by Claudius-Marian Teodorescu, presents the development of an editor for syntactic trees, to be used during the process of teaching grammar in universities or for research purposes. It complies with the Government and Binding (GB) model, but there is the possibility of extending it to support various other grammar models. The editor was designed after a comprehensive analysis of the existing software products for editing or generating syntax trees. The functionality of the tree editor and its user-friendly interface are presented in detail.

The next chapter (Chapter 8) "Cartesian Visual Cosmology: Ways Towards a Digital Platform", co-authored by Mihnea Dobre, Ovidiu Babeş and Ioana Bujor, details the work of collecting, cataloguing, and presenting in a digital form a variety of early modern cosmological images. The corpus is based on early modern prints, already digitized, but never collected as "cosmological illustrations". It offers an entry point in the study of the imagery associated with the philosophical system of René Descartes, and details how a Digital Humanities approach to the subject can enrich early modern scholarship. The chapter includes a discussion of several digital tools, and open research questions about Cartesian natural philosophy, but also about the use of images at the time of the scientific revolution of the early modern period.

The last chapter of the section (Chapter 9), "An Evaluation of the *Ithaca* Tool Performance for Restoring Lost Texts (Ancient Greek)", co-authored by Alexandra Liţu and Valentin Bottez, aims to evaluate the performance of the *Ithaca* tool on a funerary inscription, coming most probably from Callatis, a Greek colony on the Western shore of the Black Sea, that was fully preserved and published recently by the authors. To overcome the requirement of having at least 50 characters in order to use *Ithaca*, they performed some text augmentation. However, these augmentations might have proved influential for geographical and chronological attribution. One of the salient features of *Ithaca* seems to be its receptiveness to context. It also proved itself very sensitive to slight changes in the input text, even on the level of basic punctuation.

The third and last section of the volume, **Computational Methods Analysis, Classification, and Clustering** comprises five chapters that present work ranging from language relatedness methods like Parametric Comparison Method to quantitative and qualitative analysis and from traditional clustering and classification methods like support vector machines to transformer models like BERT.

The first chapter of the section (Chapter 10), "At the Boundaries of Syntactic Prehistory: Metric and Non-Metric Distances", by Andrea Sgarro, presents a language phylogeny method based on syntax, which assesses relatedness between linguistic families against chance, in situations when *etymological evidence is missing*. This method is based on the pioneering work of the linguist Giuseppe Longobardi and his school. Some controversial language clusters are supported, like, for instance, Altaic and Uralo-Altaic, while others test negatively, such as Indo-Uralic or Basque-Northeast Caucasian.

The following three chapters deal with various classification problems. The first one in the group (Chapter 11), entitled "Automatic Authorship Attribution in the Work of Tirso de Molina", by Miguel Cavadas Docampo and Pablo Gamallo Otero, aims to find the most probable authors of five plays that were traditionally attributed to Tirso de Molina, but which have controversial paternity, involving also the possible authors Andrés de Claramonte, Mira de Amescua and Luis Vélez de Guevara. Clustering and ensemble strategies that use the mean of four different profile-based strategies, in addition to an instance-based one, have been applied to the controversial plays, with good results.

The next chapter (Chapter 12), "Computational Analysis and Author Detection for Political Discourses of Romanian Presidents", by Anca Dinu, Dan Ioan Dobre, Andreea-Codrina Moldovan and Elena-Daniela Nicolescu, puts forth a new corpus composed of the speeches of the last four Romanian presidents. The authors perform a comparative analysis based on quantitative parameters such as the vocabulary density, the mean sentence length, or part of speech frequencies among the discourses of the four presidents. Also, topic modelling was employed to discover the predominant speech topics for each president. Finally, the speeches of the four presidents were automatically classified using a variety of methods. The best accuracy, of 96 %, was obtained by the Support Vector Machine method, which outperformed the Romanian BERT transformer model.

The last of the classification problems group (Chapter 13), the chapter "Contemporary Chronological Classifications of Hafez Poetry and Influences on French Literature", by Arya Rahgozar, Mehran Rahgozar and Diana Inkpen, presents a new set of chronological scholarly labels of Hafez's poetry, based on two annotators: scholars from different time periods, Houman and Raad. The authors measured the inter-agreement between the two, before and after automatic classification. They show that the elimination of inconsistent labels enhances the accuracy of the chronological classification. Support Vector Machine outperformed some other machine learning algorithms.

The fifth and last chapter in this section (Chapter 14), "On the Use of Knowledge Graphs for Representing Past Classification Schemes for Various Genres of Literature", by Thierry Declerck, describes work on folkloristics and is based on the results of a series of Bachelor/Master theses and software projects conducted by students of the Computational Linguistics Department of the Saarland University. The creation of multilingual (English, German, Russian, Bulgarian) ontologies, based on well-established studies proposed by "classical" folklorists is supporting the availability of a huge amount of digital and structured knowledge on folktales to digital humanists.

3. Volume audience

The volume addresses a wide range of scholars interested in the use of digital tools and methods in the Humanities. It offers a collection of chapters that can be read independently, detailing sometimes more technical approaches, while other times acknowledging the broader implications derived from the use of computational models in scholarly work. Readers can find examples of new tools and workflows, which are useful in their own right, as they attest to successful applications of the Digital Humanities techniques to some (traditional) problems in the scholarship of several disciplines. The variety of approaches is also due to the variety of disciplines and topics covered by the volume. This is another strength of the collection, as it expresses the plurality implied by the term *Digital Humanities*. In addition, the focus on Romance language applications, while capturing specific language processing and analysis challenges, turns this volume into a valuable reference work. In brief, the volume can offer useful insights to advanced scholars in the field, it provides examples to be discussed in the classroom, but it can also help newcomers in the study of Digital Humanities and a more general public to become aware of the general significance of this discipline for the Humanities at large.

Aknowledgements

The publication of the volume was supported by the CODHUS Research Centre (*Centre for Corpus Related Digital Approaches to Humanities*) of the Faculty of Letters, History and Theology at the West University of Timisoara. Besides financial support, the assistance during the editing process offered by the CODHUS research assistant Raluca-Andreea Petruş (PhD candidate) is highly appreciated. Work on this volume was also supported by a grant of the Ministry of Research, Innovation and Digitization, CNCS/CCCDI UEFISCDI, project number 108, COTOHILI, within PNCDI III.

Section 1: Resources and Digitalisation

Annamaria Goy, Cristina Re, Davide Colla and Marco Leontino

Chapter 1 Turning 1968 Memories into Usable Texts

Abstract: In this paper we present the OCR processing of historical documents referring to the protest events that took place in the years 1968–1969 in Italy. In particular, we discuss the peculiarities of this type of documents (mainly leaflets with poor-quality typewritten text and manual notes) and the potential usage of the obtained full texts within the prototype annotation platform developed in the PRiSMHA project, where automatic Information Extraction techniques are applied to support users in building semantic representations needed to annotate documents. This work represents a first step to show that, starting from paper documents characterized by challenging features for an OCR system, OCR, coupled with suited pre- and post-processing actions, could provide good enough texts to be processed by automatic Information Extraction tools.

Keywords: archives, digital curation, historical documents, OCR

1. Introduction

PRiSMHA (Providing Rich Semantic Metadata for Historical Archives) is a project funded by Fondazione Compagnia di San Paolo and Università di Torino that started in 2017. The partners of the project are the Computer Science and the Historical Studies Departments (University of Torino), in collaboration with Fondazione Istituto Piemontese Antonio Gramsci (www.gramscitorino.it), member of Polo del '900 (www.polodel900.it), a cultural consortium headquartered in Torino, that provides several institutions, related to historical and social fields, with the opportunity to merge their libraries and archives, as well as their cultural initiatives. In particular, the largest part (25 %) of the Polo del '900 archive (www.polodel900.it/9centro) is represented by Ist. Gramsci's collections.

The main goal of PRiSMHA is to design and develop a proof-of-concept prototype platform enabling a community of users to annotate documents from the library and archive of the Polo del '900. The core idea underlying the PRiSMHA approach is that, to offer an effective and "intelligent" access to historical archives, a digital catalog is not enough: the access system needs to be aware of the content of the available documents. In order to provide the system with such knowledge, a formal, machine-processable, semantic representation of the content of archival documents is required.

The strategy adopted to reach this goal is based on the synergy between:

- A rich formal ontology (Gruber 1993), based on a careful ontological analysis of the domain, carried out by ontologists and historians, taking into account historical documents and existing ontologies (see Goy et al. 2019). As a test domain for the proof-of-concept prototype, we selected the historical events that took place in the years 1968–1969 in Italy (see Section 2). The result of the ontological analysis is HERO (Historical Event Representation Ontology) – available at https://w3id.org/hero/ a reference ontology modelling general concepts (e.g., *event*, *object*, *physical person*, *role*, *organization*, *collective*), coupled with a domain ontology (HERO – 900) characterizing notions useful to describe the history of the 20th century, and, in particular, the 1960s and the 1970s.
- Automatic Information Extraction technologies (see, for instance, Nanni and Dietz 2017), namely Named Entity Recognition (NER) and Time Expression Recognition (TER) tools, in order to process texts (when available) to identify persons, organizations, places, and time intervals useful to grasp the document content (see Colla et al. 2021). The Named Entity Recognition tool exploited in PRiSMHA is based on the work presented in Carducci (2019) and includes two modules, relying on: (a) The TINT Named Entity Recognition Tool (Aprosio and Moretti 2016), based on a machine learning approach; (b) BabelFy (Moro, Raganato and Navigli 2014), based on a semantic approach, and exploiting BabelNet (Navigli and Ponzetto 2010) to perform word-sense disambiguation. The Temporal Expressions Recognition tool uses Heideltime (Strötgen and Gertz 2010) to recognize temporal expressions and normalize them.
- A collaborative annotation platform that enables users to read archival documents, identify relevant text fragments, build the semantic representations of their content, and link them to document fragments (see Goy et al. 2020). For example, Fig. 1 shows the platform page displaying the biography of Emilio Pugno (an Italian Trade Union

leader). Text fragments are highlighted in light blue, while entities identified by automatic tools are highlighted in orange, if they appear within a fragment, or displayed in orange font, if they occur outside any fragment.

Fig. 1. The biography of E. Pugno on the annotation platform

The ontology drives the user interface (see Goy et al. 2020 for details), while NER/TER supports users in the annotation activity, in particular in identifying text fragments, recognizing relevant entities, and building semantic representations (see Colla et al. 2021 for details).

To assess the feasibility of our approach, we used the proof-of-concept prototype to annotate digital full-text documents, e.g., biographies of well-known people related to the historical period in focus (like the one displayed in Fig. 1). However, one of the most challenging aspects of the project is represented by the archival documents available in the Ist. Gramsci's collections and related to the selected period: we will describe such documents and the process they underwent in Sections 2 and 3, respectively.

2. The documents: 1968 memories

Within the project, we selected 200 paper documents, on the basis of an analysis of both their form and content (see Goy et al. 2019). They are mainly leaflets, often with poor-quality typewritten text and manual notes or drawings, or multi-column newspaper articles. The first step has been their digitization, following the guidelines of the Minerva Project (www.minervaeurope.org); (see De Francesco 2006). In particular, we carried out the following activities: definition of naming and metadata rules; metadata production; image acquisition; master file production (uncompressed TIFF 6.0, 600 dpi); other format images generation (JPEG2000, PNG, GIF, PDF); watermarking and quality check; archiving; online publication (on the 9centRo archival platform: www.polodel900.it/9centro).

The second step has been the OCR (Optical Character Recognition) processing of the digital documents (Hamad and Kaya 2016). The automatic recognition of characters in historical texts is a challenging task (see, for instance, Reul et al. 2019), due to the poor quality of the original image, complex layout, old fonts, old lexicon. The evaluation of the performance of OCR, in particular on historical texts, strongly depends on the goals of the project. In PRiSMHA, the availability of full texts supports users of the annotation platform, mainly because it enables the exploitation of NER/TER tools, which provide useful suggestions for semantic annotation (see Section 1).

3. The OCR process

3.1. Document analysis

All documents were original paper sheets, in the majority of cases with yellowed backgrounds, often stained. The pool of selected documents includes two main typologies: typewritten leaflets and newspaper articles.

Typewritten leaflets were produced by a typewriter or by a mimeograph. An example is shown in Fig. 2. These documents are characterized by a very low-quality printing, containing a lot of inking flaws, manual corrections, spelling errors, missing blanks, or inaccuracies due to defective typewriters (causing, for instance, not aligned or overlapping characters). Moreover, these leaflets – in particular those produced by a mimeograph – typically contain manual notes, drawings, and graphical titles.

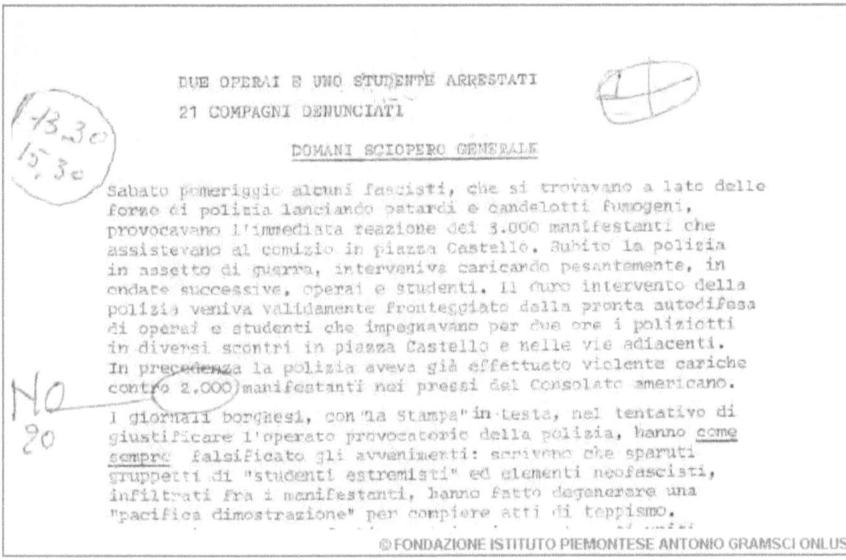

DUE OPERAI E UNO STUDENTE ARRESTATI

21 COMPAGNI DENUNCIATI

DOMANI SCIOPERO GENERALE

Sabato pomeriggio alcuni fascisti, che si trovavano a lato delle forze di polizia lanciando petardi e candelotti fumogeni, provocavano l'immediata reazione dei 3.000 manifestanti che assistevano al comizio in piazza Castello. Subito la polizia in assetto di guerra, interveniva caricando pesantemente, in ondate successive, operai e studenti. Il duro intervento della polizia veniva validamente fronteggiato dalla pronta autodifesa di operai e studenti che impegnavano per due ore i poliziotti in diversi scontri in piazza Castello e nelle vie adiacenti. In precedenza la polizia aveva già effettuato violente cariche contro 2.000 manifestanti nei pressi del Consolato americano.

I giornali borghesi, con "la Stampa" in testa, nel tentativo di giustificare l'operato provocatorio della polizia, hanno come sempre falsificato gli avvenimenti: scrivono che sparuti gruppetti di "studenti estremisti" ed elementi neofascisti, infiltrati fra i manifestanti, hanno fatto degenerare una "pacifica dimostrazione" per compiere atti di teppismo.

Fig. 2. A leaflet with manual notes [*Fondo Vadacchino*; copyright: *Fondaz. Ist. piemontese A. Gramsci onlus*]

Besides leaflets, the pool of selected documents includes newspaper articles, in which the main challenges for the OCR tool are represented by multiple columns, often very close to each other, and boxes focusing on related topics. Fig. 3 shows an example.

Scaglia: assemblee? Sì, ma addomesticate

La circolare del ministro della Pubblica Istruzione - Cortei a Milano e a Monza per una scuola più democratica - Migliaia di giovani in sciopero a Ravenna - Manifestazione di 5000 a Verona - Cariche della polizia a Chieti e a Terni - In sciopero a Torino i «serali»

Una lettera dell'on. Daniele Mattalia

Gli scrutini del primo trimestre

Fig. 3. A newspaper article, with multiple columns and a box [*Fondo Arian Levi*; copyright: *Fondaz. Ist. piemontese A. Gramsci onlus*]

3.2. Selection of the OCR tool

To choose the most suitable tool for our goal, we built a ground truth reference text by manually transcribing seven documents from our corpus, with heterogeneous features with respect to length, layout, and quality. We then selected six candidate tools (namely, Readiris 17, Tesseract v. 4.1.1, Adobe Acrobat Pro DC, FreeOCR v. 2.6, Prizmo 4, CuneiForm v. 1.1) and exploited Ocreval (github.com/eddieantonio/ocreval#ocreval-1) to evaluate their performance (Rice and Nartker 1996; Santos 2019). Tab. 1 shows the results, by providing Character Error Rate (CER; basically, the number of wrong characters in the output text) and Word Error Rate (WER; the number of wrong words) for each tool; see Santos (2019) and Rice and Nartker (1996) for details about the output of Ocreval.

Tesseract (see github.com/tesseract-ocr/tesseract) clearly obtained the best results: both CER and WER are definitely lower than those obtained by other tools (Smith 2007). In particular, in PRiSMHA, full-text documents are exploited to perform Named Entity and Temporal Expression Recognition; thus the correct identification of words is even more important than the less controversial character-level measure.

Tab. 1. Evaluation of OCR Tools with Ocreval

OCR software	CER	WER
Readiris 17	40.13 %	71.62 %
Tesseract v. 4.1.1	07.85 %	20.72 %
Adobe Acrobat Pro DC	14.03 %	37.55 %
FreeOCR v. 2.6	12.72 %	32.56 %
Prizmo 4	13.75 %	25.41 %
CuneiForm v. 1.1	58.70 %	98.44 %

Moreover, by analysing the evaluation reports, we discovered that Tesseract's accuracy is higher, especially with multi-column articles that represent an important part of our pool of documents. Therefore, Tesseract turned out to be the best OCR tool for our project.

However, considering the WER obtained by Tesseract in the evaluation (20.72 %), analysing its outputs, and taking into account that even CER is not below the threshold for a quality full-text search (5 %) (Holley 2009), manual corrections of the OCR outputs are clearly needed in order to obtain high-quality texts to be used in the PRiSMHA platform.

3.3. Pre-processing, OCR, and post-processing

Pre-processing actions, in particular on historical documents, aim at enhancing source quality and represent a key task in order to improve OCR accuracy (Holley 2009). Therefore, we performed a careful analysis of the original images representing the output of the digitisation process that highlighted specific faults (e.g., inking flaws, missing blanks, overlapping characters, spelling errors, manual corrections, and notes). Based on such an analysis, the following pre- processing actions resulted in being the most useful, in order to improve the final text quality:

- white characters, black background: colour inversion;
- colour background: convert to gray scale;
- noise (stains and faded zones): convert to gray scale;
- crooked alignment: align text, rotate image;
- borders with stains, creases, or staples: remove borders.

Moreover, the information gathered during the analysis of the original images, together with the errors (displayed in the terminal window) and the confidence values (provided in a .tsv file and referring to each word or character, depending on configuration) reported by Tesseract, enabled us to select those documents that needed manual post-processing and to identify the following actions:

- faded characters or missing ink: add missing characters;
- manual notes, underlined parts: remove additional characters, add missing ones, correct incorrect ones;
- splitting elements: remove additional characters.

The final results of the OCR process on the PRiSMHA documents are definitely satisfactory: Only 13 out of 200 documents resulted not to be suited for the OCR process, thus producing 187 full-text documents that can be annotated through the PRiSMHA platform. In most cases, the failure of the OCR is due to the very poor quality of the original image (e.g., very faded characters), or to the presence of prevalent drawings and handwritten parts; in some cases, these features are coupled with an unusual layout, like, for instance, the document shown in Fig. 4, for which OCR was not possible (Tesseract reports an error message, and no output is produced).

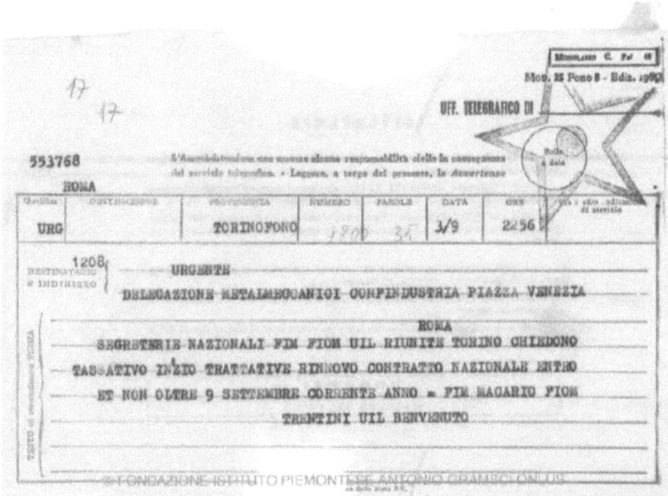
UFF. TELEGRAFICO DI

553768
ROMA

URG TORINOFONO 1208 35 3/9 2256

1208
URGENTE
DELEGAZIONE METALMECCANICI CONFINDUSTRIA PIAZZA VENEZIA
ROMA
SEGRETERIE NAZIONALI FIM FIOM UIL RIUNITE TORINO CHIEDONO
TASSATIVO INIZIO TRATTATIVE RINNOVO CONTRATTO NAZIONALE ENTRO
ET NON OLTRE 9 SETTEMBRE CORRENTE ANNO = FIM MAGARIO FIOM
TRENTINI UIL BENVENUTO

Fig. 4. A telegram, for which OCR was impossible [*Fondo FIOM*; copyright: *Fondaz. Ist. piemontese A. Gramsci onlus*]

The pre-processing and post-processing actions, identified on the basis of a detailed analysis of both the original images and the specific errors of the OCR tool, represent the backbone of a set of future guidelines for the usage of OCR in historical archives that host direct testimonies of social movements belonging to the (Italian) history of the 20th century.

4. Conclusions and future work

The main purpose of OCR within the PRiSMHA project is to enable the semantic annotation of the selected archival documents, and, in particular, the possibility of performing Named Entity and Time Expression Recognition on such documents (Section 1). Fig. 5 shows the result of the NER/TER functionality of the prototype annotation platform on the text produced by the OCR process for the document shown in Fig. 2.

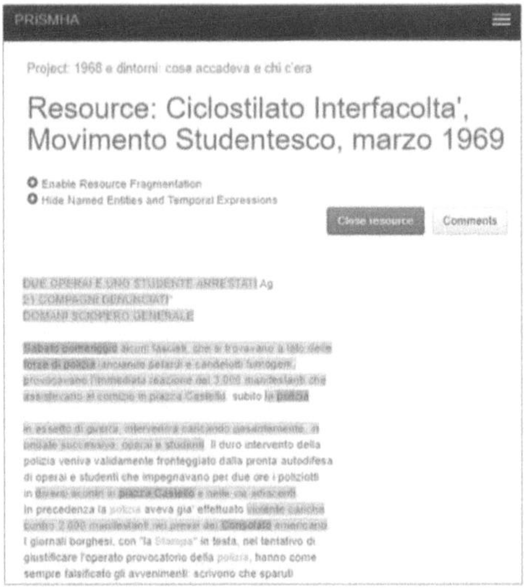

Fig. 5. NER/TER on the text produced by the OCR process for the document displayed in Fig. 2 [*Fondo Vadacchino*; copyright: *Fondaz. Ist. piemontese A. Gramsci onlus*]

The perspective is encouraging: The system recognizes references to temporal entities like “sabato pomeriggio” (Saturday afternoon), places like “Piazza Castello” (Castello Square), and also “polizia” (police) as an organization. A user evaluation of our prototype, described in (Colla et al. 2021), shows that NER/TER support is definitely useful in the annotation process, when users have to identify new entities.

In the future, we will extensively analyse the output of the NER/TER tools on the full-text version of the documents, in particular by asking users to evaluate it within the annotation context. Our goal is to demonstrate that, starting from paper documents characterized by challenging features for an OCR system, OCR, coupled with suited pre- (and post-) processing actions, is feasible and could provide good enough texts to be processed by automatic Information Extraction tools. Moreover, since a significant number of documents require post-processing manual correction, we will evaluate the possibility of involving users of the annotation platform in the correction activity, a solution that could enable larger-scale projects.

Acknowledgments

This research was funded by Fondazione Compagnia di San Paolo and Università di Torino within the PRiSMHA project (CSTO168023). We would like to thank all PRiSMHA collaborators, and in particular Diego Magro, Rossana Damiano, and Daniele Paolo Radicioni for their valuable support in the project.

References

Aprosio, A.P. and Moretti, G. (2016) "Italy goes to Stanford: A collection of CoreNLP modules for Italian". Available from: *arXiv preprint arXiv:1609.06204*. (Accessed: 14 February 2022).

Carducci, G., Leontino, M., Radicioni, D.P., Bonino, G., Pasini, E. and Tripodi, P. (2019) "Semantically aware text categorisation for metadata annotation". *Italian Research Conference on Digital Libraries*, 315–330. Cham: Springer.

Colla, D., Goy, A., Leontino, M., Magro, D. and Picardi, C. (2021) "Bringing Semantics into historical archives with computer-aided rich metadata generation". *ACM Journal on Computing and Cultural Heritage*. https://doi.org/10.1145/3484398. (Accessed: 14 February 2022).

De Francesco, G. (ed.) (2006) *Linee guida tecniche per i programmi di creazione di contenuti culturali digitali* 1(8). Ministero per i Beni e le Attività Culturali, Progetto Minerva.

Goy, A., Accornero, C., Astrologo, D., Colla, D., D'Ambrosio, M., Damiano, R., Leontino, M., Lieto, A., Loreto, F., Magro, D., Mensa, E., Montanaro, A., Mosca, V., Musso, S., Radicioni, D.P. and Re, C. (2019) "Fruitful synergies between computer science, historical studies and archives: The experience in the PRiSMHA project". In Bernardino, J., Salgado, A., Filipe, J. (eds.): *Proceedings of the 11th Int. Joint Conf. on Knowledge Discovery, Knowledge Engineering and Knowledge Management, Vienna, Austria, 17–19 September*, 3, 225–230. Setúbal: Scitepress.

Goy, A., Colla, D., Magro, D., Accornero, C., Loreto, F. and Radicioni, D. P. (2020) "Building semantic metadata for historical archives through an ontology-driven user interface". *Journal of Computing and Cultural Heritage* 13(3), 1–36.

Gruber, T.R. (1993) "A translation approach to portable ontology specifications". *Knowledge Acquisition* 5(2), 199–220.

Hamad, K. and Kaya, M. (2016) "A detailed analysis of optical character recognition technology". *International Journal of Applied Mathematics, Electronics and Computers* 4, 244–244.

Holley, R. (2009) "How good can it get? Analysing and improving OCR accuracy in large scale historic newspaper digitisation programs". *D-Lib Magazine* 15(3). https://www.dlib.org/dlib/march09/holley/03holley.html. (Accessed: 14 February 2022).

Moro, A., Raganato, A. and Navigli, R. (2014) "Entity linking meets word sense disambiguation: A unified approach". *Transactions of the Association for Computational Linguistics* 2, 231–244.

Nanni, F., Ponzetto, P. and Dietz, L. (2017) "Building entity-centric event collections". *Proceedings of the ACM/IEEE Joint Conference on Digital Libraries*, 1–10.Toronto: IEEE.

Navigli, R. and Ponzetto, S.P. (2010) "BabelNet: Building a very large multilingual semantic network". *Proceedings of the 48th Annual Meeting of the Association for Computational Linguistics*, 1, 216–225. Uppsala: Association for Computational Linguistics.

Reul, C., Christ, D., Hartelt, A., Balbach, N., Wehner, M., Springmann, U., Wick, C., Grundig, C., Büttner, A. and Puppe, F. (2019) "OCR4all – An open-source tool providing a (semi-) automatic OCR workflow for historical printings". *Applied Sciences* 9(4853).

Rice, S.V. and Nartker, T.A. (1996) "The ISRI analytic tools for OCR evaluation". *UNLV/Information Science Research Institute*, *TR-96*, 2.

Santos, E.A. (2019) "OCR evaluation tools for the 21st century". *Proceedings of the 3rd Workshop on the Use of Computational Methods in the Study of Endangered Languages* 1, 23–27. Honolulu, Hawai'i: Association for Computational Linguistics.

Smith, R. (2007) *An Overview of the Tesseract OCR Engine*. IEEE. https://doi.org/10.1109/ICDAR.2007.4376991. (Accessed 14 May 2022).

Strötgen, J. and Gertz, M. (2010) "Heideltime: High quality rule-based extraction and normalization of temporal expressions". *Proceedings of the 5th Int. Workshop on Semantic Evaluation*, 321–324.

Valentina Mureşan, Roxana Rogobete, Ana-Maria Bucur, Mădălina Chitez and Andreea Dincă

Chapter 2 Phraseology in Romanian Academic Writing: Corpus Based Explorations into Field-Specific Multiword Units

Abstract: At present, the writing particularities of the academic genres in the Romanian language are not well established. The lack of language-specific research, especially in the areas investigating expert academic writing, such as research articles, overburdens the efforts of young researchers to share their findings effectively with their research community. Our study aims to fill the gap in available research-based outcomes concerning expert academic writing production in Romanian and proposes a computational linguistics approach for the extraction and analysis of discipline-specific multiword units using academic writing corpora. We test our method on two self-compiled corpora of academic writing, with two levels of expertise (i.e., ROGER for novice academic writing and EXPRES for expert academic writing), and we identify co-occurring words, collocations / n-grams, which can be further processed to build academic wordlists. Such lists can be consulted by academic writers during the text production processes, but they can also be used to detect possible inaccuracies, given the scarcity of resources that define academic writing norms in Romania.

Keywords: academic writing in Romanian, corpus-based academic writing in Romanian, discipline-specific multiword units in Romanian academic writing, Corpus of Romanian Academic Genres, Corpus of Expert Writing in Romanian and English

1. Introduction

Investigating academic writing in Romanian is not an easy endeavour. First of all, "academic writing" in Romanian seems to be the result of a "mixture of European influences" (Baniceru et al. 2012: 332), starting with the French model in the 19th century, which emerged alongside the French influence on the entire Romanian educational system, and reaching a point, after the Fall of the Soviet Curtain, when the Anglo-Saxon model started to gain momentum (ibid.). The influence of multiple writing cultures makes it difficult for researchers to define the "Romanian academic style" (Bercuci and Chitez 2022 *in press*).

Another challenge when investigating this topic is posed by the lack of representative linguistic data, in the form of large corpora that have the potential to shed light on the linguistic and rhetorical features of academic writing in Romanian. While general Romanian language corpora, like The Reference Corpus of the Contemporary Romanian Language – CoRoLa (Mititelu et al. 2014), have been compiled, they do not allow register-specific or discipline-specific searches. It is therefore rather difficult to extract linguistic characteristics, such as academic phraseology, from heterogeneous databases.

In this chapter, we rely on self-compiled academic writing corpora, created in the framework of two research projects, ROGER and DACRE, conducted at the Centre for Corpus Related Digital Approaches to Humanities (CODHUS), at the West University of Timişoara. We use the two corpora (see Section 4), ROGER – *Corpus of Romanian Academic Genres* (Chitez et al. 2021), a learner academic writing corpus, and EXPRES – *Corpus of Expert Writing in Romanian and English* (Chitez et al. 2022), an expert academic writing corpus, to analyse the phraseological profile of academic writing in Romanian, in four disciplinary fields (Linguistics, Information Technology, Economics and Political Sciences). We decided to conduct exploratory analyses on the use of phraseology, in Romanian, in the above-mentioned fields, based on preliminary results from previous investigations, using the ROGER and EXPRES corpora, which analysed multiword units for academic writing in English L2. Our studies indicated field-specific, multilevel, linguistic differences concerning, for example, various levels of lexical complexity, with articles from the field of Political Sciences displaying higher lexical complexity than articles from the fields of Economics and IT (Bucur et al. 2022). Another analysis demonstrated that, in the case of academic writing texts in English L2, "IT students used considerably more content-related phrases (both 4- and 5-grams) than discourse organizing phrases compared to the Literature Studies students" (Dinca and Chitez 2021: 82). Since such findings seem to be specific to the language of the academic texts (i.e., L2 English), the

Romanian counterpart for the same datasets is expected to confirm or contradict the hypothesis that the same type of field-specific linguistic features is encountered, irrespective of the language in which academic texts are produced. At the same time, by exploring the two datasets from the perspective of academic writing level (i.e., novice academic writing versus expert academic writing), our objective is also to draw conclusions on the distribution of academic phraseological disciplinary differences into writing expertise categories (see Hyland 2008a; 2008b).

2. Theoretical background

2.1. General framework: Research on phraseology in English

Language is largely composed of "combinations of words that customarily co-occur" (Kjellmer 1991: 112). It is rather challenging to put forward a clear definition of phraseology, the emerging approach concerned with the study of multiword units, due to its conceptual and methodological complexity. Broadly speaking, phraseology is concerned with the "the study of the structure, meaning and use of word combinations" (Cowie 1994: 3168), one of its aims being to propose criteria which are used to differentiate "phraseological units from non-phraseological ones" (Granger and Paquot 2008: 27). This has led to two main approaches to phraseology:

1. The Phraseological Approach, also called the "traditional approach to phraseology" (Granger and Paquot 2008: 28), has laid the foundation for phraseology as a discipline. This approach acknowledges the most restricted multiword units, such as idioms or proverbs, to best represent phraseology, arguing that the combinations of words which only have "syntactic and semantic restrictions" are not part of phraseology, and are called free combinations, e.g., *drink coffee* (Granger and Paquot 2008: 38). In this approach, phraseological units are selected using a top-down, corpus-based technique, where researchers usually produce a list of predetermined multiword units, compiled based on intuition or by selecting certain multiword units that are considered "perceptually salient or theoretically interesting" (Gray and Biber 2015: 126); thus the corpus may be consulted to find examples of usage for those units. While this approach is appreciated for its depth and attention to

details, one major weakness is that it can become restrictive in identifying a wide range of phraseological units.

2. The more recent Frequency-Based Approach relies on the study of electronic linguistic corpora using computational tools since these revealed that "words are not isolated but rather combine with each other in preferred syntagmatic patterns to acquire meaning" (Paquot 2015: 460). This approach relies on a bottom-up, corpus-driven technique to identify multiword units, various types of recurrent phraseological units being identified in linguistic corpora according to their frequency and distribution (with no predefined lists of phraseological units being used), often through the application of statistical algorithms to extract relevant multiword units. Consequently, new types of phraseological units have been identified, such as N-grams (see Biber et al. 2004) or discontinuous lexical frames (see Gray and Biber 2013). In addition, the study of other more traditional categories of multiword units, such as collocations (also referred to as co-occurrences), has benefited considerably from the frequency-based approach (see Xiao 2015).

The frequency-based approach offers an effective way of automatically identifying new types of multiword units. However, one important limitation lies in the fact that, while it is easy to retrieve multiword units automatically, the findings might not be easy to interpret qualitatively (Ebeling and Hasselgård 2015: 210). One consequence of this is that there is considerable ambiguity in defining and categorizing all the new types of phraseological units (Granger and Paquot 2008: 29). Nowadays, the quantitative corpus-assisted automatic methods of extraction are combined with the more qualitative types of analyses to get the best results (see Frankenberg-Garcia et al. 2019; 2021), which is also reflective of our study's intention.

2.2. Multiword units under investigation

Since the aim of our research was to identify typical multiword units for field-specific academic writing in Romanian, by relying on co-occurrence frequencies, we have to clarify the typology of multiword units under close investigation. Biber, Conrad and Leech (2002) refer to several categories of "sequences of words that behave as a combination" (2002: 18) and distinguish between multiword units ("a sequence or orthographic words which functions as a single grammatical unit" [2002: 18]), idioms and collocations ("the relationship between two or more independent words which commonly appear together (or co-occur)" [2002: 18]), but later explain the use of the term lexical bundle to refer to "a sequence of words which co-occur frequently, especially when the sequence consists of more than two words" (2002: 19), in other words an extended collocation, also referred to as N-grams.

N-grams

This category of phraseological units originates from the frequency-based approach to phraseology. N-grams, also called lexical bundles, are recurrent multiword sequences of a given length, usually between two and five words (2-Grams, 3-Grams, etc.). They are automatically extracted from a corpus by applying various quantitative parameters. To ensure the relevancy of the extracted N-grams, several extraction parameters are set, such as the size of the N-grams, and thresholds for frequency and dispersion in the corpus.

Usually, most of the extracted N-grams are neither complete structural units, nor idiomatic in meaning, but it was proved that they are very frequent in language and are considered "important building blocks in discourse" (Biber and Barbieri 2007: 268–270). For example, in a corpus of academic prose, a list of frequent 3-grams might include sequences such as *according to the*, *on the basis of*, *the fact that*, *there is a* etc. After extraction, lexical bundles can be categorized using various structural and functional taxonomies (for English, see Biber et al. 1999; 2004).

Collocations

Halliday and Yallop (2007: 15) define collocations as words which tend to "keep company with each other", and therefore some semantic relationship is expected, while Jackson and Zé Amvela (2007: 131) highlight the property of these co-occurring words to contract meaning relations. Although there are numerous possible definitions, Benson, Benson and Ilsen (2010) propose a more specific distinction between two classes of collocations: lexical and grammatical. While the first includes combinations between two major parts of speech (verb + noun/ pronoun/ noun phrase, adjective + noun, noun + verb, nouns + noun, adverb + adjective, verb + adverb), the grammatical collocations are defined as phrases which are composed of "a dominant word (noun, adjective, verb) and a preposition or a grammatical structure such as an infinitive or clause" (2010: XIX), for which 19 patterns are described. In our study, we have included both grammatical collocations and lexical ones, as our interest lies with identifying the stable combination patterns for Romanian language.

2.3. Terminological issues in Romanian phraseology

Terminological ambiguity and overlap in Romanian language has already been reported by Cernea (2009), who explains the "rich terminology" (2009: 12) used to refer to the object of research concerned with phraseology – "unitate frazeologică, frazeologism, locuţiune, locuţiune frazeologică, grup sintactic stabil, izolare, idiomatism, discurs repetat, formula fixă, expresie, perifrază, expresie idiomatică, îmbinare stabilă/ constantă de cuvinte, grup sintactic stabil, unitate sintagmatică, ormula/ combinaţie fixă, sintagmă" [our translation – phraseological unit, phrase, locution, phraseological locution, stable syntactic group, tournure, idiom, repeated discourse, functional idiom, expression, periphrase, idiomatic expression, stable combination of words, stable structure, syntagmatic structure, formula, syntagm] (2009: 12). As can be seen above, there is no clear distinction between these sub-classes of multiword units in the Romanian language and they are often used in enumerations that function as all-encompassing umbrella terms (see the more recent dictionaries Pănculescu and Nijloveanu 2015), or they may occur under larger categories of "stable structures" (Avădanei 2000; Ţeghiu 2004), or Romanian expressions (Bucă 2014). It is only recently that recognition emerged of such standardized combinations for the Romanian language, known as *collocations* in English lexicology: Groza (2005) attempts a definition for *collocation*, in Romanian, as a unit composed of a node ("bază" [2005: 20]) and a collocate ("colocativ" [2005: 20]), which functions as a "probable and frequently used combination of words" (Cernea 2009: 20) [our translation].

However, reference works admit that the use of collocations is still isolated within the Romanian terminology (see Bidu-Vrănceanu et al. 2005), which tends to be rather cyclical and self-referenced, instead of setting clear delineations (see Trantescu 2010).

3. Previous research

Few studies describe the computational methods used for Romanian to automatically extract collocations – most of them apply or test algorithms or pipelines provided for other languages. Although collocations are one of the most common types of multi-word expressions, researchers almost unanimously recognize that they "require a special, holistic treatment in NLP systems" (Seretan 2014: 12). For instance, Seretan (2014) details the automatic extraction of collocations in the context of syntactic parsing and machine translation by following multiple steps (syntactic analysis of the primary texts, preprocessing texts with the Fips multilingual parser) and eventually "coupling the collocation identification and the parsing tasks". However, the Romanian language is only subject to a marginal note. Todirascu et al. (2007) focus on a comparative perspective (Romanian vs French) in automated extraction of collocations, emphasizing the need for several filtering stages and the difficulties triggered by contextual features of the Romanian constructions. Hence, various hybrid approaches are often adopted by researchers interested in low-resourced languages such as Romanian.

It must be mentioned here that, if collocations have slowly taken centre stage in more recent research, N-grams are still somewhat of a novelty for the Romanian academia. Thus, in Romanian Linguistics relatively little research has been carried out on N-grams. However, there seems to be a surge of interest regarding N-grams in Romanian, especially in computational fields of study, such as Natural Language Processing (see Chiru et al. 2010; Inkpen and Islam 2010; Tufiş et al. 2013).

4. Data and methods

4.1. Data

ROGER: The ROGER corpus (*Corpus of Romanian Academic Genres*) (Chitez et al. 2021) is a bilingual comparable corpus ROGER containing learner discipline-specific academic writing samples in Romanian L1 and

English L2. Unlike other learner academic writing corpora, ROGER is freely available via a corpus query interface (ibid.), accessed through a simple login account. The platform allows for user-friendly searches of terms/phrases, filtered by language (English, Romanian), student genre (currently 20 genres), study year (1 through 4), level (BA, MA or PhD), discipline (currently 8 disciplines) and gender (male, female or unknown). The Romanian sub-corpus size at the time of the current analysis is 904 883 words.

EXPRES: The EXPRES Corpus (*Corpus of Expert Writing in Romanian and English*) (Chitez et al. 2022) is composed of research articles in the disciplines (Linguistics, Political Sciences, Economics, IT), compiled using online resources. The profile of the corpus is "expert academic writing corpus" since all articles have been published in peer-reviewed journals. The EXPRES corpus has a dedicated corpus query platform which allows for the search and extraction of desired linguistic items (words, phrases, patterns, n-grams) and statistical visualizations of data. The Romanain sub-corpus at the time of the current analysis is 1 437 886 words.

The corpora selected for this study have a comparable number of texts: 111 texts focusing on Linguistics, 132 on Political Sciences, 96 on Economics, 42 on the IT field. Since the ROGER corpus contains texts written by novice writers (mostly during certain courses or as gradable assignments in specific disciplines), and EXPRES contains articles elaborated by expert researchers, EXPRES' larger extension is justified. Another difference between the corpora concerns the academic genres included: if EXPRES consists solely of scientific articles, the ROGER corpus is a multi-genre text corpus, containing BA or MA papers, reviews, scientific and seminar papers, essays, etc.

4.2. Method

The SpaCy library was used for tokenizing the texts and extracting the Universal Part of Speech (POS) tags from the EXPRES and ROGER corpora, with the "ro_core_news_sm" pipeline available for the Romanian language. To compute the percentages of specific POS tags for each field from the two corpora, all the texts were concatenated for each field. The percentages were computed as the number of apparitions of the POS tag (e.g., NOUN) in a field divided by the total number of words in the texts from that field.

Collocations were identified by training a Phraser model from the Gensim library (Rehurek and Sojka 2010) using the Normalized Pointwise Mutual Information (NPMI) metric (Bouma 2009). The NPMI metric was chosen because it is less biased towards collocations with a lower frequency than Pointwise Mutual Information (PMI). PMI measures how much the probability of co-occurrence of certain words differs from the expected probability of occurrence of the individual words and the assumption of the independence of words. An NPMI score equal to 1 means that the words from the collocation only occur together, a score equal to 0 means that the words are distributed as expected under independence, while a score can be -1 if the words occur only separately in the corpora. We chose to extract collocations of two and three words. We then analysed in more detail collocations with specific part-of-speech-tag combinations, such as verb and preposition (see Fig. 2).

Another instrument used for this study is Sketch Engine, since the corpus management system developed within the platform and the POS tagger performs rather well for Romanian corpora (in comparison with other corpus linguistics tools such as LancsBox or Antconc, Sketch Engine supports tokenization, lemmatization and tagging). The specific lists generated with Sketch Engine were Wordlists and N-grams.

4.3. Limitations

Even if the Part of Speech Tagger for Romanian language from SpaCy has a 93 % accuracy for Universal POS and it successfully detects the POS for the most common words such as nouns, verbs, adjectives and adverbs, its performance is reduced when trying to detect the POS for particles, interjections, auxiliary verbs and other less frequent POS.

5. Analysis and discussion

a. Novice versus expert academic phraseology use in the disciplines: N-Gram analysis

In general, the most frequent N-Grams generated by Sketch Engine (Kilgarriff et al. 2014) for the analysed corpora were structures overused in Romanian academic writing. We compared the results for each discipline and took into account the first 5 to 10 N-grams based on their frequency, regardless of the POS combinations: data results were not filtered by any attributes such as word, lemma, or regular expressions, but the size of N-grams was set to the range of 3–4.

For Linguistics, we noticed that expert writers (i.e., EXPRES data) tend to compare and analyse several perspectives, using structures such as "on the one hand" (*pe de o parte*), "on the other hand" (*pe de altă parte*), "while" (*în timp ce*) to signal transition. Also, more references are included in the scientific articles: "see..." (*a se vedea*). In ROGER, on the contrary, data indicate that novice students' writing does not show a consistent argument flow when moving from one topic to another, since students tend not to indicate contrast or addition, but they simply list their ideas: "in terms of X" / "as far as X is concerned", "from the point of view of" (*în ceea ce priveşte, din punct de vedere*).

Both sub-corpora (novice and expert writing), containing texts from the Economics field, have fewer argumentative connectors than those in the Linguistics field – as expected, both experts and novice writers in the field of Philology tend to produce more elaborated statements (in terms of discursive practices). The ROGER subcorpus includes more assertions which list examples ("such as" – *cum ar fi*), instead of using a diversified vocabulary and of arguing the relevance of those exemplifications: "creativity factors such as: inventiveness, operability, versatility, ability to notice unusual relationships" (*factori de creativitate, cum ar fi: ingeniozitatea, operativitatea, plasticitatea, abilitatea de a sesiza relaţii neobişnuite*).

The Political Sciences sub-corpora have a high similarity degree with those related to Linguistics/Philology: comparing and contrasting are more frequent in EXPRES (analysing multiple perspectives: "on one hand", "on the other hand"). An interesting aspect within this field is that novice writers tend to express a very confident tone: "has to be" (*trebuie să fie*, 4.203 hits pttw). Several examples are relevant for students' tendency to make absolute judgements: "the absolute truth must be something accessible and easy to identify" (*adevărul absolut trebuie să fie ceva accesibil şi uşor de identificat*), "the support and legitimacy of a proposal should be assumed by a large audience" (*susţinerea şi legitimitatea unei propuneri trebuie să fie asumată de un public numeros*).

As for the IT field, both sub-corpora have the same most frequent N-gram: "such as" (*cum ar fi*), but we noticed that the expert corpus tends to include more discursive connectors ("in terms of X" / "as far as X is concerned" – *în ceea ce privește, din punct de vedere*), while, in ROGER, novice writers focus on describing processes and data without giving commentaries or explanations, since the next N-grams used are "dataset", "database", "automated learning" (*setul de date, baza de date, de învățare automată*). The students have a more telegraphic style, which indicates that they are rather unaware of the relevance of the factors related to writing and composition. Moreover, references are not as present in ROGER as in EXPRES: the lack of novice writers' expertise can also be a consequence of the poor discipline-specific bibliography in Romanian (as shown in Rogobete et al. 2021: 11–12, there is a lack of valuable resources in Romanian for the field of IT). Another interesting aspect revealed by the analysis is that expert writers are more interested in "real-time" processes – this N-gram is the third most frequent in EXPRES, occurring in concordances such as "real-time analysis (streaming)" (*analize în timp real (streaming)*), "real-time extraction of frequencies" (*extragerea în timp real a frecvențelor*), "real-time integration and synchronisation" (*integrare și sincronizare în timp real*).

b. Novice versus expert writing in the disciplines: POS distribution

In order to verify the grammatical profile of the writing samples in the corpus, representing different disciplines and levels of writing expertise, we conducted an automated POS-tag distribution analysis (see Fig. 1).

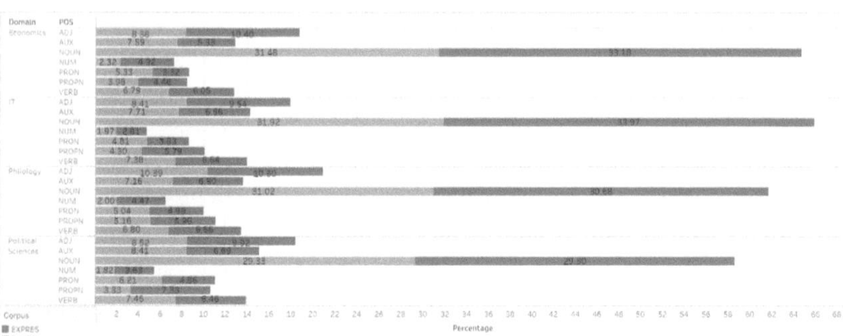

Fig. 1. Main POS percentages in the two corpora

Even though the noun category distribution is comparable, in terms of proper nouns present in the corpora (PROPN), EXPRES has a higher percentage. This can be justified by the fact that expert authors tend to analyse or mention official positions of certain institutions (especially for Political Sciences and Economics), but they also refer more frequently, in their articles, to documents issued by certain authorities. In addition, a stronger bibliographic background present in EXPRES shows a larger number of in-text or indirect references (for Philology/Linguistics, IT) or that authors focus on explaining the context for economic or political phenomena.

Verb categories are more frequent in ROGER, owing to a more frequent use of gerund or analytical forms by novice writers (the last aspect explains the higher percentage of auxiliary verbs – AUX). On the other hand, expert writers tend to choose shorter, clearer sentences instead of more elaborated phrases, thus including more nominalizations. The use of adjectives (ADJ) is systematic in EXPRES, since expert writers are more evaluative, their "voice" is appraisal oriented, while novice writers are not confident enough to make appreciations. However, experienced researchers are less subjective than students, and this can be noticed in the lower percentages of pronouns (PRON) used in EXPRES. Research articles are written in a more objective tone, whereas novice writers tend to express their subjective opinion quite frequently (either using the singular or plural form of the first-person pronouns). Another feature demonstrating the scientific and well-documented character of the EXPRES corpus is exemplified by the larger numeral forms (NUM) present in the texts. This shows that expert writers base their arguments on statistics, reports, and more precise data in general.

c. Novice versus expert academic phraseology use in the disciplines: POS-based collocation patterns

Collocation patterns were identified starting from corpus frequencies of headwords (nouns, verbs and adjective lemmas), used to identify possible collocative nodes. Based on that, target searches were performed using combination patterns imported from English lexicographic studies (mentioned in Section 2.2) or references to Romanian phraseological structures (mentioned in Section 2.3). This was decided considering that there is no research-supported classification of academic phases / multi-word units / collocations for the Romanian language.

The investigative method (similar to the one mentioned by Frankenberg-Garcia et al. 2019; 2021) is a starting point for future categorization of collocation patterns for the Romanian language, i.e., 2-word or 3-word collocations. Several categories proved to be relevant for the extraction of discipline-specific multi-word units: verb+preposition, preposition+verb, noun+preposition, noun+adjective, preposition+noun, preposition+noun+preposition, preposition+noun+adjective, adjective+preposition+noun, preposition+noun+noun, noun+adjective+preposition, verb+preposition+noun were considered. These were also tested in this study. Other patterns, such as noun+adjective+preposition, adjective+preposition+noun, were excluded from the analysis because they did not lead to productive functional academic phases. Categories such verb+preposition+noun or preposition+noun+noun were considered stable combinations to be further explored. Due to the linguistic particularities of Romanian, some other collocation patterns, such as adjective+noun, were not considered relevant to investigate for now, as adjectives typically occur in post-position of the noun they modify. They may prove relevant for detecting possible inaccuracies.

As other e-lexicographic studies reveal (Frankenberg-Garcia et al. 2021), a thorough analysis of nodes and collocates is necessary to extract and define academic collocations in Romanian and to establish reliable academic phrase indexes. However, several salient observations emerged from the present study. First, some collocation patterns prove to have a higher degree of relevance for academic writing practice improvement since they have a dominant functionality. For example, collocations constructed around noun nodes (especially 3-word combinations) are rather content-related and field-specific.

Then, one of the most productive 2-word POS sequence is represented by verb+preposition collocations, which are often employed with a specific discursive function (e.g., information organization – summing up, adding a comment, exemplification etc.). The ten most frequent verb+preposition sequences (VP) are illustrated in Fig. 2 below and allow for the lemmatization of the verb.

ROGER Linguistics	EXPRES Linguistics	ROGER Economics	EXPRES Economics
opri asupra (0.5988)	oprim asupra (0.6342)	orientate spre (0.7022)	cuprinsă între (0.6471)
vorbi despre (0.5584)	formată dintr- (0.6248)	orientată spre (0.6591)	clasificate drept (0.6278)
bazează pe (0.5184)	vorbi despre (0.5809)	vorbim despre (0.6528)	bazată pe (0.5644)
caracterizat prin (0.5111)	vorbim despre (0.5593)	avem de- (0.5899)	bazează pe (0.5385)
optează pentru (0.5001)	format dintr- (0.5504)	efectuate până (0.5877)	bazate pe (0.5332)
referă la (0.498)	caracterizează printr- (0.5416)	cunoscut sub (0.551)	adecvate privind (0.5178)
bazată pe (0.4699)	bazată pe (0.5275)	bazează pe (0.5347)	bazat pe (0.5127)
redate prin (0.4628)	vorbeşte despre (0.5191)	bazată pe (0.5324)	află intr- (0.4971)
formată din (0.4373)	bazate pe (0.4979)	caracterizează prin (0.5308)	referă la (0.4932)
provenit din (0.4316)	avem de- (0.493)	caracterizată prin (0.5231)	duce la (0.463)
ROGER IT	**EXPRES IT**	**ROGER Political Science**	**EXPRES Political Science**
bazate pe (0.6336)	bazate pe (0.6242)	orientat înspre (0.7569)	îndreptate împotriva (0.6423)
bazat pe (0.5919)	bazat pe (0.6101)	orientate spre (0.6526)	durat până (0.594)
bazată pe (0.5911)	bazată pe (0.5959)	cuprinsă între (0.5956)	îndrepta spre (0.5654)
bazează pe (0.5559)	bazează pe (0.5423)	cuprinse între (0.5938)	orientat spre (0.5555)
concentrează pe (0.499)	referă la (0.5138)	vorbim despre (0.5834)	vorbi despre (0.5491)
referă la (0.4736)	conduce la (0.4738)	vorbit despre (0.5603)	discută despre (0.5286)
formate din (0.47)	centrate pe (0.4712)	vorbi despre (0.554)	îndreptat împotriva (0.5277)
stau la (0.4697)	compusă din (0.466)	formată dintr- (0.5483)	vorbim despre (0.5274)
ajunge la (0.4431)	provenită din (0.466)	bazează pe (0.5218)	bazate pe (0.5006)
adaptate la (0.4386)	entităţi cu (0.4583)	bazată pe (0.5059)	discuta despre (0.4914)

Fig. 2. A comparison of the most frequent verb+preposition collocations in the the two corpora

What can be remarked here is that there is little variation at the level of writing expertise (ROGER versus EXPRES corpus), the most frequently occurring combinations being identical or with a similar discursive function in the two categories of texts and even across several disciplines. For the field of Linguistics, the most frequent VP collocation is *opri asupra* ("concentrate on", usually followed by a specific case/ example – e.g., *merită să ne oprim asupra fenomenului*), with a similar discursive function as *bazate pe* ("focus on") in the field of IT, or *orientate spre* ("focus on", "discuss") in Economics and Political Science ROGER corpora. For the field of Economics in the EXPRES corpus the most frequent VP collocation is *cuprinsă între* ("range between"), typical of reference to statistical reports, while, in the case of expert texts in the field of Political Science (EXPRES corpus), the most frequent VP collocation is *îndreptate împotriva* ("(aimed) against") used for examples of various consequences of political/social actions, for example *acţiunile îndreptate împotriva românilor* ("actions (aimed) against Romanians").

Regardless of the frequency rank in the VP collocation index, there is a rather high frequency of VP collocations which are used for introducing examples and specifications – *bazate pe*, *centrate pe*, *orientate spre*, *opri asupra* ("focus on"), followed by a large number of collocations used to introduce an argument – *vorbi despre*, *discută despre* ("talk about"), *se referă la*, *contribuie la*, *avem de (-a face)* ("deal with"), with some VP collocations used for information classification – *format din* ("consist of"), ("*caracteriza prin*").

Although a focus on 2-word or 3-word multi-word units, or collocations, does not cover exhaustively the particularities of academic writing distinctions between writing proficiency levels (i.e., novice versus expert writers), our findings highlight some linguistic preferences or choices according to the writing expertise level. The results also point towards potential misuse patterns of some standard collocations (e.g., *orientate înspre* which refers to a direction rather than *orientate spre* which implies a focus, combination which occurs exclusively in ROGER). Corroborating the analysis of POS multiword frequencies and N-grams, it was demonstrated that EXPRES data are indicative of a higher standard of "academic writing style" (e.g., "from my point of view" occurs exclusively in novice-writing ROGER data, regardless of the field). Also, authorial voice expression displays a distinctive pattern in expert writing: the first person plural is rarely used in Linguistics and Political Sciences research articles ("from our point of view" or "in our study"), while in the texts from Economics or IT there are no authorial markers. This demonstrates that impersonal writing is a salient feature in expert academic writing.

5. Conclusions

Our research presents and exemplifies a first methodological stage in the identification of 2- and 3-word structures which are frequently encountered in Romanian academic writing. The study also shows how the method can be further used for the development of linguistic inventories, such as academic word or collocation lists, non-existant for the Romanian language. The overlap of computational and applied corpus linguistics methods for the extraction of the phraseological units in the Romanian language (N-grams, POS co-occurrence patterns) accounts for greater reliability and replicability of the proposed approach. Additionally, the use of two representative academic writing corpora (ROGER and EXPRES), allows for the identification of academic writing features that characterize different levels of writing expertise (novice versus expert). With the help of corpus-based frequencies, it is possible to observe functionality patterns within the multiword unit categories, thus emphasizing their role as general use or filed-specific writing phrases. The study can be exploited pedagogically to support academic writers who, although familiar with the general use of a particular lexical item in Romanian, could exploit the findings to acknowledge its functionality within complex collocation patterns. However, follow-up analyses are necessary in order to compile academic word / collocation / phrase lists (see Frankenberg-Garcia 2021) which can be used by text producers to improve their academic writing in the disciplines.

Acknowledgements

This work was supported by a grant of the Ministry of Research, Innovation and Digitization, CNCS/CCCDI – UEFISCDI, project number 158 / 2021, within PNCDI III, awarded to Dr Habil Madalina Chitez (PI), from the West University of Timişoara, Romania, for the project DACRE (*Discipline-specific expert academic writing in Romanian and English: corpus-based contrastive analysis models*, 2021–2022).

References

Avădanei, C. (2000) *Construcţii idiomatice în limbile română şi engleză.* Iaşi: Editura Universităţii "Al. I. Cuza".

Băniceru, C., Borchin, M.I., Doroholschi, C. and Tucan, D. (2012) "Academic writing in Romania: A contrastive analysis of BA thesis introductions in Romanian and English". *Quaestiones Romanicae*, 1, 331–344.

Benson, M., Benson, E. and Ilson, R. (2010) *The BBI Combinatory Dictionary of English. Your Guide to Collocations and Grammar* (2nd ed. revised by R. Ilson). Amsterdam/ Philadelphia: John Benjamins Publishing Company.

Bercuci, L. and Chitez, M. (2022, *in press*) "The influence of the Romanian academic style on student writing in English". In Vránová, M. (ed.) *New to the LSP Classroom? A Selection of Monographs on Successful Practices*. Wilmington: Vernon Press.

Biber, D., Johansson, S., Leech, G., Conrad, S. and Finegan, E. (eds.) (1999) *Longman Grammar of Spoken and Written English*. London: Longman.

Biber, D., Conrad, S. and Leech, G. (2002) *Longman Student Grammar of Spoken and Written English*. Harlow, Essex: Pearson Education Limited.

Biber, D., Conrad, S. and Cortes, V. (2004) "If you look at …: Lexical Bundles in University Teaching and Textbooks". *Applied Linguistics*, 25, 371–405. https://doi.org/10.1093/applin/25.3.371. (Accessed: 10 March 2022).

Biber, D. and Barbieri, F. (2007) "Lexical bundles in university spoken and written registers". *English for Specific Purposes*, 26, 263–286.

Bidu-Vrănceanu, A., Călărașu, C., Ionescu-Ruxăndoiu, L., Mancaș, M. and Pană Dindelegan, G. (2005) *Dicționar de științe ale limbii*. București: Nemira.

Bouma, G. (2009) "Normalized (pointwise) mutual information in collocation extraction". *Proceedings of GSCL*, 30, 31–40.

Bucur, A.-M., Chitez, M., Muresan, V., Dinca, A. and Rogobete, R. (2022). "EXPRES Corpus for A Field-specific Automated Exploratory Study of L2 English Expert Scientific Writing". In Calzolari, N. et al. (eds.): *Proceedings of the 13th Conference on Language Resources and Evaluation- LREC 2022*, Marseille, France, June 20–25, 2022. pp. 4739–4746. Available at: http://www.lrec-conf.org/proceedings/lrec2022/LREC-2022.pdf. Accessed June 22, 2022.

Bucă, M. (2014) *Marele dicționar de expresii românești*. București: Meteor Press.

Cernea, M. (2009) *Unități frazeologice în limba română*. Târgu Mureș: Editura Kreativ.

Chiru, C., Hanganu, A., Rebedea, T. and Trausan-Matu, S. (2010) "Filling the gaps using Google 5-grams corpus". *Proceedings of the 5th International Conference on Software and Data Technologies*, Athens, 22–24 July, 438–443. DOI: 10.5220/0002932204380443. (Accessed: 10 March 2022).

Chitez, M., Bercuci, L., Dincă, A., Rogobete, R. and Csürös, K. (2021) *Corpus of Romanian Academic Genres* (ROGER). West University of Timisoara. Available at https://roger-corpus.org/. (Accessed: 10 March 2022).

Chitez, M., Rogobete, R., Muresan, V. and Dinca, A. (2022) *Corpus of Expert Writing in Romanian and English* (EXPRES). West University of Timisoara. Available at <https://dacre.projects.uvt.ro/research/?lang=en>. (Accessed: 10 March 2022).

Cowie, A.P. (1994) "Phraseology". In Asher, R.E. (ed.) *The Encyclopedia of Language and Linguistics*, 3168–3171. Oxford: Oxford University Press.

Dinca, A. and Chitez, M. (2021) "Assessing learners' academic phraseology in the digital age: A corpus-informed approach to ESP texts". *Journal of Teaching English for Specific and Academic Purposes*, 9(1), 71–84.

Ebeling, S.O. and Hasselgård, H. (2015) "Learner corpora and phraseology". In Meunier, F., Gilquin, G. and Granger, S. (eds.) *The Cambridge Handbook of Learner Corpus Research, Cambridge Handbooks in Language and Linguistics*, 207–230. Cambridge: Cambridge University Press. https://doi.org/10.1017/CBO9781139649414.010.

Frankenberg-Garcia, A., Lew, R., Roberts, J.C., Rees, G.P. and Sharma, N. (2019) "Developing a writing assistant to help EAP writers with collocations in real time". *ReCALL*, 31(1), 23–39. DOI: 10.1017/S0958344018000150.

Frankenberg-Garcia, A., Rees, G.P. and Lew, R., (2021) "Slipping through the cracks in e-lexicography". *International Journal of Lexicography*, 34(2), 206–234. https://doi.org/10.1093/ijl/ecaa022. (Accessed 16 May 2022).

Halliday, M.A.K. and Yallop, C. (2007) *Lexicology. A Short Introduction*. London: Continuum.

Hyland, K. (2008a) "Academic clusters: Text patterning in published and postgraduate writing". *International Journal of Applied Linguistics*, 18, 41–62. DOI: 10.1111/j.1473-4192.2008.00178.x.

Hyland, K. (2008b) "As can be seen: Lexical bundles and disciplinary variation". *English for Specific Purposes*, 27, 4–21. doi: 10.1016/j.esp.2007.06.001.

Granger, S. and Paquot, M. (2008) "Disentangling the phraseological web". In Granger, S. and Meunier, F. (eds.) *Phraseology: An Interdisciplinary Perspective*, 27–50. Amsterdam/Philadelphia: John Benjamins Publishing Company.

Gray, B. and Biber, D. (2013) "Lexical frames in academic prose and conversation". *International Journal of Corpus Linguistics*, 18(1), 109–136. https://doi.org/10.1075/ijcl.18.1.08gra9/SPED.2009.5156184. (Accessed 10 March 2022).

Gray, B. and Biber, D. (2015) "Phraseology". In Biber, D. and Reppen, R. (eds.) *The Cambridge Handbook of English Corpus Linguistics, Cambridge Handbooks in Language and Linguistics*, 125–145. Cambridge: Cambridge University Press. https://doi.org/10.1017/CBO9781139764377.008. (Accessed 10 March 2022).

Groza, L. (2005) *Dinamica unităţilor frazeologice în limba română contemporană*. Bucureşti: Editura Universităţii din Bucureşti.

Inkpen, D. and Islam, A. (2010) "Unsupervised approaches to text correction using Google N-grams for English and Romanian". In Tufis, D. and Forascu, C. (eds.) *Multilinguality and Interoperability in Language Processing with Emphasis on Romanian*, 270–285. Bucharest: Romanian Academy Publishing House.

Jackson, H. and Zé Amvela, E. (2007). *Word, Meaning and Vocabulary. An Introduction to Modern English Lexicology*. (2nd ed.) London: Continuum.

Kjellmer, G. (1991) "A mint of phrases". In Aijmer, K. and Altenberg, B. (eds.) *English Corpus Linguistics. Studies in Honour of Jan Svartvik*, 111–127. London: Longman.

Mititelu, V.B., Irimia, E. and Tufiş, D. (2014 May) "Corola – the reference corpus of contemporary Romanian language". *Proceedings of the Ninth International Conference on Language Resources and Evaluation* (LREC'14), 1235–1239.

Paquot, M. (2015) "Lexicography and phraseology". In Biber, D. and R. Reppen (Eds). *The Cambridge Handbook of English Corpus Linguistics*, 460–477. Cambridge: Cambridge University Press.

Pănculescu, D. and Nijloveanu, I. (2015) *Dicţionar de colocaţii, locuţiuni şi expresii populare româneştii*. Craiova: Aius.

Rehurek, R. and Sojka, P. (2010) "Software framework for topic modelling with large corpora". *Proceedings of the LREC 2010 Workshop on New Challenges for NLP Frameworks*, Valetta, Malta, 22 May 46–50.

Rogobete, R., Chitez, M., Mureşan, V., Damian, B., Duciuc, A., Gherasim, C. and Bucur, A.-M. (2021) "Challenges in compiling expert corpora for academic writing support". *Conference Proceedings. 11th International Conference the Future of Education, Virtual Edition, 1–2 July 2021*, 409–414. Florence: Filodiritto Editore.

Seretan, V. (2014) "On collocations and their interaction with parsing and translation". *Informatics*, 1, 11–31. DOI: 10.3390/informatics1010011. (Accessed: 10 March 2022).

Todirascu, A., Gledhill, C. and Stefanescu, D. (2007) "Extracting collocations in context: The case of Romanian VN constructions". *Proceedings of RANLP*, Borovets, Bulgaria, 27–29 September, 594–598. https://hal-univ-paris.archives-ouvertes.fr/hal-01220405. (Accessed 10 March 2022).

Trantescu, A.-M. (2010) "Probleme terminologice în definirea unităţilor frazeologice în română şi engleză. O perspectivă contrastivă". *Analele Universităţii "Dunărea de Jos" din Galaţi*, 1 (3), 103–115. Galaţi: Europlus.

Tufiş, D., Ion, R. and Boroş, T. (2013) "Filtering, normalizing and spell-checking the Romanian N-grams from Google's Web 1t 5-grams". in Tufiş, D., Rus, V. and Forăscu, C. (eds.) *Towards Multilingual Europe 2020: A Romanian Perspective*, 123–142. Bucureşti: Romanian Academy Publishing House.

Ţeghiu, L. (2004) *Structuri stabile în limba română*. Timişoara: Marineasa.

Xiao, R. (2015) "Collocation". In Biber, D. and Reppen, R. (eds.) *The Cambridge Handbook of English Corpus Linguistics, Cambridge Handbooks in Language and Linguistics*, 106–124. Cambridge: Cambridge University Press. https://doi.org/10.1017/CBO9781139764377.007. (Accessed 10 March 2022).

Digital tools

Adam Kilgarriff, Vít Baisa, Jan Bušta, Miloš Jakubíček, Vojtěch Kovář, Jan Michelfeit, Pavel Rychlý, Vít Suchomel. The Sketch Engine: ten years on. *Lexicography*, 1: 7–36, 2014.

Tommaso Spinelli

Chapter 3 The Latin Diachronic Database: A New Digital Tool for the Study of Latin

Abstract: This article discusses the creation of an innovative digital toolkit for studying the frequency and the chronological development of the use of words in a very large corpus of Latin literature and epigraphy. By using original algorithms and the capabilities of recent open source lemmatising technologies, this new toolkit can query a 14-million-word-corpus that includes the works of 308 Latin authors and 521 000 inscriptions covering the 4th century BCE to the 6th century CE. In doing so, it empowers scholars and students to explore the usage of Latin lemmas (including their variants and homographs) across different time periods and linguistic registers for the first time, offering crucial statistical information to support philological, linguistic, and literary analysis.

Keywords: digital tool, digital tool for Latin, Latin diachronic database

1. Introduction

This paper discusses the creation of an innovative digital toolkit for studying the frequency and the chronological development of the use of words in a very large corpus of Latin literature and epigraphy. Designed to bridge teaching and research, the toolkit is currently accessible through the website of the University of St Andrews. Some of its data are also accessible through a Latin diachronic frequency dictionary that is forthcoming in the series *Digital Classics Books* (*Propylaeum*) (Spinelli, Fenzi, Short and Leslie forthcoming) edited by the Universities of Leipzig and Heidelberg.[1]

By using original algorithms, this toolkit empowers scholars and students to both detect interactions between literary and epigraphical texts, and explore the usage of Latin words (including their variants and

1 The Database can be accessed at https://doi.org/10.5281/zenodo.2562829.

homographs) across different time periods and linguistic registers for the first time, thus offering crucial statistical information to support philological, linguistic, and literary analysis. After providing a concise overview of the programme and previous attempts to study the frequency of Latin words in literary texts, this paper will discuss the methodological and practical issues faced by the creation of the toolkit, while also offering insights into the future developments of this project and its impact on research.

2. Theoretical background

Recent scholarship has increasingly emphasised the benefits of incorporating a diachronic perspective into research on Latin, as well as the necessity of setting elite literary texts in dialogue with documentary sources (e.g., inscriptions).[2] While grammarians and scholars have always used intuitions about the frequency of words to make stylistic claims, frequency information has begun to play a significant role in modern computational linguistics, in language pedagogy, in philology (where the rarity of a lemma is often considered a sign of authenticity for textual conjectures), and in literary studies because it provides statistical support for hypotheses about intertextuality.[3] In this perspective, scholars have stressed the importance of developing comprehensive chronologically annotated corpora that allow for diachronic analyses.[4] At the same time, studies on intermediality and intertextuality in different genres and media indicate that a considerable percentage of intertexts can be identified between literary and epigraphical

2 On intermediality, see König, Langlands and Uden 2020: 16 who propose the expansion of the concept of intertextuality to include references to the "material aspects of empire". See also Spinelli 2019 and Spinelli and Gregori 2019: 242–267. On diachrony, see McGillivray and Kilgarriff 2013.

3 On the use of the concept of word frequency in ancient authors, see Denooz 2010: 1–2. On the role of frequency in computational linguistics, see Dee 2002, Kornai et al. 2006, and Denooz 2010. On the role of frequency in language pedagogy, see Sinclair 1991; in philology, see Tov 1982; in literary studies, see Coffee 2018: 209.

4 See, for instance, McGillivray and Kilgarriff 2013.

texts, although these interplays tend to be based on similarities of meaning in the absence of explicit verbal allusions.[5]

In the last decade, several digital tools for the study of classical texts have been developed, but none of them, so far, has combined a comprehensive textual corpus with robust chronological, lexical and statistical analysis tools. In fact, existing digital technologies have so far tended to treat documentary and literary texts separately (cf. http://www.manfredclauss.de/; https://www.hs-augsburg.de/~harsch/augustana.html; https://www.degruyter.com/document/doi/10.1515/btl/html) and to offer only limited corpora to intertextual analysis (cf. https://tesserae.caset.buffalo.edu/; http://mizar.unive.it/mqdq/public/index). Some of these tools (e.g., https://latin.packhum.org/index) permit querying the occurrences of a stem or a specific inflected form in literary texts without any awareness of lemmas, while others require advanced technological knowledge (https://eureka.utexas.edu/project/quantitative-criticism-lab).[6]

However, some exceptions must be acknowledged. For example, the *Corpus Corporum* (http://www.mlat.uzh.ch/MLS/), offers the possibility of querying a large chronologically annotated corpus of Latin texts by lemma or word-form but only shows the texts in which the lemma or word-form appears without providing statistical data on its usage.[7] Leveraging the Latin corpus *LatinISE*, the premium programme *Sketch Engine* (https://www.sketchengine.eu/) offers the possibility of querying a large corpus of Latin texts broadly divided by era (e.g., "*era Romana antiqua*") in order to explore the frequency of Latin words, their synonyms, and collocations, though currently a proper diachronic analysis is not available for Latin texts.[8] Similarly, the few modern studies on the frequency of Latin lemmas have all been based on circumscribed corpora of only "highly representative", "golden-age" authors, and thus struggle to meet the demands of

5 See Rajewsky 2005, O'Gorman 2006, Coffee et al. 2012, and Milnor 2014. On the interactions between epigraphical and literary texts, see Cugusi 1996 and Gregori and Bianchini 2017: 8–10.

6 See also https://github.com/pjheslin/diogenes and https://outils.biblissima.fr/en/collatinus-web/.

7 See Roelli 2014.

8 For LatinISE and an overview of other Latin corpora, see McGillivray and Kilgarriff 2013.

modern researchers who are increasingly shifting their attention to the margins of literature of the early Republican, late Imperial, and Christian Eras.[9] The first of these studies was published by Gonzalez Lodge (1907) under the title *Vocabulary of High School Latin*. It used a corpus of only 77 142 words, yielding a list of 4 650 entries, excluding proper names. The second is Paul Diederich's *Frequency of Latin Words and their Endings* (1939), based on a corpus of 202 158 terms and featuring a list of 3 800 lexical entries. More recently, the *Laboratoire d'Analyse Statistique de la Langue Latine* of the University of Liège has published two editions (Delatte et al. 1981; Denooz 2010) of a Latin frequency dictionary created with the aid of digital technologies. While the first edition (*Dictionnaire Fréquentiel et Index Inverse de la Langue Latine*) used a corpus of 794 662 words, resulting in 13 077 lexical entries, the second edition (*Nouveau Lexique Fréquentiel de Latin*) includes some works of nineteen authors and a corpus of circa 1.7 million words resulting in 26 940 lexical entries.[10] Nevertheless, its corpus is still very much focused on texts of the so-called *saeculum aureum* and omits certain linguistically fundamental poems, such as Ovid's *Metamorphoses*. Thus, existing studies only record the number of occurrences of Latin words in their chosen corpus, but they do not provide any information on the historical development of the use of a term or how to interpret the statistical data they collect. Similarly, the still incomplete *Thesaurus Linguae Latinae* records only the

9 These studies are Lodge 1907, Diederich 1939, Delatte et al. 1981, and Denooz 2010. Although it represents the first attempt to provide a comprehensive and chronological analysis of Latin word-forms, the Thesaurus Formarum Totius Latinitatis published by Paul Tombeur in 1998 cannot be considered a frequency lexicon because it records inflected and non-lemmatised word-forms. Instead, the dictionary by Dee 2002 (which is no longer available) used to be a digital collation of two former dictionaries (Lodge 1907; Diederich 1939).

10 The corpus assembled by the Laboratoire between 1961 and 1981 included: Catullus; Caesar, Bell. Gall.; Cicero, Catil., Manil., Nat. Deorum 3, Rabir., Tusc. Disp. 5; Hor. Od.; Juvenal; Ovid, Met. (selected passages); Persius; Propertius; Quintus Curtius; Sallust, Catil., Jug.; Seneca, Philosophica, Tragoediae; Tacitus, Agric., Ann., Dial., Germ.; Tibullus; Livy, (selected passages); Vergil, Buc., Georg., Aen. 1–6; Vitruvius, Arch. 1, 9, 10.

most significant occurrences of Latin lemmas.[11] At this critical juncture, the *Latin Diachronic Database* aims to align with recent developments in the fields of computational linguistics, intertextuality, and intermediality, by offering historical, statistical (and soon semantic) information for Latin texts within a wide-ranging, inclusive corpus.

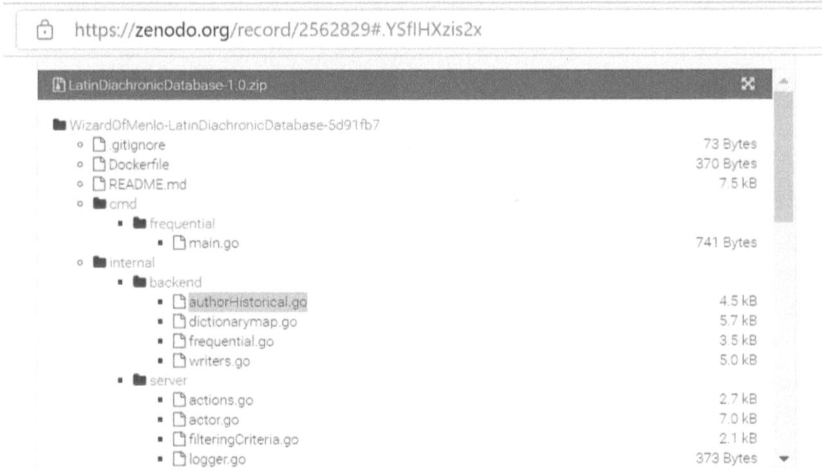

Fig. 1. The Database's repository

3. The Latin Diachronic Database

The *Latin Diachronic Database* and its forthcoming user-friendly web application offer several unique features to meet modern scholarly needs. The most striking feature of this resource is its attempt to be comprehensive. Currently, the *Latin Diachronic Database* permits users to search a generically and chronologically diverse set of texts spanning the 4th century BCE to the late 5th century CE. Based on a textual database yielding some 14 000 000 words, which represents most of extant Latin classical

11 Cf. the ThLL Praemonenda (p. 30): "only in the case of rare words can an article cite all the examples contained in the archive… the commonest usages are illustrated as a rule only a few further examples".

literature, this corpus covers the works of 308 authors, fragmentary and anonymous texts, works that are usually considered "secondary" by scholastic curricula, and 521 532 epigraphs. The choice of using such a variety of texts is motivated by methodological concerns. Replacing editorial selection of a small group of supposedly "highly representative" texts with a larger textual corpus that provides more empirical data is fundamental to ensuring that the analysis of a language is scientific and unbiased. Moreover, only an extensive corpus allows the accurate exploration of the chronological evolution of the use of a word, without the risk of prioritising the literature of the so-called *aureum saeculum*. Thus, moving beyond this practical and methodological limit of past frequency studies, the *Latin Diachronic Database* tries to deliver a more realistic and empirical history of the Latin language, but also offers the opportunity to explore if and to what extent the computerised analysis of a "Big Data" corpus produces results that are significantly different from those deriving from the small and hand-curated corpora of former frequency dictionaries.

The basic function performed by the database is calculating the frequency of Latin lemmas in literary and epigraphical texts, or in selected centuries, authors and works. As we shall see better in the following section, because Latin is a highly inflected language, this function involves parsing, lemmatising, and categorising the data directly from the sources. In this respect, the database is able not only to count different inflected word-forms under their appropriate lemma, but also to recognise the presence of homographic forms (i.e., graphically identical forms belonging to different lemmas) so as to signal the number of "certain" occurrences of a lemma and the number of "ambiguous" occurrences of a lemma, due to the presence of potential homographs.

Another innovative feature of the *Latin Diachronic Database* is its attention to diachronic development of the Latin language. While Latin frequency dictionaries tend to record the occurrences of Latin lemmas without providing information on their chronological development, the *Latin Diachronic Database* leverages a unique chronologically annotated corpus in which authors and works are divided by century. Divisions by century have been chosen because this provides the most accurate and easy-to-read summary of the history of a word: other organising principles such as a statistic-based division into linguistic eras (e.g., archaic, classical, late) or a division on the basis of the chronology of single classical texts would provide a less consistent presentation of the diachronic data, as the precise date of composition of many classical texts is unknown and the division between different linguistic "eras" is inevitably arbitrary. Leveraging these chronological annotations, the programme calculates not only the number of authors and epigraphs in which a Latin lemma occurs, but also the occurrences of the lemma in each century, or in the centuries selected by the user. Moreover, original algorithms allow the programme to calculate the relative frequency of the lemma in individual authors, who are named in Latin (e.g., *Gaius Suetonius Tranquillus*) following the convention of the *PHI* corpus.[12] These historical data provide invaluable help to linguistic and literary analysis by affording the possibility of obtaining frequency information for lemmas in different authors over the history of Latin literature.

This is helpful for both high-frequency words, for which the *ThLL* does not always provide complete listings of occurrences, and for low-frequency and rare words. In the latter case, rare use of a term by authors might suggest meaningful literary interactions.

The *Latin Diachronic Database* can also perform a more complex statistical analysis on the use of Latin lemmas. For example, it can be used to calculate the "rate of incidence" of a word in the works of an author or in a century. The rate of incidence per century provides information on the

12 The Packard Humanities Institute (PHI) corpus is one of the widest open-source Latin corpora currently available online (https://latin.packhum.org/) and, although it does not match our corpus perfectly, it can be effectively used to doublecheck the information provided by the Latin Diachronic Database and to look up the large majority of the Latin passages in which our lemmas or their inflected forms appear. However, while our programme lemmatises every inflected form, the PHI searching tool performs a simple pattern-matching query. Thus, if one searches "ultor" the programme shows also results like "multorum", unless the search is made for a specific form like "ultor". In this case the programme displays only the occurrences of this specific graphic form and not of the lemma ultor and of its inflected forms.

ratio (out of a thousand) of occurrences of the lemma in the given century to the total number of occurrences of the forms of that word. This figure gives an immediate idea of the popularity of the lemma in each century. Similarly, the rate of incidence for each author indicates the percentage of occurrences of a given word out of a thousand in the extant texts of that author – information crucial for understanding the significance of the statistical data.

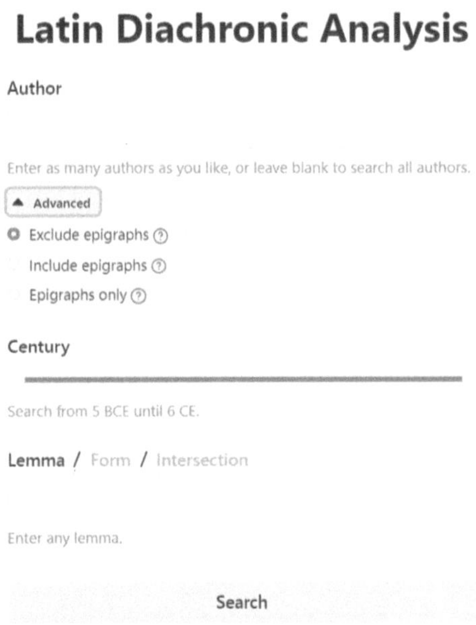

Fig. 2. The Database's web application

For instance, the 14 308 occurrences of the lemma *ut* in Cicero mean that the word is used around 9 times every thousand words, while the 5 occurrences of the same form in the *Laus Pisonis* mean that, on average, the word is used 2 times every thousand words. This is because the simple number of occurrences of a word in the works of an author is not necessarily significant, insofar as its significance largely depends on the number of words preserved for that author in the *Latin Diachronic Database*. In other words, it would be misleading to think that 100 occurrences of a form in the attested corpus of the works of Cicero have the same statistical significance as 100 occurrences of the same form in a much smaller text such as the *Laus Pisonis*. The rate of incidence has thus been introduced to give an immediate indication of how often a term is used in comparison to the extent of an author's surviving *oeuvre*. This information could inform stylistic as well as textual-critical research, as it provides crucial information on which terms are more likely to be used by an author and, therefore, what conjectural readings might represent the *lectio facilior* or *difficilior* for a text.

Finally, while the programme is currently available only to expert users, our corpus will soon enable complex statistical analysis through a simple, intuitive web application. Through the interface, users will be presented with an intuitive search box where the names of the authors that they want to include in their query can be selected. An "advanced search" button will allow users to specify limitations on the search parameters, such as using an interactive timeline to limit the chronological range of a query. A text search bar then allows the user to specify the lemma or inflected word-forms to find in the selected texts. For word searches, the programme will return the total number of occurrences of the specified lemma or word-form; the number of potentially homographic forms; the authors, works and centuries in which the word appears; and the "incidence" of that word in the extant corpus of each author (i.e., the percentage of occurrences of the given word out of a thousand, based on the number of extant words for that author). Users will then be able to view the specific passages of text in which the word occurs.

4. Technologies

The technologies used to develop the program underpinning the *Latin Diachronic Database* are highly advanced and closely tailored to its aims and function. This complex program is organised in different packages that govern, respectively, the chronological mapping of authors and texts, the lemmatisation of the textual corpus, and the frequential statistics of the words most commonly attested in Latin literature, and their visualisation through a user-friendly web app.[13] This section discusses the most important technologies and methodological issues concerning the backend.

---

13 These packages are freely accessible through the program's repositories: https://doi.org/10.5281/zenodo.2562829, https://github.com/WizardOfMenlo/LatinDiachronicDatabase/tree/1.0.

The first stage of the development of the *Latin Diachronic Database* was the creation of a standardised digital corpus of Latin texts. This corpus was created at the University of St Andrews using different opensource textual databases available online such as *Perseus*, the *PHI* database, and the *Bibliotheca Augustana*, while the epigraphical corpus was kindly provided by Manfred Clauss.[14] Both the Latin diachronic frequency dictionary and the *Database*'s web application will allow users to query the data derived from the corpus without making the corpus itself publicly available or downloadable in accordance with its distribution licence. However, users can feed into the programme a personalised textual corpus on which they can run our program by using, for example, the textual databank provided by *Perseus*, or the *Packard Humanities Institute* both online and on CD.

The most challenging aspect of the creation of the database was counting and lemmatising Latin words. Due to Latin being a highly inflected language, elaborating frequential data on the usage of Latin words through the centuries involved parsing, lemmatising, and categorising the data from the sources, which means scanning the pre-assembled and standardised textual corpus in order to identify the different inflected forms of each Latin lemma. While most previous studies have relied on a manual processing of texts, the *Latin Diachronic Database* uses original algorithms and the capabilities of the open source lemmatisation service offered by *Lemlat*.[15] Lemmatisation is the process through which the variants of a term, and its inflected or graphically different forms (e.g., *amat, amant, amas, amavi, amatum*; to love), are attributed to their lemma: the standard form of the word (e.g., *amo*) as it appears in a dictionary. Many programmes can perform this task on Latin texts quite successfully (e.g., the Schinke algorithm, the *Perseus* lemmatiser, *PROIEL*, *Parsley*, *Morpheus*, Whitaker's *Words*, *LatMor*), but none of these technologies provides entirely correct data.[16] Among them, we have chosen to use a freely adapted version of

---

14 On Perseus see http://www.perseus.tufts.edu/hopper/; the Bibliotheca Augustana can be accessed at http://www.hs-augsburg.de/~harsch/a_impressum.html.

15 Cf. http://www.ilc.cnr.it/Lemlat/Lemlat/index.html

16 See, for instance, LatMor (http://cistern.cis.lmu.de), Words (http://archives.nd.edu/words.html), Parsley (https://github.com/goldibex/parsleycore), PRO IEL(https://github.com/mlj/proielwebapp/tree/master/lib/morphology), and

Lemlat2.0.[17] Based on a database of 40 014 lexical entries and 43 432 lemmas including many late antique and medieval terms, *Lemlat* adopts the standards of the *Oxford Latin Dictionary* (Glare 1982). Being able to recognise over 97 % of Latin terms including many anthroponyms and toponyms, it successfully lemmatises 319 725 lexemes into 30 413 lexical entries (around 3 500 more than the modern Liège dictionary by Denooz). Moreover, its automatic analysis is very accurate and takes into account many spelling variations and even rare or archaic forms of a lemma which the former frequency dictionaries neglect. However, this technology is still undergoing further development and cannot disambiguate homographic forms that are therefore counted (as potentially ambiguous) under all the lemmas which they can belong to.

The most important element of this package of the programme is the lemmatiser itself. The lemmatiser is a "csv" file directly exported (with adaptations) from *Lemlat* to specify the lemmatisation bases that are used to operate on the texts. This package also contains an original "runner" program that is in charge of the full *GraphQL* endpoint, being used to query the text through the generic command: "*cargo run--bin {program_name}--- aAUTHORS_FILE-dDATA_DIR-lLEMM_FILE*". There, the options *authors_file, data_dir, lemm_file* are used to specify the data files on which to operate. Another folder (*author_historical*) contains a database with the chronology of Latin authors which can be used to perform diachronic linguistic searches on specific centuries. The data can be then exported using the "csv" function. Conceptually, this system works as a "forest" of sorts, with one tree for each lemma, one leaf for each form, and each form with a collection of occurrences. The data obtained from this system is semi-structured (data is fully tagged, but its structure is not rigidly defined, allowing for great flexibility in terms of exporting it), and the entire system operates without interacting with the disk. Leveraging this core system, two applications can query the relational databases (texts,

---

Morpheus (https://github.com/tmallon/morpheus). On these technologies, see Springmann, Schmid and Dietmar 2016.

17 The programme is available at http://www.ilc.cnr.it/Lemlat/Lemlat/index.html. See also https://github.com/CIRCSE/LEMLAT3. On its features and assessment see Passarotti et al. 2017: 24–31 and Springmann, Schmid and Dietmar 2016.

lemmatiser, and chronological authors map), and generate the results requested by users in different formats (e.g., Json, txt, Excel).[18]

5. Implementation

The *Latin Diachronic Database*'s web application will offer an innovative feature that is being currently developed to further support literary research. Called "intersection", this new functionality will allow users to compare specific texts or authors. Using this function, users will be able to create lists of rare words used only by the user-selected authors (e.g., Ovid and Statius) within a chosen timeframe, or generate a list of potential verbal and semantic similarities (based on very low-frequency words) between selected works (e.g., Virgil's *Aeneid* and epigraphs composed after the 1st century CE).

These lists of words shared only by two authors in selected centuries may reveal meaningful intertexts, spurring new insights into Latin literature and its interconnections: for example, although the author Statius is famous for his allusions to Vergil (e.g., *Theb.* 12.816), a preliminary test of our tool has revealed that he used a large number of lemmas (e.g., *anguicomus, inamoenus, oblectamen*, etc.) whose only prior attestation is in Ovid, suggesting that scholarship has – unwittingly – ignored a potent source of literary inspiration. Moreover, this function can help identify epigraphical allusions to literary works that are corrupted in the manuscripts, facilitating reconstruction of the lost text (e.g., *in/ad undas*, Ov. *Met.* 3.272, 1st cent. C.E.; *ad undas*, *CIL* 06, 21521, 1st cent. CE; *ad undas*, *CIL* 11, 06435, 2nd cent. CE).

A future development of the programme will involve the creation of a new function to query the texts semantically. Leveraging the lists of Latin synonyms offered by Tommaso Spinelli's *Online Dictionary of Latin Synonyms* and by William Short's *Latin Wordnet* project, this new functionality will enable users to search not only for a Latin word like *bellum* ("war") to see all of its occurrences across the corpus but also (by concept)

18 Samples of potential results are available at https://github.com/latineloquamur/Latineloquamur-toolkit-IPA-transcriber-and-App/blob/master/src/sample_frequency_list_data.txt and https://latin.netlify.com/.

for the English word "war", which will produce results for all Latin words of the same or similar meaning: e.g., *bellum*, *proelium*, *dimicatio*, *luctus*, *conflictus*, and even (figuratively) *Mars*.

6. Conclusion

Overall, in its interdisciplinary focus on the development of innovative resources for the study of classical texts, the *Latin Diachronic Database* brings immediate benefits to scholarship by providing scholars and students with a reliable digital tool to query a very large corpus of Latin literary and epigraphical texts, and to consult chronological and statistical data that can support their literary, philological, and intertextual research. More specifically, by showing which authors or inscriptions have used a Latin term and in which century, this tool provides commentary-writers with invaluable information about the usage of words in a given period, genre, author or specific work. By indicating how often a term is used in comparison with other works, authors, or periods, this information could inform stylistic as well as textual-critical research, as it enables statistically informed inferences to be made about what terms are more likely to be used by an author and, therefore, what conjectural readings might represent the *lectio facilior* or *difficilior* for a given text at a given point in the language's history.

More generally, the current pandemic has shown the importance of reliable digital corpora and research tools that enable scholars to conduct their research while having limited access to physical libraries. In allowing a more flexible, inclusive and sustainable way of doing research, the *Latin Diachronic Database* will play a critical role in post-pandemic world to make classical studies more inclusive and available to scholars and students from disadvantaged areas and backgrounds. The successful development of this project also shows the vitality, potential and forward-looking attitude of classical studies in a moment in which their suitability for students' intellectual and professional growth tends to be questioned.

References

Coffee, N. et al. (2012) "Intertextuality in the digital age". *TAPA* 142(2), 383–422.

Coffee, N. (2018) "An agenda for the study of intertextuality". *TAPA* 148, 205–223.

Cugusi, P. (1996) *Aspetti letterari dei* Carmina Latina Epigraphica. Bologna: Pàtron.

Dee, J. (2002) "The first downloadable word-frequency database for classical and medieval Latin". *CJ*, 98, 59–67.

Delatte, L. et al. (1981) *Dictionnaire Fréquentiel et Index Inverse de la Langue Latine*. Liège: L.A.S.L.A.

Denooz, J. (2010) *Nouveau Lexique Fréquentiel de Latin*. Hildesheim/Zürich/New York: Georg Olms Verlag.

Diederich, P. (1939) *The Frequency of Latin Words and Their Endings*. Chicago: University of Chicago Press.

Glare, P. G. W. (1982) *Oxford Latin Dictionary*. New York: Oxford University Press Oxford.

Gregori, G. L. Bianchini, G. (2017) "Tra epigrafia, letteratura e filologia". In Dondine-Payr, M., *Esclaves et Maîtres dans le Monde Romain*, 141–159. Rome: École Française de Rome.

König, A., Langlands, R. and Uden, J. (Eds.) (2020). *Literature and Culture in the Roman Empire, 96–235: Cross-Cultural Interactions*. Cambridge and New York: Cambridge University Press.

Kornai, A. et al. (2006) "Web-based frequency dictionaries for medium density languages". *Proceedings of the 2nd International Workshop on Web as Corpus*, Trento, Italy, 1 April, 1–8.

Lodge, G. (1907) *The Vocabulary of High School Latin: Being the Vocabulary Of: Caesar's Gallic War, Books IV; Cicero Against Catiline, on Pompey's Command, for the Poet Archias; Vergil's Æneid, Books I-VI; Arranged Alphabetically and in the Order of Occurrence (No. 9)*. NewYork: Columbia University Press.

McGillivray, B. and Kilgarriff, A. (2013) "Tools for historical corpus research, and a corpus of Latin". In Bennett, P., Durell, M., Scheible, S. and Whitt, R. J. (Eds.), *New Methods in Historical Corpus Linguistics* 1(3), 247–257. Tübingen: Gunter Narr Verlag.

Milnor, K. (2014) *Graffiti and the literary landscape in Roman Pompeii*. Oxford: Oxford University Press.

O'Gorman, E. (2006) "Intertextuality, time and historical understanding". In Macfie, A. (Ed.), *The Philosophy of History*, 116–137. London: Palgrave Macmillan.

Passarotti, M. et al. (2017) "The 'Lemlat3.0' package for morphological analysis of Latin". *Proceedings of the NoDaLiDa* 133(6), 24–31.

Rajewsky, I. (2005) "Intermediality, intertextuality, and remediation: A literary perspective on intermediality". *Intermédialités* 6, 43–64.

Roelli, P. (2014) "The *Corpus Corporum*, a new open Latin text repository and tool". *Archivum Latinitatis Medii Aevi-Bulletin du Cange* 72, 289–304.

Sinclair, J. (1991) *Corpus, Concordance, Collocation*. Oxford: Oxford University Press.

Spinelli, T. (2019) "The Argos narrative in Statius' *Thebaid*: A New Ovidian Perseid?". *American Journal of Philology* 140(2), 291–315.

Spinelli, T. and Gregori, G. L. (2019) "(Un)damning sub-plots: Re-reading the principate of Domitian in light of fresh material evidence". *Illinois Classical Studies* 44(2), 242–267.

Spinelli, T., Fenzi, G., Short, W. M. and Leslie, J. (forthcoming). *The Diachronic Frequency of Latin Words*. Digital Classics Books. Propylaeum.

Springmann, U., Schmid, H. and Dietmar, N. (2016) "LatMor: A Latin finite-state morphology encoding vowel quantity" *Open Linguistics – Topical Issue on Treebanking and Ancient Languages: Current and Prospective Research* 2(1), 386–392.

Tombeur, P. (Ed.) (1998) *Thesaurus formarum totius Latinitatis: a Plauto usque ad saeculum XXum*. Turnhout: Brepols.

Tov, E. (1982) "Criteria for evaluating textual readings: The limitations of textual rules". *Harvard Theological Review* 75(4), 429–448.

Cecilia Mihaela Popescu and Oana-Adriana Duță

Chapter 4 A Proposal for a Multilingual E-Glossary of Discourse Markers

Abstract: Our paper aims to describe a proposal to design a multilingual electronic glossary of discourse markers in English and several Romance languages – French, Spanish and Romanian. Discourse and pragmatic markers are functional units, universally present in human language, that deictically relate text fragments, propositions, utterances, and discourse chunks to the context of the speech, managing the interaction of the discourse participants in the speech situation and facilitating successful communication (Remberger 2021). Concretely, our approach aims to outline the main linguistic features that are valid for each type of use of the relevant discourse markers, presenting a general frame that will focus on linguistic, etymological, and pragmatic-discursive aspects.

Keywords: multilingual e-glossary, discourse markers in English, discourse markers in Romance languages

1. Introduction

This article aims to present a proposal to design a multilingual electronic glossary of discourse markers in Romanian and in several foreign languages – English, French and Spanish. Due to their wide array of pragmatic meanings and values, the translation of discourse markers from one language into another is a particularly challenging task as shown, among others, by Crible et al. (2019: 139–155) or Iliescu et al. (2021: 1385–1349). Hence, a multilingual resource would be especially useful not only for translation studies, but also for foreign language acquisition as well.

After a theoretical overview of the notion of *discourse markers* (in Section 2), with the purpose of outlining the main features of this pragma-linguistic category of items, and after a contextualization of similar projects existing in the literature (such as, for instance, Briz, Pons and Portolés [2008] or Vorobey [2011]) (see Section 3), we propose, in Section 4, starting from concrete examples, a general frame of lexicographical operation, that would emphasize etymological aspects, as well as the functional and pragmatic-discursive behaviour of lexical-pragmatic units that may be included in such a multilingual glossary.

2. Discourse markers – An overview

The study of units with a discursive-pragmatic meaning is a recent research trend in linguistic pragmatics and the use of the relevant terminology is not unequivocal, as also outlined by Ştefănescu: "There are multiple classifications, a wide variety of terminological choices and the effects of connectors are extremely diverse" (Ştefănescu 2007: 260).[1] Indeed, linguists have been dealing with a variation between notions such as *pragmatic marker/discourse marker/connector*, with the second one being the most widely used in scientific literature.

Discourse markers (hereinafter referred to as DMs) generally refer, *in extenso*, to a wide array of items, most often morphologically invariable and belonging to secondary morphological categories (adverbs, interjections, conjunctions) or being represented by entire phrases. The category of DMs includes, for instance: Rom. *însă, atunci, deci, bine, păi, iată, hai, de fapt, cu alte cuvinte, pe de altă parte, care va să zică, ştii, hai, mă rog*; Fr. *mais, alors, donc, ben, voilà, en fait, voyons*; Engl. *then, now, so, furthermore, eventually, actually, I mean, on the other hand, however*. These units reflect discursive-pragmatic information, i.e., they have textual and/or communicative meaning and they carry at least one of the following functional features:

(i) they are non-referential units, with no contribution to the global meaning of the sentence; their presence or absence in the sentence does not change the informative propositional content: *Ne vedem **atunci** la ora 3! '**Then** let's meet at three o'clock'* vs. *Ne vedem Ø la ora 3! 'Ø Let's meet at three o'clock!'*;

(ii) They provide some "guidance" on how the discourse was drawn up and/or must or can be interpreted (see Bazzanella 1995: 225; Ghezzi and Molinelli 2014). In other words, such units have a *procedural function* according to O. Ducrot and the Geneva School, i.e., they

1 Unless otherwise mentioned, all the translations into English belong to the authors of this article.

serve to guide "las inferencias que se producen en la comunicaciones y (...) facilitar, en consecuencia, el proceso cognitivo" ("the inferences that occur in communication and, consequently, facilitate the cognitive process", Sainz 2012: 735).

Besides these major features, discourse markers frequently form independent prosodic units, properly outlined by means of intonation or other paraverbal methods. They are speech parts and belong to a macro-syntax of discourse, they belong to both written and spoken style and are highly mobile at the sentence level, i.e., they can appear at the beginning, middle or end of a sentence. Additionally, they are multifunctional units, having various functions and argumentative roles on an intra-discursive and cross-discursive level. Discourse markers are the outcome of pragmaticalization processes, as they frequently migrate from the lexical – more seldom from the grammatical – area to the pragmatic area, generally retaining their "core meaning" (see Bazzanella 1994; Doestie and Pusch 2007: 3–4).

There is a more or less clear distinction in scientific literature between *discourse markers* and *pragmatic markers* (e.g., Schiffrin 2001). According to this dichotomic perspective, a *discourse marker* acquires a restricted meaning, referring to marks of cohesion and consistency, with a procedural function on the discourse and/or text level, ensuring:

> "legătura formală şi semantică dintre componentele enunţului, participând la coeziunea şi coerenţa tematică a textului şi orientează interpretarea lecturii enunţului, facilitând configurarea sensului textual" [a formal and semantic link between the elements of the sentence, participating in the thematic cohesion and consistency of the text and guides the interpretation of the sentence, facilitating the configuration of the textual meaning]
>
> Chiorean (2013: 298).

Moreover, Chiara Ghezzi (2014: 5) offers a similar perspective:

> "[...] the term *discourse marker* [our emphasis] is mainly used to refer to elements that index the structure of discourse, functioning as discourse-cohesive devices that stress intra-discourse relations and specify how the message, or its content is related to the preceding and following discourse or the extralinguistic situation"
>
> Ghezzi (2014: 15).

In *Enciclopedia Treccani*, Carla Bazzanella (2011) proposes a detailed functional classification of DMs, which can be synthesized into: (a) interactional functions; (b) metatextual functions (*delimitation markers*, *focalization markers, rephrasing markers*) and (c) cognitive functions of DMs (*procedural markers, epistemic markers, intensity mechanisms*) (Bazzanella 2011).

Similarly, H. Rosén outlines four types of functions for discourse markers in the age of Classical Latin: (a) production of textual coherence; (b) discourse organization and communication management; (c) modalization and illocutionary identification; (d) focus marking (Rosén 2009: 326).

On the other hand, the notion of *pragmatic marker* could also be used either with a restricted meaning, derived from the above-mentioned dichotomic perspective, i.e., units (particles, adverbs, conjunctions, interjections, vocatives, quantifiers, intensifiers, etc.) whose meaning is constructed based on the communicative context, or as an umbrella concept, an archi-lexeme having the same meaning as the extended meaning of a *discourse marker*. For instance, Fraser classifies pragmatic markers into the following categories: (i) basic (illocutionary force) markers; (ii) commentary pragmatic markers; (iii) parallel markers; (iv) discourse markers (Fraser 1996: 167), while Portolés proposes a similar classification of markers into: (i) information structuring markers; (ii) reformulation markers; (iii) discursive operators; (iii) contact control markers (Portolés 1998).

Thus, we observe from the latter classifications that DMs represent a distinct category of pragmatic markers, probably because their discursive values often generate pragmatic meanings/interpretations, so that the same item can have both types of functions, or because both categories of markers (discursive and pragmatic) depend on the context/co-text from which they extract their meaning.

In our proposal, DMs are defined based on the previously presented extended definition, which means that we focus on non-referential discursive units that have a textual or communicative procedural function on the intra- and inter-discursive level.

3. State of the art

Recent attempts to create glossaries of discourse markers have focused mostly on monolingual data. These resources are nevertheless instrumental in our endeavour since they provide us with an inventory of words and their meanings/definitions. Moreover, these glossaries are drawn up based on various methodologies and envisaging a variety of purposes, which results in their heterogeneity.

In their *Diccionario de partículas discursivas del español* (2008), Briz, Pons and Portolés propose a fully online resource of Spanish discourse particles, in which an entry has the following structure: *editor, definition (the basic or fundamental meaning, which is the same for all uses, illustrated with an example), geographical distribution (if applicable), further examples, translations (into English, Italian, Portuguese), prosody and punctuation, further uses, position, syntax, register, less frequent variants, conversational formulae, similar particles*. Although the entries do include a *translation* heading, the basic approach is not fully cross-linguistic, but mostly focuses on explaining the Spanish term to foreign natives. For instance, the *translation* heading for the Spanish phrase *al final* includes the following text: *Le marqueur espagnol « al final » présente le membre du discourso ù il apparaît comme le terme d'un processus ou d'une situation qui se produit après une suite d'événements* (Briz, Pons and Portolés 2008).

Kobozeva and Zakharov discuss dictionaries of Russian DMs and argue that the available resources present several drawbacks. They consider that a fully-fledged dictionary of DMs should include the following types of information: *graphic information (spelling, punctuation), phonetic information (transcription, prosodic information, sound files), syntactic information (linear position, possibility of independent use, argument structure), semantic information (explication, paradigmatic relations), communicative information, pragmatic information, paralinguistic information, derivational information, bibliography* (Kobozeva and Zakharov 2004).

Giampieri (2018) reviews the presence of discourse markers in dictionaries for Italian learners of English as a second language and proposes a frame that first classifies these units into one-word discourse markers and multi-word discourse markers and then inventories their functions in alphabetical order according to literature. For instance, for the discourse marker *right*, Giampieri proposes the following entry:

> "*RIGHT* = an interactive and flow-sustaining tool (...) aimed at: eliciting a reaction from or exercising control over the addressee(s); signalling the end of the topic or to move on – when marked by falling intonation"
>
> Giampieri (2018)

while the proposed entries for the cross-linguistic dimension take into consideration information from both lexicographic (Cambridge, Collins, Oxford Learners', Hoepli) and online-based sources (Reverso.com), as well as possibilities of back translation, in order to ensure the full rendition of all possible valences (Giampieri 2018).

Finally, Vorobey (2011) offers a contrastive analysis of *pragmatemes*[2] from several languages from the point of view of their onomasiological classification. The French-Spanish-Russian pragmatemes dictionary proposed by her is designed for foreign languages teaching/learning and is divided into 14 thematic groups, with an entry being structured according to the following headings:

Conceptual representation	**Situation of communication**	**Pragmateme in French**	**Variant of pragmateme**	**Synonym of pragmateme**
Il faut conserver le produit au frais (It is necessary to keep the product cold)	[sur un emballage] (On the package)	*Conserver au frais* (Keep in cold)	*Garder au frais* (Save in cold)	*A conserver à l'abri de la chaleur* (Keep away from heat)

Tab. 1. The structure of an entry for a French pragmateme in Vorobey's dictionary (2011)

4. Our approach

Against this background and given the importance of these lexical units in terms of speech production, but also in terms of foreign language acquisition and translation, a dictionary of discourse markers becomes a strong necessity. Our linguistic approach envisages two phases of elaboration.

2 Defined by Vorobey as discursive units resulting from a pragmaticalization process.

A first phase will imply the selection of DMs and a description of each unit on a monolingual level in Romanian, similarly to the models presented above – on the one hand in terms of the traditional etymological-phonetic and semantic-syntactic description, as detailed by Kobozeva and Zakharov (2004) or Briz, Pons and Portolés (2008) on the other hand, in terms of the specific discursive-textual and pragmatic meanings, as proposed by Giampieri 2018. The second phase will consist of a cross-linguistic corpus-based approach, again with Romanian as a starting point and equivalences in English, French and Spanish.[3]

On a macro-structural level, the glossary[4] will be structured alphabetically, with Romanian as a starting point, similarly to Briz, Pons and Portolés (2008). The glossary is intended to be searchable and allow cross-referencing.

On a micro-structural level, each entry will include – besides morphological, etymological and syntactic data – the primary, secondary and pragmatic values of each Romanian DM, which are centralized and illustrated with examples from corpora of contemporary spoken language. The corpus of Romanian texts to be used includes CoRoLa (The Reference Corpus of the Contemporary Romanian Language 2014), the SWARA speech corpus (2017) and roTenTen (2016) (a Romanian corpus made up of texts collected from the internet, belonging to the TenTen corpus family, which includes all the Romance languages envisaged in our approach). Additionally, we will also consult samples of Romanian language in use, such as CLRVN (*Corpus de limbă română vorbită actuală nedialectală*), CORV (*Corpus de română vorbită 2002*) and IVRLA II (*Interacţiunea verbală în limba română actuală 2002*). These resources provide an accurate image of today's written and spoken Romanian. Thereafter, the excerpted examples will be translated into three foreign languages: English, French and Spanish. The translations will be done by linguists specialized in each of the above-mentioned foreign language, based on their professional and

---

3 This approach could subsequently be extended for other languages, such as Italian and Portuguese.

4 We propose the term "glossary" instead of its partial synonym "dictionary", since our approach envisages a specific domain of knowledge, i.e., discourse markers.

linguistic expertise. The translators will analyse the value of the DM in each selected context and will look for the optimal equivalences in the target languages. The resulting equivalences will also be verified by means of searches in corpora of contemporary spoken language for each of the three languages : e.g., the British National Corpus (2009) for English, CEFC (n.d.) for French and the CREA (n.d.) corpus for Spanish. As for the electronic interface and the software programmes, they will be decided when the team will be extended with computational linguists and IT specialists.

However, the approach faces a significant range of challenges, since the meaning of discourse markers is derived from their context, and such communication contexts are generally quite diverse. This means that such a glossary would have to be comprehensive enough to encompass a wide array of values and meanings, also keeping in mind the principles of economy and achievability. Furthermore, a Romanian discourse marker may have several equivalents (not only discourse markers, but also paraphrastic structures) in a foreign language.

In the following table, we present an indicative frame for the entry of the Romanian adverb *cică* in the proposed glossary, as a sample of the work algorithm.

Tab. 2. The entry for the Romanian adverb *cică* in our proposed glossary

***cică*. Adv. First attested in Romanian in 1850, in the works of Vasile Alecsandri (see RDW 1986–1989, vol. I, s.v. *cică*). It originates from the apheresized agglutinated structure [[se zi]ce+că], formed by the dicendi verb *a zice* "to say" < Lat. *dicere* used in the 3rd person singular of the present of indicative and the complementizer *că*.**					
Values	**Functions**	**Examples of use**	**Equivalences**		
			English	French	Spanish
I. reportative evidential meaning	complex sentence/ phrastic adverb with an impersonal meaning, frequently used at the beginning or in the middle of the sentence and, most often, right next to the predication	***Cică*** *era odată un om însurat, și omul acela trăia la un loc cu soacră-sa.* (Ion Creangă, *Prostia omenească*, in Archeus.ro 2006–2020)	***They say/It is said*** *that a married man once lived, and that he lived with his mother-in-law.*	*Ø Il y avait une fois un homme marié, et cet homme vivait avec sa belle-mère.*	***Dizque*** *había una vez un hombre casado, y ese hombre vivía con su suegra.*
	predicative adverb (similarly to "probably", "of course", etc.), with an expressed or deducted subject (frequently human), indicating the exact source of information and having the value of a dicendi verb followed by a complementizer (v. Cruschina, Remberger 2008: 109; Zafiu 2020)	***Cică*** *ar fi reclamat cineva că în bloc se aude muzică popular* (https://www.digi24.ro/stiri/actualitate/social/mama-unei-fetite-de-2-ani-sanctionata-de-politisti-din-cauza-ca-micuta-face-zgomot-in-apartament-1306345)	***Allegedly*** *someone complained about folk music being heard in the building.*	***Prétendument*** *quelqu'un s'est plaint de la musique folk entendue dans le bâtiment.*	***Dizque*** *alguien se habría quejado de que en el edificio se oía música folclórica.*

(*Continued*)

Tab. 2. Continued

***cică.* Adv. First attested in Romanian in 1850, in the works of Vasile Alecsandri (see RDW 1986–1989, vol. I, s.v. *cică*). It originates from the apheresized agglutinated structure [[se zi]ce+că], formed by the dicendi verb *a zice* "to say" < Lat. *dicere* used in the 3rd person singular of the present of indicative and the complementizer *că*.**					
II. modal-epistemic meaning	doubt, lack of commitment, lack of trust in an opinion	*Se pare că și sufletul tău va avea parte de odihna veșnică din rai în care,* ***cică****, nu se muncește.* *<u>Dar</u> pe pământ trebuie să….* (Cu Dumnezeu înainte, by Emil Wagner, in CoRoLa)	*Apparently, your heart will also get the eternal rest in heaven where,* ***they say****, one does not work.* *<u>But</u>, on earth, one must…*	*Apparemment, votre cœur obtiendra aussi le repos éternel au ciel où,* ***disent-ils****, on ne travaille pas.* *<u>Mais</u>, sur la terre, il faut…*	*Parece que tu alma también obtendrá su descanso eterno en el paraíso, donde* ***dizque*** *uno no tiene que trabajar.* *<u>Pero</u> en la tierra hay que…*
		Și au venit unii, ***cică*** *[de la Protecția Consumatorilor] și ne-au amendat.*(CoRoLa, in Zafiu 2020)	*And some people came,* ***apparently*** *[from Consumer Protection] and fined us.*	*Et certaines personnes sont venues,* ***apparemment*** *[de la Protection des consommateurs] et nous ont imposé une amende.*	*Y ciertas personas aparecieron,* ***dizque*** *[de Protección de consumidores] y nos pusieron una multa.*
III. pragmatic-discursive meaning	used in the opening formulae of fairy tales (20) or anecdotes/jokes (21), also functioning as an indicator of the fictionality of certain types of discourse (Pop 2017)	*Amu* ***cică*** *era odată într-o țară un crai, care avea trei feciori* (Ion Creangă, *Povestea lui Harap-Alb*, in archeus.ro 2006–2020).	*Now,* ***they say*** *there was once, in a country, a king who had three sons.*	*Maintenant,* ***ils disent qu****'il était une fois, dans un pays, un roi qui avait trois fils*	*Ahora,* ***dizque*** *había una vez un rey que tenía tres hijos.*

	a marker of non-paraphrastic rephrasing	*Amu o scornit <u>alta</u>:* ***cică** să-i aducă pe fata împăratului-Roș!* (Creangă, *Povestiri*, in DLRLC1955–1957).	*Now he wants <u>something else</u>:* ***he says** he wants the daughter of the Red Emperor!*	*Maintenant il veut <u>autre chose</u> :* ***il dit** qu'il veut la fille de l'Empereur Rouge!*	*Ahora quiere <u>otra cosa</u>: **¡dizque** le traiga a la hija del Emperador Rojo!*
	an objection marker (mostly appearing at the end of the sentence when it has such a meaning, showing the speaker's full disagreement and irritation)	*(…) ca să-și construiască/ definească personalitatea, **cică**! Da?* (Să nu se împiedice apa în care a plâns Dumnezeu, in CoRoLa 2014).	*(…) so that they can build/define their personality, **they say**! Right?*	*(…) pour qu'ils puissent construire /définir leur personnalité, **disent-ils**!* N'*est-ce pas?*	*(…) para que ellos puedan construir/definir su personalidad, **supuestamente**! ¿Sí?*
	a marker of accumulation and pursuit of the discursive topic (metatextual value)	*Aceluia îi dă fata; ba **cică**-i mai dă și jumătate din împărățialui* (Creangă, *Povestiri*, in DLRLC 1955–1957).	*He'll give his daughter to that one; even more, **they say** he'll also give that man half of his kingdom.*	*Il donnera sa fille à celui-là, et plus encore, **on dit** qu'il donnera aussi à cet homme la moitié de son royaume.*	*A ése le entregará su hijo; además, **dizque** le dará también mitad de su reino.*
	an indicator of astonishment	*E oare cu putință? auzi! Apoi **cică** să nu te strici de rîs!* (Creangă, *Povestiri*, in DLRLC1955–1957).	*Is it possible? Hear that! Then **Ø** how could one not laugh like hell!*	*Est-ce possible? Entends ça! Alors Ø comment ne pas rirecomme l'enfer!*	*¿Será posible? ¡Oye eso! ¿Cómo Ø no partirse de la risa?*

The examples above show that Rom. *cică* has diverse functions (modal-epistemic and evidential uses, as well as pragmatic-discursive uses – see Popescu and Duță 2022), mostly not registered and, especially, not sufficiently explained/defined in the explicative dictionaries of this linguistic system.

As can be seen in the table above, among the analysed foreign languages only Spanish has a corresponding lexical unit, while French and English resort to various paraphrases in order to render the contextual meaning of the Romanian word.

Finally, Tab. 2 shows that pragmatic-discursive meanings (the 3rd category) are the most difficult to convey in other languages, either typologically related or not. This will be the greatest challenge of our approach since, in order to provide most accurate contextual meanings in the target languages, we should not limit our endeavour to providing descriptions of the pragmatic functions of Romanian discourse markers, but we should also try to emphasize other phonological or non-verbal, paratextual clues (such as punctuation marks, emoticons, images).

5. Conclusion

We postulate that a multilingual glossary of discourse markers, starting from Romanian, would be a useful tool both for translation activities and for the teaching and learning of Romanian as a foreign language. It is, undoubtedly, a complex project, which implies forming an interdisciplinary team of researchers, including linguists (even native speakers for each analysed language), specialists in pragmatics and phonetics, and experts in IT and computational linguistics, in order to effectively achieve all the envisaged goals. Such interdisciplinary research could nevertheless entail a wide range of challenges, which are mostly due, as outlined above, to the fact that, from a pragma-linguistic perspective, some Romanian DMs, such as *cică*, do not always have full lexical equivalents in other languages. Therefore, a wide range of discursive strategies (such as the use of impersonal phrases) are needed in order to accurately render their meaning. However, these challenges could be overcome through the proposal of/by means of using a comprehensive and clearly structured frame (not only linguistically, but also computationally) that would eventually provide added value to the cross-linguistic study of discourse markers.

References

Bazzanella, C. (1994) *Le facce del parlare. Un approccio pragmatico all'italiano parlato*. Firenze: La Nuova Italia.

Bazzanella, C. (1995) "I segnali discorsivi". In Renzi, L., Salvi, G. and Cardinaletti, A. (eds.) *Grande grammatica italiana di consultazione*, III, 226–257. Bologna: Il Mulino.

Bazzanella, C. (2011) "Segnali discorsivi". *Enciclopedia dell'Italiano* [online]. Roma: Istituto della Enciclopedia Italiana Giovanni Treccani. Available at: https://www.treccani.it/enciclopedia/segnali-discorsivi_(Enciclopedia-dell%27Italiano)/ (Accessed: 4 April 2022).

Briz, A., Pons Bordería, S. and Portolés Lázaro, J. (coords.) (2008) *Diccionario de partículas discursivas del español* [online]. Available at: www.dpde.es. (Accessed: 4 April 2022).

Chiorean, L. (2013) "Despre conectorii textuali. Cu referire la adverb". *The Proceedings of the European Integration – Between Tradition and Modernity Congress*, 22–23 October, Târgu- Mureș, 5, 295–305.

Crible, L. et al. (2019) "Functions and translations of discourse markers in TED Talks: A parallel corpus study of underspecification in five languages". *Journal of Pragmatics*, 142, 139–155.

Cruschina, S. and Remberger, E.-M. (2008) "Hearsay and reported speech: Evidentiality in Romance". *Rivista de Grammatica Generativa*, 33, 95–116.

Doestie, G. and Pusch, C. (2007) "Presentation. Les marqueurs discursifs. Sens et variation". *Langue française* 154(2), 3–12.

Fraser, B. (1996) "Pragmatic markers". *Pragmatics* 6(2), 167–190.

Ghezzi, C. (2014) "The development of discourse and pragmatic markers". In Ghezzi, C. and Molinelli, P. (eds.), *Discourse and Pragmatic Markers from Latin to the Romance Languages*, 10–26. Oxford: Oxford University Press.

Ghezzi, C. and Molinelli, P. (eds.). *Discourse and Pragmatic Markers from Latin to the Romance Languages*. Oxford: Oxford University Press.

Giampieri, P. (2018) "Assessing discourse markers in dictionaries for Italian learners of English as L2". *Linguistics Journal* 13(1), 101–125.

Iliescu, M., Costăchescu, A. and Popescu, C.M. (2021) "L'italien *anzi* et ses équivalences romanes: une analyse sémantique comparée". *Actes du XXIXe Congrès International de Linguistique et de Philologie Romane* (Copenhague, 1–6 juillet 2019) sous la direction de Lene Schøsler et Juhani Härmä avec la collaboration de Jan Lindschow, Bibliothèque de Linguistique Romane 17, 1. Strasbourg: Société de Linguistique Romane (SLiR) & Éditions de Linguistique et Philologie (ELiPhi), II., 1385–1399.

Kobozeva, I.M. and Zakharov, L.M. (2004) "Types of information for the multimedia dictionary of Russian discourse markers" [online]. *SPECOM'2004: 9th Conference Speech and Computer St. Petersburg, Russia September 20–22, 2004*. Available at: http://www.isca-speech.org/archive. (Accessed: 2 February 2022).

Pop, L. (2017) "Du marqueur discursif à marqueur textuel: *cică* ('on dit que, dit-on') du roumain". *Pragmalingüística monográfico* 1, 171–185.

Popescu, C.M., Duță, O.A. (2022) "From evidential to discursive and/or pragmatic markers: An insight on Romanian *cică* and Spanish *dizque*". In Marín-Arrese, J., Hidalgo Downing, L. and Zamorano, J.R. (Eds.), *Stance and Subjectivity in Discourse*. Berlin: Peter Lang.

Portolés, J.L. (1998) *Marcadores del discurso*. Barcelona: Ariel.

Remberger, E.-M. (2021) "Discourse and Pragmatic Markers in the Romance Languages". *Oxford Research Encyclopedia of Linguistics*: Oxford: Oxford University Press. https://oxfordre.com/linguistics/view/10.1093/acrefore/9780199384655.001.0001/acrefore-9780199384655-e-675. (Accessed: 12 March 2022).

Rosén, H. (2009) "Coherence, sentence modification, and sentence-part modification – The contribution of particles". In Baldi, P. and Cuzzolin P. (eds.), *New Perspectives on Historical Latin Syntax*, 1, *Syntax of the Sentence*, 17–442. Berlin–New York: Mouton de Gruyter.

Sainz, E. (2012) "*Anzi*: dal italiano al español". In Cassol, A., Guarino, A., Mapelli, G., Matte Bon, F. and Taravacci, P. (eds.), *Metalinguaggi e metatesti. Lingua, letteratura e traduzione, XXIV Congresso AISPI (Padova, 23–26 maggio 2007)*, 735–746. Padova: AISPI Edizioni.

Schiffrin, D. (2001) "Discourse markers: Language, meaning, and context". In Schiffrin, D., Tannen, D. and Hamilton, H.E. (eds.), *The Handbook of Discourse Analysis*, 54–75. Oxford: Blackwell.

Ştefănescu, A. (2007) *Conectori pragmatici*. Bucureşti: Editura Universităţii din Bucureşti.

Vorobey, M. (2011) "French-Spanish-Russian pragmatemes dictionary". *Proceedings of the 5th International Conference on Meaning-Text Theory*, Barcelona, September 8–9, 2011, 287–294.

Zafiu, R. (2020) "Biografia gramaticală a unui cuvânt: 'cică'". In Pană Dindelegan, G. (coord.), *Dicţionar de interpretări gramaticale. Cuvinte mici, dificultăţi mari*. Bucureşti: Univers Enciclopedic.

Corpora and dictionaries

Archeus.ro (2006–2020). *Resurse electronice pentru limba română*. http://www.archeus.ro/lingvistica/CautareTextWikisource?query=MERSI&pageNo=1. (Accessed: 14 March 2022).

BNC. *British National Corpus*. (2009) https://www.english-corpora.org/bnc/. (Accessed: 14 March 2022).

CLRVN (2013) Hoarţă Cărăuşu, L. (coord.) *Corpus de limbă română vorbită actuală nedialectală*. Iaşi: EdituraUniversităţii A. I. Cuza.

CoRoLa. (2014) *Corpus computational de referinţă pentru limba română contemporană*, https://corola.racai.ro/. (Accessed: 14 March 2022).

CORV. Dascălu Jinga, L. (2002) *Corpus de română vorbită. Eşantioane*. Bucureşti: Oscar Print.

CEFC (n.d.) *Corpus d'etude pour le français contemporain*. https://repository.ortolang.fr/api/content/cefc-orfeo/4/documentation/site-orfeo/index.html. (Accessed 14 March 2022)

CREA (n.d.) *Corpus de referencia del español actual*. https://corpus.rae.es/creanet.html. (Accessed: 12 March 2022).

DLRLC. (1955–1957) Macrea, D., Petrovici, E. (coord.) Al. Rosetti et al. (authors), *Dicţionarul limbii române literare contemporane*. Bucureşti: Editura Academiei Române.

IVRLA. (2002) Ionescu-Ruxăndoiu, L. (ed.) *Interacţiunea verbală în limba română actuală. Corpus (selectiv). Schiţă de tipologie*, Bucureşti: Editura Universităţii din Bucureşti.

RDW. (1986–1989) Tiktin, H., Miron, P. *Rumänisch-Deutsches Wörterbuch*, Wiesbaden, Harrassowitz.

RoTenTen. (2016) https://www.sketchengine.eu/rotenten-romanian-corpus/. (Accessed: 12 March 2022).

SWARA speech corpus.(2017) *A Large Parallel Romanian Read Speech Dataset*, https://speech.utcluj.ro/swarasc/. (Accessed: 12 March 2022).

Eugen Istodor

Chapter 5 The Meme That Brings About the Roar. Then, Discredit. The Tismăneanu Case in Pandemic Times

Abstract: The culture that shares, that is transmitted and transmits, the copy-paste culture (Dawkins 1976) is reduced, in the online environment, to one syllable: *meme*. No matter its type, of studies, the meme selects in the receiver a formula of coexistence, more precisely, a level of identification, one of emotional reaction: euphoria/ fear and, of course, an immediate result, catharsis-fun/ disgrace-anxiety (Carroll 2014). In social media, these processes amplify, accelerate and impose the sharing of this state of exuberance, without discernment (Lanier 2018). Of course, reinforced, reinterpreted, a meme posted on your own Facebook page becomes an assumption and, at the same time, a reason to judge closed groups or social media users. The annulment of free will, its own lack of discernment (Lanier 2018), becomes social media lynching. The automatic distribution process becomes an individual one of assumption. And this can be transformed again into a public one of catharsis/ disgrace. It is Vladimir Tismăneanu's case. Politologist and sociologist, professor at Maryland University, USA, he becomes a victim of social media. Sharing a private message on Facebook, Vladimir Tismăneau walks into the cancel culture manifestations firefight (Laidlaw 2017; Leidner 2019). A simple meme transmitted in 2020, during full Covid expansion, became immediately online, the downloading of multiple forms of shaming (Posner 2015), vigilantism, bullying, bigotry, and gossiping. The present endeavour tries to identify the way in which intergenerational social codes have changed and the way in which humour functioned in pandemic times, between January and April 2020.

Keywords: cancel culture, COVID-19, gender/ race, humour, Vladimir Tismăneanu, offensive/ hate speech, social media

1. Introduction: The meme, from technical guilt to collective catharsis

A meme has its guilt. Its construction of a visual or a visual text is done with a purpose; it does not leave anybody indifferent, in any case (Shifman 2013). Even the technique plays the part of guilt. It is easy to technically identify it. The meme is an extremely familiar form of communicating in a syncretic, multimodal, intertextual way on social networks (Shifman 2013). The meme belongs to everybody that sees and shares it and, at the same time, belongs to nobody, its author is lost in collective memory. The online collective behaviour is one of the automatic gestures (cognitive shortcuts, Lanier 2018: 98). The meme becomes more "guilty" through its online maintained behaviour, not only through the significance of the distributed message. Its significance and its permanent semantization are conferred by the users. By the habitus (Bourdieu 2012: 157) and the immediate individual or group reaction. Shifman (2013: 367) calls Internet memes "units of popular culture that are circulated, imitated, and transformed by Internet users, creating a shared cultural experience".

Under these circumstances, the meme is a symbolic artefact, a pretext of semantization and sociability, of online group unity assertion. Once generated, the meme becomes a form of reaffirming and adhesion of an extended group's way of being. The meme, through the popularity of the message, appeals to an emotional reaction and, in this way, it may become a detonator of the forms inhibited in time, ingrained individually or in a group. Invested with such a vibration, the meme transcends the group borders or those of classical differences in sex, studies, and religion.

The meme performed became prolific in the public discourse during the period when COVID-19 began to spread, in January-April 2020. During the incertitude created by the spread of the coronavirus and belated answers of the authorities, memes and gifs functioned in humorous formulas. Humour was consecrated as an antidote to diminishing incertitude and reducing social anxiety (Carroll 2014).

Humorous memes were easy to accomplish (there are a lot of applications that generate memes) and easy to spread (taking into account the diversity of social networks). The global village (McLuhan 1962) under the epidemiological circumstances was debating the medical, social, political dimensions through these easy manipulate visuals, remedies against anxiety. These memes also had another quality: they were versatile, they responded to a momentary need, and they did not establish a long-term cognitive report.[1]

1 See the research done by Child, Petronio, Agyeman-Budu and Westermann (2011); especially on the topic of the online contents erased by the social media users.

The online performers, sheltered or not from the COVID-19 effects, spread such popular and multimodal comments, entering public debates. Instead of some certitudes, the meme was a comment, it meant active participation. Lacking an efficient official information, the meme became a spreading vehicle. Finally, under the tense COVID-19 moment circumstances, the memes became forms of catharsis (Carroll 2014: 141). Under the sanitary situation of global proportions circumstances, the meme functioned globally, and its humour, under certain circumstances, became one of global proportions (Robertson 1995).

2. Social media and incertitude

After a moment of confusion, the global spread of COVID-19 surpassed the official communication force. The special cases competed with the official health rhetoric. Also, fake news became a greater concern than the lack of official solutions. Finally, the effect was not felt only physically (contamination, death), but also psychically, emotionally, etc. (Jetten, Reicher et al. 2020: 45). The main remedies and the consequent legislation were the mask, the closing of the frontiers and withdrawal in private space.

The only borders that remained open and free were those of social media. The physical and psychical pressure of the virus added to the compulsive behaviour of social media. One in three people in the world uses social media platforms, and more than two-thirds of all internet users do (ourworldindata.org). The surpassing of physical borders converted into excessive and expansive behaviour on the internet. Lanier's (2018) plea to erase the social media accounts was refuted by the reality itself. The social networks proved their utility. The second argument as to "quitting social media is the most finely targeted way to resist the insanity of our times" (Lanier 2018: 25) can be rephrased as "the lack of social media isolates you from the insanity of the moment, but also from social relations".

In fact, Lanier's arguments for giving up social media, launched before the pandemic, turned into their opposites. His sixth argument, "social Media is destroying your capacity for empathy" (Lanier 2018: 73) and the seventh, "Social Media is making you unhappy" (Lanier 2018: 81), became irrelevant during the pandemic, despite a solid theoretical support developed before the health crisis.

The lack of determination, the uncertainty transformed the seeking engines and social media into real “friends”. The pandemic had a true contestant in the individual psychic. This was dominated by uncertainty. The late mobilization and answer of the authorities and the monotonous public communication gave a new dimension to the collective uncertainty and anxiety. The official scarce communication, the social media pressure dictated by the unpredictable sanitary phenomenon created an instantaneous link with social media, an automatic, but handy, “friend”, through various devices and helped by the internet.

The unpredictable (Berger and Calabrese 1975) built its own virtual identity determining the development of relationships between friends and unknown people. The interpersonal relationships in moments of psychical pressure diminished the uncertainty spectrum (Berger and Calabrese 1975: 96; Berger 1979: 25). The users’ behaviour was constantly unpredictable, vacillating between the official rules and the individual faith of “The Others”, strangers or friends.

The individual/collective behaviours engaged in various strategies of avoiding uncertainty (Berger et al. 1976): (1) passive strategies through which the information seeker collects information about a target person by observing his or her behaviour; (2) active strategies that involve proactive efforts to gain knowledge about another person, usually by asking a third party about the target person; and (3) interactive strategies that require direct communication with a target of information seeking. Interpersonal communication, in one or another form, is the primary means of uncertainty reduction. As uncertainty levels decline, information-seeking behaviour decreases. The reactions included those researched by Antheunis et al. (2012), online interaction may take place even with those recently met, thus without sharing a relationship past.

The tense moment of the pandemic extended the relationships and melted the differences. The dyadic effect became more pregnant (Parks and Floyd 1996; Ramirez, Walther, Burgoon and Sunnafrank 2002). Entire series of friends in suffering were included online “in the family”, beyond prior online strategies and the users’ will. It allowed the generalization of information seeking, and of trustworthy information suppliers, the generalization of online projecting your own person (Berger et al. 1976), your own moods, feelings, personal experiences, and hopes – all these became a *sine qua non* condition for becoming a part of the "family".

3. The Țăndărei Airport meme

The visual consists of 14–15 crows seated on a fence in different positions. The positioning of the crows confers the sensation of reality. The visual in itself would not have a racial-humorous connotation if it were not accompanied by a text, split in two tranches: "The Țăndărei Airport" and "All the flights are cancelled". The visual and the text orientate and select the receiver. They appeal to the individual and collective habitus (Bourdieu 2012: 134). The symbolics of the text-image collage functions according to the individual's disposition to react in certain ways (Bourdieu 2012: 134) and generates an immediate reaction according to the behavioural pattern in social media (Larnier 2018: 45).

The text-visual symbolics identifies crows with the Roma people, and Țăndărei with poverty, pointing to their departures to the West in search for a better life. For those familiar to the socio-political situation in 2020's Romania, the message can be humorous or racist, depending on which "echo chambers" one belongs to (Sunstein 2007b).

The viewer recognizes an official information through the text and the visual. Taking into account the epidemiological situation of the moment, the viewers are reminded that "the airports are closed". Technically, the viewers will identify a meme, a formula easy to achieve and an extremely familiar form of communicating in a syncretic, multimodal and intertextual way on social networks (Shifman 2013). For those familiar with the social situation the significance of this message is created. In both cases, we identify automatic gestures (i.e., cognitive shortcuts) related to the online behaviour of the user (Lanier 2018).

More than that, the meme appeared in a sanitary, emotionally, and psychically tense moment of the local and national community, according to Digi24 (Digi24 2020a):

> "There is an alert in Țăndărei, Ialomița district. The approximately 450 inhabitants, all of Roma origin, recently returned from Italy, Spain, France, Germany, and Great Britain transformed the city in the epicentre of coronavirus contamination in Bărăgan. Some of the people quarantined at home went for a

walk and were fined. Because of them, the other people in the city are scared and ask for their city to be quarantined".

4. The value of Vladimir Tismăneanu's share. Resemantization and feeling

From the whole range of visualizations and shares, the most valuable for the network is the one belonging to the Facebook user Vladimir Tismăneanu. He shared the meme (Tismăneanu 2020). More than that, he personalized this gesture by posting a short text: "Awesome Denisa Comănescu", which indicates that the meme does not belong to the user Tismăneanu. By sharing the meme on his Facebook page, he assumed the content of its publication and ulterior viralization. Simultaneously, Tismăneanu also undertook the public opprobrium, considering that one characteristic of social media is participatory digital culture (Jenkins 2006). Sharing means identity and a form of continuous changes in meaning, "process of semiotic change in the circulation and flow of discourses across social and cultural boundaries" (Leppänen et al. 2013: 8). The change in meaning is done by direct comments to the post, shares, likes, etc., but also through sanctions from the authorities. The meme without a precise emitter, a clearly determined creator, becomes viral in different social media, without any control from the emitter.

Nonetheless, looking at the importance of Tismăneanu's position in the Facebook "small world" structure, (Hâncean 2018: 74, apud Dunbar 1997, Watts and Strogatz 1998, Watts 1999), his post, meme and share could not leave anybody indifferent. The more so, as the egonetwork on Tismăneanu's Facebook overlaps, through that "Awesome Denisa Comanescu", with the informal offline network (Hâncean 2018: 76). The dyadic effect of the society was disclosed. The user Denisa Comănescu is part of the family and of the network and family regulars.

The dyadic effect, the self-disclosure provokes another situation: the social reward, social attraction in return (Sheldon and Pecchioni 2014). Public sharing under such circumstances opens the way to reward. Jourard (1959) says the act of self-disclosure is personally rewarding and cathartic, and such positive feelings lead to liking. Public sharing is a form confidence, and, at the same time, even of predictability (Sheldon and Pecchioni

2014). It is clear, online or offline, that one expects to be rewarded according to one's gesture.

But the meme detonated unpredictably for the user Tismăneanu. A "populist" meme and an automated gesture within Tismăneanu's "small world" quickly became a public accusation and guilt. The discrepancy between Tismăneanu, well known for his well–balanced public position, of a reputed politologist and professor in a strict academic environment in the United States, and the meme was immediately noticed. The comments of other Facebook users instantaneously analysed and re-evaluated Tismăneanu's private life and "family" life.

A meme becomes popular because it conveys a community meaning in a fragmented world (Shifman 2014: 342). This is what happened in the Țăndărei Airport case, but in a negative sense. Thus, Tismăneanu's share was popular and solidary as to the message with "his small world" (Dunbar 1997), of which Denisa Comănescu was a part, but also with his own echo chamber. Outside of this group, the multiplication of this share can produce – and it has produced – unexpected consequences. This sort of "vernacular creativity" (Burgess 2007) depends on this sort of personalities like Tismăneanu to act as gatekeepers of socially accepted values.

5. Private-public in the pandemic

As long as the message was in his echo chamber, in his small world, Tismăneanu did not have any reason to worry about the sharing. It was about a private choice. More than that, as it was during the pandemic, there was solidarity against the common enemy. In this respect, the opposition between the public space and the private one is best illustrated by the talk "According to Boyd (2010), 'a conversation you might have in the hallway is private by default, public through effort,' but on the Facebook wall 'the conversation is public by default, private through effort.' In other words, information shared face to face is something people easily forget, whereas information shared online is stored and archived and is easily replicated" (Sheldon 2015: 13). Under COVID-19 circumstances, private space becomes essential.

It is not only a physical space, but mostly a union with the virtual one, as the public one became harming. More than that, symbolically, the virtual space became one of solidarity. One of the mental constructs of the moment being: we all share the same tragedy, we are all in the same situation, we all forgive our errors. Resilience and empathy were "the common traits" of a world that was living the incertitude of the moment. The strictly private space was extended into the one of the online suffering "family". Looking in retrospect and re-reading the messages that followed the sharing, we notice that Tismăneanu lived in such a mental construct. He thought that the message would have the effect and the reward "in the family", as between friends in suffering.

In this respect, Tismăneanu might have thought that he was protected in this global space of sufferance. But the network automations and the pandemic social constructs did not stop here. Tismăneanu considered himself aggrieved for a while. For a long time, he had posted different messages reminding him that he was part of an ethnic minority, accusing official institutions, but also the misunderstanding of his contemporaries. In the end, he apologized to those targeted (Digi24 2020b). His succession of posts in those days shows the fact that he had difficulty in understanding the complex game he had started with a simple meme.

6. Critical thinking – emotion

Not understanding how his online gesture functions symbolically, Vladimir Tismăneanu abolished exactly the functioning of what constituted his own personality: critical thinking. The emotions of momentary confinement surpassed the critical posture, the obvious one, taking into account his academic position. Critical thinking (Calvin 1996; Kahnman 2011), in the sense of observing the details of the discourse, meditating on the discourse, was replaced by an excessive emotional state (Mayer, Salovey and Caruso 2004). When seeing the meme, Tismăneanu failed to evaluate his civic situation and did not have the capacity to refrain from his own emotions. Believing that we all are in the same situation of crisis buddies, Tismăneanu acted without discernment. In this way, Tismăneanu personalized excessively a simple meme transmitted by Denisa Comănescu, a close friend also offline.

It is important to add a few details about how such memes are seen in academic North America (in Yoon 2019): racial and ethnic humour have significant consequences in the current American context, which can be named as the era of political correctness and colorblindness (Rosenberg 2004; Bonilla-Silva 2006; Ullucci and Battey 2011). Racial or ethnic humour is defined as "humour directed at racial and nationality groups, denigrating alleged attributes of those groups" (Schutz 1989: 167). Weaver (2010: 537), on the other hand, uses the term "racist humour" instead of racial and ethnic humour. He explains that "where humour has a racist potential, in relation to stereotype and inferiorisation used, it remains accurate to label it racist humour".

The meme x-rayed and underlined social stratifications and racial prejudices (Castells 2009; 381–428). The Țăndărei meme anonymously got through Tismăneanu and then became a personalized tsunami. Political correctness artisans, academic media, politicians, journalists noticed the discrepancies between the politology professor and the racist message. The ones in any way affected by the pandemic lost their humour. The empowered institution to sanction discrimination took notice. Emotion and global pandemic solidarity gave Tismăneanu the appearance of protection. In fact, global emotion and solidarity thus detonated their states so virulently personalized.

7. Humour

Attardo (2001) suggests that the simplest structure of a joke includes a configuration, a discrepancy and a resolution and he states that the overlap of the scenarios (or of the outlines) is essential for humour. Goatly (2012: 22) imposes punchline as essential for the structure of the joke. The punchline introduces the discrepancy and forces the changing of the outline underlined in the initial configuration. More than that, Goatly argues that there should be a connector that functions as a bridge between the outlines or scripts in order to obtain a resolution. The one that visualizes the meme starts from the visual and, heading to the text, symbolically reconstructs the meme. The punchline is the crows visual and its second significance, the one indicated as naming the Roma people in a racist way.

This was not an isolated meme produced under pandemic circumstances. The memes about those involved in the pandemic – heroes, victims, authorities, those reticent – circulated in social media even from the beginning of the epidemiological situation, in January-February 2020. Taking into account the restrictions imposed by the pandemic, the meme was one of the online communication forms "for surviving" and interacting with the external world. Information, restrictions, states of mind, similarities with previous events were communicated. The memes were humour formulas. The memes were one of the instant products that brought along collective catharsis (Carroll 2014) in physical, psychic and emotional isolation.

Humour is a conscious classification/ interpretation/ immediate reaction, and through laughter catharsis means freeing from tension, a way out of ambiguity, misunderstanding, lack of determination (Carroll 2014).

This time, humour/ an automatic gesture that contained humour came in a moment of public crisis, of sanitary incertitude and created irritation, prompted the state of incertitude that was lived. Populist, racist, the shared meme dispersed through various "echo chambers" (Sunstein 2007a) and was top of the bill for a few days. Not only the contrast between the person and the professor was underlined in the comments, but also Vladimir Tismăneanu's private space was scanned. The meme about Țăndărei said much more about Vladimir Tismăneanu.

More than that, by sharing a private message on Facebook, Vladimir Tismăneau walks into the cancel culture manifestations firefight (Laidlaw 2017; George and Leidner 2019). A simple meme became a radical manifestation of multiple forms of shaming (Posner 2015), vigilantism, bullying, bigotry, and gossiping.

8. Conclusion

Vladimir Tismăneanu shared a cognitive shortcut, a prejudice, an online/ offline way of being that was not compliant with his academic status and with the new global configuration. Despite the closing of national borders, the hybridizations, the delocalizations, the interbreedings, relocalizations (Ferreol and Jucquois 2003) had taken place at a global level. These globalization formulas had reconfigured identities, a heterogenous Together resulting, with an obvious respect for differences, for people's and societies' cultural identities (Wolton 2012: 21). In a public space concentrated on debating cultural mixtures, hybrid practices, the gentrification of city centres and territories, the emergence of some idyllic hyper places or, on the contrary, the trivialization of the suburbs, Tismăneanu's meme isolates and points to the victims of economic inefficient policies and, at the same time, to the marginal beneficiaries of globalization (Agier 2014; Guidikova 2014; Boltanski and Esquerre 2017; Lussault 2017). Tismăneanu, in a world of connected individualism (Flichy 2004), proved, individually and in his dyadic group, connected to global emotions, disconnected from the socio-political reality.

In 1955, John Austin suggested that an utterance can also be used to perform an act (Austin 1962). A meme about the Roma people in Țăndărei turned against Vladimir Tismăneanu doubting his competence, his professionalism, his authentic relation with his country of origin. The politologist Valdimir Tismăneanu managed one single thing: to share a meme. Besides that, he lost his way among social codes, including the identity in social media, the division between private and public life, the humour, and not least, discrimination.

References

Agier, M. (ed.) (2014) *Un monde de camps*. Paris: La Découverte.

Antheunis, M.L. et al., (2012) "Interactive uncertainty reduction strategies and verbal affection in computer-mediated communication". *Communication Research* 39(6), 757–780.

Attardo, S. (2001) *Humorous Texts: A Semantic and Pragmatic Analysis*. Berlin and New York: Mouton de Gruyter.

Austin, J.L. (1962) *How to Do Things with Words*. Cambridge: Harvard University Press.

Berger, C.R. (1979) "Beyond initial interaction: Uncertainty, understanding, and the development of interpersonal relationships." In Giles, H. and St. Clair, R. (eds.), *Language and social psychology*, 122–144. Oxford: Blackwell.

Berger, C.R. and Calabrese, R.J. (1975) "Some explorations in initial interaction and beyond: Toward a developmental theory of interpersonal communication". In *Human Communication Research, 1*(2), 99–112. https://doi.org/10.1111/j.1468-2958.1975.tb00258.x. (Accessed: 14 March 2022).

Berger, C.R. et al. (1976) "Interpersonal epistemology and interpersonal communication". In *Explorations in Interpersonal Communication*. London: Sage, 149–172.

Boltanski, L. and Esquerre, A. (2017) *Enrichissement. Une critique de la marchandise*. Paris: Gallimard.

Bonilla-Silva, E. (2006) *Racism without Racists: Color-blind Racism and the Persistence of Racial Inequality in the United States*. 2nd edn. Lanham, MD: Rowman & Little eld.

Bourdieu, P. (2012) *Language and Symbolic Power*. trans. by Laura Albulescu and Bogdan Ghiu. Bucharest: Editura Art.

Boyd, D. (2010) "Making sense of privacy and publicity". *SXSW*. Austin, Texas, March 13. https://www.danah.org/papers/talks/2010/SXSW2010.html (Accessed: 15 March 2022).

Burgess, J. (2007) *Vernacular Creativity and New Media*. Unpublished PhD thesis. Brisbane, Australia: Queensland University of Technology.

Calvin, W.H. (1996) *How Brains Think: Evolving Intelligence, Then and Now*. New York: Basic Books.

Carroll, N. (2014) *Humor*. Oxford: Oxford University Press.

Castells, M. (2009) *Communication Power*. Oxford: Oxford University Press.

Child, J.T., Petronio, S., Agyeman-Budu, E.A. and Westermann, D.A. (2011) "Blog scrubbing: Exploring triggers that change privacy rules". *Computers in Human Behavior* 27(5), 2017–2027.

Dawkins, R. (1976) *The Selfish Gene*. Oxford: Oxford University Press.

Dunbar, R. (1997) *Grooming, Gossip, and the Evolution of Language*. Cambridge, MA: Harvard University Press.

George, J. and Leidner, D. (2019) "From clicktivism to hacktivism: Understanding digital activism". *Information and Organization* 29(3). https://doi.org/10.1016/j.infoandorg.2019.04.001. (Accessed: 16 March 2022).

Goatly, A. (2012) *Meaning and Humour: Key Topics in Semantics and Pragmatics*. Cambridge: Cambridge University Press.

Guidikova, I. (2014) *Cultural Diversity and Cities – Intercultural Integration Approach*. Fiesole: EUI RSCAS Policy Paper.

Digi24. (2020a) "Orașul Țăndărei intră în carantină." Available: https://www.digi24.ro/stiri/actualitate/decizie-oficiala-orasul-tandarei-intra-in-carantina-128652 (Accessed 2 January 2022).

Digi24. (2020b) "Vladimir Tismăneanu își cere scuze pentru meme-ul rasist, dar amintește că atunci când el a fost atacat, CNCD nu a intervenit." Available at: https://www.digi24.ro/stiri/actualitate/social/vladimir-tismaneanu-isi-cere-scuze-pentru-meme-ul-rasist-dar-aminteste-ca-atunci-cand-el-a-fost-atacat-cncd-nu-a-intervenit-1290509 (Accessed: 2 January 2022).

Ferreol, G. and Jucquois, G. (2003) *Dictionnaire de l'altérité et des relations interculturelles*. Paris: Armand Colin.

Flichy, P. (2004) "L'individualisme connecté entre la technique numérique et la société". In *Réseaux* 124(2), 17–51. (translated by L.C. Libbrecht). DOI: 10.3917/res.124.0017. (Accessed: 14 March 2022).

Hâncean, M.G. (2018) *Rețelele sociale în era Facebook. O analiză sociologică [Social networks. A sociology approach]*. Iași: Polirom.

Jenkins, H. (2006) *Convergence Culture: Where Old and New Media Collide*. New York: New York University Press.

Jetten, J. and Reicher, S. et al. (eds.) (2020) *Together Apart. The Psychology of COVID-19*. London: Sage Publications.

Jourard, S.M. (1959) "Self-disclosure and other-cathexis". *The Journal of Abnormal and Social Psychology*, 59(3), 428–431. https://doi.org/10.1037/h0041640. (Accessed: 14 March 2022).

Kahneman, D. (2011) *Thinking, Fast and Slow*. New York: Farrar, Straus and Giroux.

Laidlaw, E. Online Shaming and the Right to Privacy (February 8, 2017). Laws 2017, 6(1), 3. http://dx.doi.org/10.2139/ssrn.2944307. (Accessed: 14 March 2022).

Lanier, J. (2018) *Ten Arguments for Deleting Your Social Media Accounts Right Now*. New York: Henry Holt and Company.

Leppänen, S., Kytölä, S., Jousmäki, H., Peuronen, S. and Westinen, E. (2013) "Entextualization and resemiotization as resources for (dis)identification in social media". *Tilburg Papers in Culture Studies* 57, 1–46.

Lussault, M. (2017) *Hyper-lieux. Les nouvelles géographies de la mondialisation*. Paris: Éd. Le Seuil.

Mayer, J.D., Salovey, P. and Caruso, D.R. (2004) "Emotional intelligence: Theory, findings, and implications". *Psychological Inquiry* 15(3), 197–215.

McLuhan, M. (1962) *The Gutenberg Galaxy*. Toronto: University of Toronto Press.

Parks, M.R. and Floyd, K. (1996) "Making friends in cyberspace". *Journal of Communication* 46(1), 80–97.

Posner, E.A. (2015) "Human rights, the laws of war, and reciprocity". *Law and Ethics of Human Rights* 6(2), 147–171.

Ramirez, A., Jr., Walther, J.B., Burgoon, J.K. and Sunnafrank, M. (2002) "Information-seeking strategies, uncertainty, and computer-mediated communication". *Human Communication Research* 28, 213–228.

Robertson R. (1995) "The conceptual promise of glocalization: Commonality and diversity". In Featherstone, M., Lash, S. and Robertson R. (eds.) *Global Modernities*, 25–44. London: Sage.

Rosenberg, P. (2004) "Colorblindness in teacher education: An optical delusion". In Fine, M., Weis, L. Pruitt, L., and Burns, A. (eds.) *Off White: Readings on Power, Privilege and Resistance*, 257–272. New York: Routledge.

Schutz, C. (1989) "The sociability of ethnic jokes". *Humor: International Journal of Humor Research* 2(2), 165–177.

Sheldon, P. (2015) *Social Media: Principles and Applications*. Lanham: Lexington Books.

Sheldon, P. and Pecchioni, L. (2014) "Comparing relationships among self-disclosure, social attraction, predictability and trust in exclusive Facebook and exclusive face-to-face relationships". *American Communication Journal* 16(2), 1–14.

Shifman, L. (2013) "Memes in a digital world: Reconciling with a conceptual troublemaker". *Journal of Computer-Mediated Communication* 18, 362–377.

Shifman, L. (2014) *Memes in Digital Culture*. Cambridge, MA: MIT Press.

Sunstein, C.R. (2007a) "Ideological amplification". *Constellations* 14, 273–279.

Sunstein, C.R. (2007b) *Republic.com 2.0*. Princeton: Princeton University Press.

Tismăneanu, V. (2020) Vladimir Tismăneanu. *Facebook*. Available at: https://www.facebook.com/vladimir.tismaneanu (Accessed 2 January 2022).

Ullucci, K. and Battey, D. (2011) "Exposing Color Blindness/Grounding Color Consciousness: Challenges for Teacher Education". *Urban Education*, 46(6), 1195–1225. doi: 10.1177/0042085911413150. (Accessed: 14 March 2022).

Watts, D.J. (1999) "Networks, Dynamics, and the Small-World Phenomenon". *American Journal of Sociology*, 105(2), 493–527. https://doi.org/10.1086/210318. (Accessed: 14 March 2022).

Watts, D. and Strogatz, S. (1988) "Collective dynamics of 'small-world' networks". *Nature 393*, 440–442. https://doi.org/10.1038/30918. (Accessed: 14 March 2022).

Weaver, S. (2010) "Developing a rhetorical analysis of racist humour: Examining anti-black jokes on the internet". *Social Semiotics* 20(5), 537–555.

Wolton, D. (2012) *Internetul. O teorie critică a noilor media [Internet et après? Une théorie critique des nouveaux medias]*. Bucharest: Comunicare.ro.

Yoon, I. (2019) "Why is it not just a joke? Analysis of Internet memes associated with racism and hidden ideology of colorblindness". *Journal of Cultural Research in Art Education* 33, 92–123.

Section 2: Tools and Interfaces

Haifa Alharthi and Diana Inkpen

Chapter 6 Natural Language Processing for Book Recommender Systems

Abstract: Reading literary books is beneficial for individuals and societies; however, this practice is decreasing. In this work, we propose several approaches to a literary book recommender system that takes the text of the books into consideration when generating recommendations. The first approach considers the writing style of the authors by transferring the information learned by an author-identification model into a book recommender system. In the second approach, we represent books using more than one hundred linguistic features including lexical, syntactic, stylometric, and fiction-based features. To our knowledge, this is the first study to use transfer learning from an author-identification model and to consider a large number of diverse features for book recommendations. The two proposed systems are evaluated in a top-k recommendation scenario, and both provide higher recommendation accuracy compared with state-of-the-art content and collaborative filtering methods. We also qualitatively analyse both approaches and investigate the lexical, syntactic, stylometric, and fiction-based features that play a role in generating accurate recommendations.

Keywords: literary books, Recommender System, writing style

1. Introduction

Nowadays, it can be overwhelming to choose from a high volume of items. This issue can be mitigated by recommender systems (RSs) which offer personalized sets of items. There are two major categories of recommender systems, namely collaborative filtering (CF) and content-based (CB). The former makes recommendations to the target user based on the likings of the community of users whereas the latter learns patterns in one user's preferences and make recommendations accordingly. Although e-books provide an easy and inexpensive reading option, the practice of reading for pleasure is declining, particularly among young people.[1] Hence, it is

1 https://tinyurl.com/jgunwfx.

important to use state of the art technologies to recommend books of interest to target users. Many studies have shown the benefits of reading such as (Hill 2013; Mar et al. 2009; Berns 2013 and Mar and Oatley 2008) which presented that reading fiction in particular is correlated with higher empathy and social communication.

A survey on book recommender systems shows that even though book metadata (e.g., author, genre) is widely used in content-based RSs, few papers have built a recommender system based on books' actual texts. One would argue that the latter may lead to copyright issues, but there are current projects that exploit the full texts of books such as Google Books, HathiTrust Digital Library,[2] and BookLamp.[3] Furthermore, most books now come in an electronic form and there is no need to convert hardcopies to machine-readable texts.

Unlike text-based items such as news articles (Kompan and Bieliková 2010), microblogs (Gurini et al. 2013), movie plots (Bergamaschi and Po 2015) and scientific papers (Wang and Blei 2011), literary books can be very old but still relevant with features that are specific to books. For example, in libraries, reader advisory considers seven appeal factors when suggesting literary books to patrons: pacing (e.g., intense, leisurely), characterization (e.g., well-defined characters, emphasis on one vs. several characters), storyline (e.g., complex, character-driven), style (e.g., dry, poetic, or conversational), setting (e.g., descriptive, historical period), tone/mood (e.g., upbeat, creepy) and frame (e.g., atmosphere and tone) (Smith et al. 2016).

In this work, our goal is to increase the accuracy of English literary book recommendations which can be fiction or non-fiction (i.e., memoirs with story elements such as characters and plot: Brown and Krog 2011). Hence, we propose two methods to recommend books after exploiting their actual texts. In the first approach, a book is represented according to its author's style which is learned by an author-identification model. To our knowledge, this is the first work to recommend books based on extracted features learned by an author-identification model.

---

2 https://www.hathitrust.org.

3 https://tinyurl.com/3qvq8zj and https://tinyurl.com/ycpwnvze.

In the second approach, a book is represented as a list of calculated attributes including lexical, syntactical, character-based, fiction-specific (e.g., the number of fictional characters), and style-based features. One algorithm adopted is extra-trees classifier which provides feature importance values to show the features that primarily contribute to the accuracy of recommendations. Such values can benefit researchers, authors, and publishers. In previous studies, for the purpose of generating recommendations, researchers calculated a limited set of features including document length and vocabulary richness (Vaz et al. 2012a) and readability score (Pera and Ng 2014a; Pera and Ng 2014b; Pera and Ng 2015). To our knowledge, this is the first work to investigate the utilization of 120 features calculated from entire texts to make book recommendations.

The remainder of this paper is organized as follows: Section 2 presents the first approach's related work, methodology, and evaluation. Section 3 describes the second approach's most similar work, set of features, methodology, and evaluation. Section 4 concludes the discussion and highlights future work.

2. Authorship identification for literary book recommendations

2.1. Overview

It is natural to think that writing style affects reading preferences. In fact, it is one of the appeal factors considered in reading advisory (Smith et al. 2016). According to the Oxford English Dictionary, style is "The manner of expression, characteristic of a particular writer (hence of an orator) or of a literary group or period; a writer's mode of expression considered in regard to clearness, effectiveness, beauty, and the like" (Jeremy 2000). Stylometry, which emerged as a way to quantitatively analyse writing styles, is adopted in author-identification applications. Currently, with the rise of deep learning algorithms, authorship attribution can be applied without the need to calculate stylometric features.

In this section, we transfer information learned by a deep-learning-based authorship identification model to a book recommendation system. Given the user's favourite writer, Zhang and Chow (2015) suggests e-books and authors. The system develops a four-layer tree for every writer. The first layer is dedicated to the author's background information such as education and political opinions. The next three layers consist of the author's number of books, number of pages of every book, and number of paragraphs on each page, respectively. The system uses the last three layers to find similar books while using all the layers to recommend similar authors. The system gives better results compared to many state-of-the-art approaches; however, it provides the same results as Latent Dirichlet Allocation (LDA). Compared to Zhang and Chow (2015), our proposed system learns from the books' text only and does not require authors' personal information.

Also, in our evaluation, we make personalized recommendations for each user based on their previous preferences. The authorship-based recommender system consists of two main modules: authorship attribution and book recommendation. The first module uses convolutional neural network (CNN) algorithm to predict the book author given the text of the corresponding book. We follow the same approach of (Solorio et al. 2017) which was used to predict authors of tweets. After training the model, we extracted the penultimate hidden layer and treat it as the book representation (we call it book AuthId features). We compare AuthId features extracted from the dense layer and max pooling layer. We believe that CNN learns distinct elements that differentiate authors from one another. The learned elements are latent, but it is assumed that they capture distinct diction (word choices), themes, and more. Of course, style has more elements (e.g., sentence structure) that may not be captured by such an algorithm; hence, we adopt here a simplified definition of style.

The second module is a content-based recommender system that predicts each target user's ratings (e.g., 1–5 stars) using a regressor trained over book AuthId features. Finally, the target user receives a list of ranked book recommendations. We adopted Support Vector Regression (SVR) (Vapnik 1996).

2.2. Evaluation and results

One of the widely used methods of evaluating recommender systems is off-line evaluation which measures the accuracy of recommendations. In this paper, we recommend a list of ranked books; hence, to evaluate our system, we use ranking metrics, namely precision at k (P@k) and recall at k (R@k). We used Litrec dataset (Vaz et al. 2012b). After filtering out authors with fewer than two books and users with fewer than 10 books, there are 351 users who rated 1010 unique books (1–5 stars converted into binary) written by 157 unique authors. For the high memory requirement concern, we kept the first 100 000 words of each book.[4] The system is compared to many state-of-the-art content-based systems, namely LDA, latent semantic indexing (LSI), Vector space model (VSM), paragraph2vec (Doc2vec), and a collaborative filtering system: matrix factorization (MF).

As shown in 1, compared to the CB algorithms, the proposed system (using the dense layer AuthId FC or the max pooling layer AuthId MP) provides statistically significantly higher accuracy at a p-value of 0.01. In addition, the author-based RS, which is also SVR but trained over author IDs instead of book AuthId features, gives the lowest accuracy. This can be due to the large number of books authored by some writers which leads to many irrelevant book recommendations (not rated by the target user). On this note, it would be interesting to see how many unrated books exist for the authors of books recommended by AuthId FC (it is adopted in the rest of the analysis). In Fig. 2, the y-axis is the number of recommended books while the x-axis is the number of unrecommended books (not in the top ten list) written by the same people who authored the recommended books. For instance, the circle at (37,3) indicates that AuthId FC ranked three books favoured by the target user in the top-ten recommendation list when there were 37 books (irrelevant to the user) by the writers of the three recommended books. In 294 cases, AuthId FC recommended at least one relevant book to the target user when there were more than ten irrelevant books by the same authors.

We also observed that, in 17 test cases, the top-ten recommendation list had at least one relevant book (favoured by the user) by an author not seen in the training set.

We also investigated the effect of text length on the performance of AuthId FC and found that the longer the text used in the author-identification model, the higher the recommendation accuracy. Furthermore, a qualitative analysis found that books/authors with similar AuthId representations are annotated similarly by NoveList experts.

4 To download: https://tinyurl.com/y998428p.

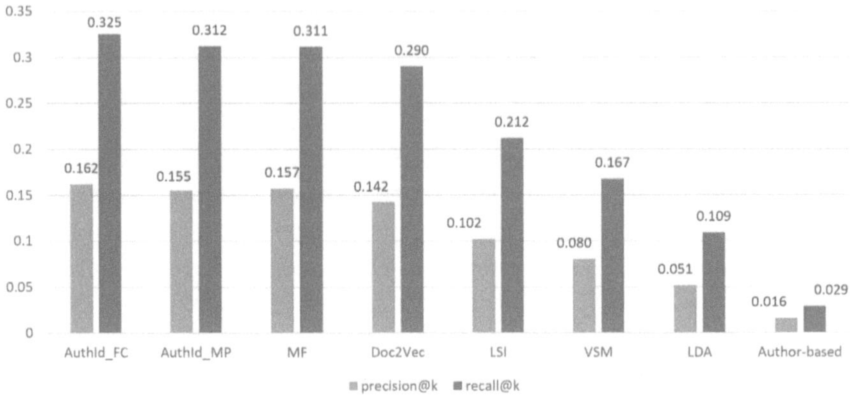

Fig. 1. Precision@10 and recall@10 generated by our system (AuthId FC and AuthId P), and the baselines

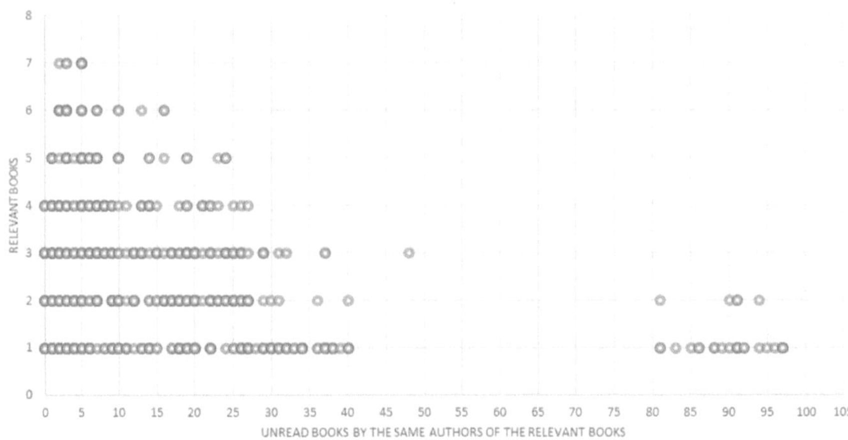

Fig. 2. Users' relevant recommended books versus unread books by the same authors

3. Study of linguistic features incorporated in a literary book recommender system

3.1. Overview

In this section, we study 120 textual features that may help improve the accuracy of book recommendations. Here, text measurements are learned from the whole text of a book and not tagged by experts, e.g., genre. The categories of the features included in the study are listed in Tab. 1. We apply two recommendation algorithms to predict the rating of the target user and provide a ranked list of recommendations. One adopted algorithm is Extra Trees which helps to calculate the variables' importance as a way to understand which factors played a role in the generation of high-quality book recommendations.

Approximately thirty published book recommender approaches were surveyed in. Of these, a few considered books' actual texts. (Vaz et al. 2012a) proposed a Stylometric content-based recommender which takes into account a list of calculated style features, namely vocabulary richness, document length, part-of-speech bigrams, and the most frequent words in a book. The set of features used to represent books in addition to topics learned by Latent Dirichlet Allocation (LDA). The study concluded that a hybrid system that combines Stylometric CB and collaborative filtering performs the best. In our work, in addition to document length and vocabulary richness, we consider a wide variety of linguistic aspects that includes syntactic, lexical, stylistic, and fiction-based features.

Our study includes the well-known dictionary LIWC 2015 (Pennebaker et al. 2015). In (Argamon et al. 2009), LIWC was used to identify an author's gender, age, and personality from the texts and in (Newman et al. 2008) to compare the writings of the two genders. The feature set was also utilized in (Nicholsa et al. 2014) which qualitatively compared three literary genres in terms of content and style. One interesting finding is that fantasy, which usually emphasizes the story settings instead of actions, contains statistically fewer auxiliary verbs. Also, fantasy, which usually discusses social elements (e.g., creatures' beliefs), has statistically higher occurrences of religious terms than science fiction. Such studies motivate the use of LIWC set for book recommendations.

We also included some text measurements which are usually used in authorship analysis such as word length (Brinegar 1963), the mean length of sentences (Smith 1988), and the average number of syllables per word (Fucks 1952).

Tab. 1. Categories of features included in our study

Category	**Feature Names**
Lexical	*Token-based*: average length of paragraph, sentence and words; average number of commas per sentence; average variance in paragraph length and in sentence length; length of book; words>6-letters; dictionary words; average syllables per word Lexical density (type-token ratio) *Word frequencies*: percent of latinate words; function words; affect words; social words; cognitive processes; perpetual processes; biological processes; core drives and needs; time orientation; relativity; personal concerns
Character-based	Numbers; all punctuation
Syntactic	Percentage of adjectives, adverbs, nouns, and verbs; comparatives, interrogatives; quantifiers
Fiction-based	Percentage of dialog text; the number of dialogues; the average length of dialog texts; the number of unique fictional characters the number of times fictional characters are mentioned; the number of unique places; the number of times places are mentioned; Percentage of dialogue by female characters; Percentage of characters which are female
Six-styles	Literary; abstract; objective; colloquial; concrete; subjective

We used GutenTag (Brooke et al. 2015) to calculate these measurements as well as the six-styles (see Tab. 1) (Brooke and Hirst 2013; Brooke et al. 2017). We also used textstat[5] to calculate Flesch reading ease score which is a readability measurement adopted in book recommender system in (Pera and Ng 2013; Pera and Ng 2014a; Pera and Ng 2014b; Pera and Ng 2015). Furthermore, we used fiction-aware named entity recognizer (LitNER) (Brooke et al. 2016) to calculate character-based features including number of fictional characters, number of their occurrences, number of dialogues, average dialogue length, percentage of female characters and percentage of their dialogues. After representing each book as a vector of 120 calculated features, we feed them into a regressor that predicts the target user ratings. We experimented with multiple machine learning algorithms, and K-nearest neighbours (KNN) and Extra Trees (ET) performed the best.

5 http://neon.niederlandistik.fu-berlin.de/en/textstat/.

3.2. Evaluation and results

In this section, we use the same dataset Litrec dataset (Vaz et al. 2012b), except that we do not filter out the authors of one book. We used the whole texts of books with an average of 91580.07 words.[6] As shown in Fig. 3, KNN and ET algorithms could rank in the top ten list more than third of the relevant books in the test sets. Compared to the CB baselines, both algorithms give statistically significantly higher performance.

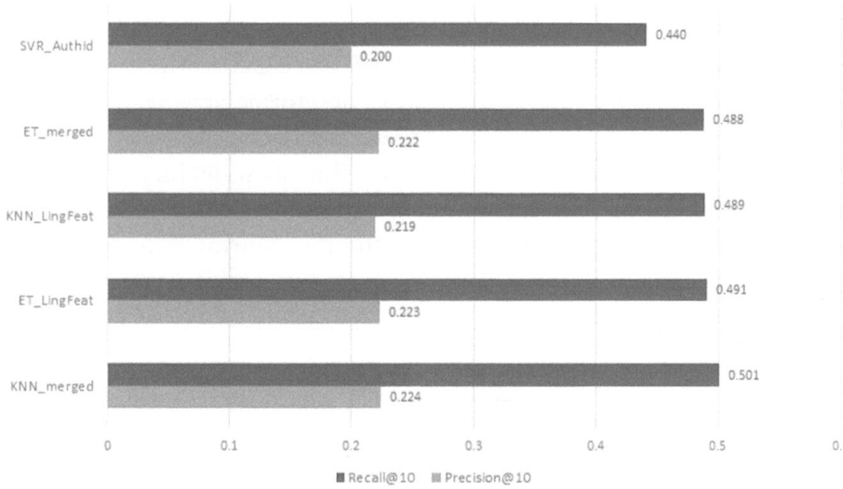

Fig. 3. Recommendation accuracy of our approach against the baselines

In addition, KNN is statistically significantly better than MF. We compared our two proposed approaches and found that lingFeat algorithms are statistically significantly higher than SVR AuthId. When combining the AuthId and lingFeat representations, the performance of KNN increased while ET decreased. However, as mentioned in 2.2, only 100 000 words are used to build AuthId representations. Since lingFeat relies on word count, it is not feasible to only consider the first 100 000 words as well.

6 To download the calculated features https://tinyurl.com/y9svvgwg.

We used 730 ET models that resulted in accurate recommendations to calculate the importance of 120 features. Fig. 4 shows the most and least important features with Seeing and author name being at the top of the list. Seeing refers to the act of observation (e.g., view). Seeing is positively correlated to concreteness (0.59) and perpetual processes (0.82), which consists of Seeing dictionary in addition to Hearing and Feeling. Concrete language is shown to be simpler and more precise to process compared to abstract language (Holcomb et al. 1999). Similar to (Hussain and Munshi 2011), we found that the Length of book is an important factor impacting reading preferences. The number of characters mentioned and the number of dialogs are also important and positively correlated with the length of book. It is not surprising that all categories of informal language including Filler, Swear, Netspeak and Informal speech are among the least important variables. This is due to the use of classic Gutenberg literary books. We used the list of most important variables to generate recommendations. As in Fig. 5, KNN's performance increased after the removal of the forty least important variables.

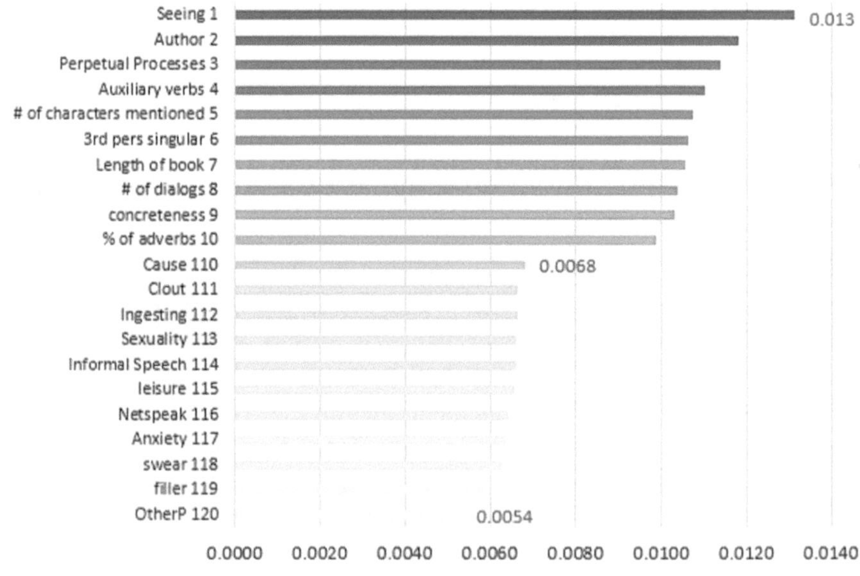

Fig. 4. Most and least influential variables in accurate ET models

Tab. 2. Top ten similar books to *Madame de Treymes* by Edith Wharton

Book name (similarity)	**Description on NoveList**
1- *Madame de Treymes* by Edith Wharton (1) 2- *The Descent of Man and Other Stories* by Edith Wharton (0.72) 3- *The Glimpses of the Moon* by Edith Wharton (0.71)	*Genre*: **Love stories,** Modern classics; *Character*: **Complex;** *Storyline*: **Character-driven;** *Writing Style*: Descriptive, Lush, Richly detailed; *Time Period*: 1920s; *Location*: Europe – Social life and customs – 20th century; *Subject headings*: Social status, Freeloaders, Americans in Europe, Honeymoons, **Married people,** Misunderstanding, **Men/women relations**
4- *Our Friend the Charlatan* by George Gissing (0.71) 5- *Denzil Quarrier* by George Gissing (0.698)	*Genre*: Psychological fiction, Domestic fiction, **Love stories,** Historical fiction, Satirical fiction; *Time Period*: 19th century; Subject headings: Women – Employment – England, Middle class women – England, Women England, Single women – England, Sisters – England, Married women – England, Self-discovery in women, Authors, Fiction writing, **Married people;** *Location*: London, England
6- *A Daughter of To-Day* by Sara Jeannette Duncan (0.697)	*Genre*: Canadian fiction; *Time Period*: 20th century; *Subject headings*: Brothers and sisters, Politicians, Romantic love, Clergy, Political science, **Men/women relations;** *Location*: Ontario
7- *In the Year of Jubilee* by Gissing (0.69)	See above
8- *The Tragic Muse* by Henry James (0.687) 9- *Sir Dominick Ferrand* by Henry James (0.682)	*Genre*: Classics, Psychological fiction; *Character*: **Complex,** Flawed; *Storyline*: **Character-driven;** *Pace*: Leisurely paced; *Tone*: Melancholy, Reflective, Thought-provoking; *Writing Style*: Stylistically complex
10- *The Tragic Bride* by Francis Brett Young (0.678)	**Genre:** Domestic fiction; *Subject headings*: Young women, Quests, Love, **Men/women relations,** Marriage, Remarriage, Self-discovery in women, Happiness in women; *Location*: Midlands, England

Furthermore, we conducted a qualitative analysis to check if books/authors with similar AuthId representations are annotated similarly by NoveList experts. In lingFeat, we include all the features except for the author's name. Tab. 2 depicts the most similar books to *Madame de Treymes* by Edith Wharton. The top retrieved books share similar descriptions as highlighted in bold.

4. Conclusion

In this work, we proposed two approaches that make book recommendations after analysing books' entire texts. The first recommends books based on extracted elements learned by an author-identification model while the second recommend books based on list of calculated attributes including lexical, syntactical, character-based, fiction-specific, and style-based features. Compared to state-of-the-art, both RSs obtained higher recommendation accuracy. This work can be extended by considering other author-identification models, applying word sense disambiguation, and calculating more textual elements.

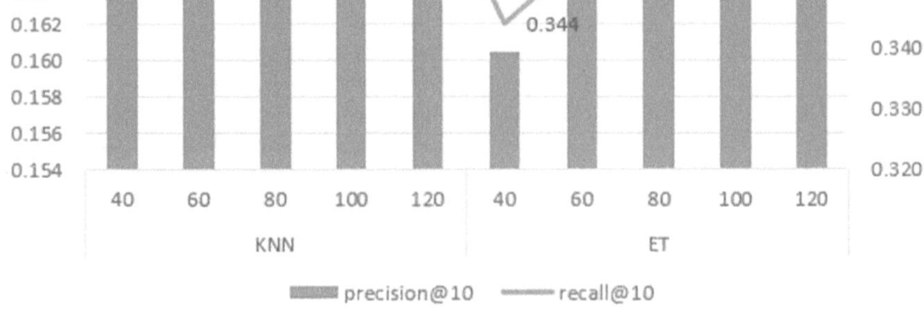

Fig. 5. The performance of ET and KNN when only top features are considered

References

Alharthi, H., Inkpen, D. and Szpakowicz, S. (2018) "A Survey of Book Recommender Systems". In: *Journal of Intelligent Information Systems* 51(1), 139–160. Springer. DOI: 10.1007/s10844-017-0489-9. URL: https://doi.org/10.1007/s10844-017-0489-9. (Accessed 3 April 2022).

Argamon, S. et al. (2009) "Automatically Profiling the Author of an Anonymous Text". In: *Communications of the ACM* 52(2), 119–123. ISSN:0001-0782. DOI: 10.1145/1461928.1461959. (Accessed 3 April 2022).

Bergamaschi, S. and Po, L. (2015) "Comparing LDA and LSA Topic Models for Content-Based Movie Recommendation Systems". In: Monfort, V. and Krempels, K.-H. (eds.) *Web Information Systems and Technologies: 10th International Conference*, WE12 H. BIST 2014, Barcelona, Spain, April 3–5, 2014, Revised Selected Papers. Cham: Springer International Publishing, 2015. 247–263. ISBN: 978-3-319-27030-2. DOI: 10.1007/978-3-319-27030-2_16. URL: http://dx.doi.org/10.1007/978-3-319-27030-2_16. (Accessed: 3 April 2022).

Berns, G.S. et al. (2013) "Short- and Long-Term Effects of a Novel on Connectivity in the Brain". In: *Brain Connectivity* 3(6), 590–600.

Brinegar, C.S. (1963) "Mark Twain and the Quintus Curtius Snodgrass Letters: A Statistical Test of Authorship". In: *Journal of the American Statistical Association* 58(301), 85–96. ISSN: 01621459. http://www.jstor.org/stable/2282956 (Accessed: 3 April 2022).

Brooke, J. and Hirst, G. (2013) "Hybrid Models for Lexical Acquisition of Correlated Styles". In: *Sixth International Joint Conference on Natural Language Processing*, 82–90. IJCNLP 2013, Nagoya, Japan, October 14–18, 2013. URL: http://aclweb.org/anthology/I/I13/I13-1010.pdf. (Accessed: 3 April 2022).

Brooke, J., Hammond, A. and Hirst, G. (2015) "GutenTag: An NLPdriven Tool for Digital Humanities Research in the Project Gutenberg Corpus". In: *Proceedings of the Fourth Workshop on Computational Linguistics for Literature,* CLfL@NAACL-HLT 2015, June 4, 2015, Denver, Colorado, USA. 2015, 42–47. URL: http://aclweb.org/anthology/W/W15/W15-0705.pdf. (Accessed: 3 April 2022).

Brooke, J., Hammond, A. and Baldwin, T. (2016) "Bootstrapped Text-level Named Entity Recognition for Literature". In: *Proceedings of the 54th Annual Meeting of the Association for Computational Linguistics*, ACL 2016, August 7–12, 2016, Berlin, Germany, Volume 2: Short Papers. 2016. URL: http://aclweb.org/anthology/P/P16/P16- 2056.pdf. (Accessed: 3 April 2022).

Brooke, J., Hammond, A. and Hirst, G. (2017) "Using Models of Lexical Style to Quantify Free Indirect Discourse in Modernist Fiction". In: *DSH 32*, 234–250.

Brown, D. and Krog, A. (2011) "Creative Non-Fiction: A Conversation". In: *Current Writing: Text and Reception in Southern Africa* 23(1), 57–70. DOI: 10.1080/1013929X.2011.572345. (Accessed: 3 April 2022).

Fucks, W. (1952) "On Mathematical Analysis of Style". In: *Biometrika* 39(1/2), 122–129. ISSN: 00063444. URL: http://www.jstor. org/stable/ 2332470.(Accessed: 3 April 2022).

Gurini, D.F. et al. (2013) "A Sentiment-Based Approach to Twitter User Recommendation". In: *Proceedings of the Fifth ACM RecSys Workshop on Recommender Systems and the Social Web co-located with the 7th ACM Conference on Recommender Systems* (RecSys 2013), Hong Kong, China, October 13, 2013. URL: http://ceur-ws.org/Vol-1066/Paper5.pdf. (Accessed: 3 April 2022).

Hawthorn, J. (2000) *A Glossary of Contemporary Literary Theory. An Arnold Publication Series*. London: Bloomsbury Academic.

Hill, K. (2013) "The Arts and Individual Well-Being in Canada" [Online; posted 13 February 2013]. February 2013. URL: http://www.hillstrategies. com/content/arts-and-individual-well-being-canada. (Accessed: 3 April 2022).

Holcomb, P.J. et al. (1999) "Dual-coding, Context-availability, and Concreteness Effects in Sentence Comprehension: An Electrophysiological Investigation". In: *Journal of Experimental Psychology. Learning, Memory, and Cognition*, 25(3), 721–742.

Hussain, I. and Munshi, P. (2011) "Identifying Reading Preferences of Secondary School Students". In: *Creative Education* 2, 6. ISSN:5. DOI: 10.4236/ce.2011.25062.

Kompan, M. and Bieliková, M. (2010) "Content-Based News recommendation". In: *E-Commerce and Web Technologies*: 11th International

Conference, EC-Web 2010, Bilbao, Spain, September 1–3, 2010. Proceedings. Berlin, Heidelberg: Springer Berlin Heidelberg, 2010, pp. 61–72. ISBN:978-3-642-15208-5. DOI: 10.1007/978-3-642-15208-5_6. URL: https://doi.org/10.1007/978-3-642-15208-5_6. (Accessed: 3 April 2022).

Mar, R.A. and Oatley, K. (2008) "The Function of Fiction is the Abstraction and Simulation of Social Experience". In: *Perspectives on Psychological Science* 3(3), 173–192. DOI: 10.1111/j.1745-6924.2008.00073. (Accessed: 3 April 2022).

Mar, R.A., Oatley, K. and Peterson, J.B. (2009) "Exploring the Link between Reading Fiction and Empathy: Ruling Out Individual Differences and Examining Outcomes". In: *Communications* 34(4), 407–428. ISSN: 0341-2059. DOI: 10.1515/comm.2009.025. (Accessed: 3 April 2022).

Newman, M.L. et al. (2008) "Gender Differences in Language Use: An Analysis of 14,000 Text Samples". In: *Discourse Processes* 45(3), 211–236. DOI: 10.1080/01638530802073712.

Nicholsa, R., Lynn, J. and Purzycki, B.J. (2014) "Toward a Science of Science Fiction". English (US). In: *Scientific Study of Literature* 4(1), 25–45. ISSN: e-issn 2210–4380. DOI: doi10.1075/ssol. 4.1.02nic.

Pennebaker, J.W. et al. (2015) *The Development and Psychometric Properties of LIWC2015*. Texas: University of Texas.

Pera, M.S. and Ng, Y.-K. (2013) "What to Read Next?: Making Personalized Book Recommendations for K-12 Users". In: *Proceedings of the 7th ACM Conference on Recommender Systems*. RecSys '13. Hong Kong, China, 12–16 October, ACM, 2013, 113–120. ISBN: 978-1-4503-2409-0. DOI: 10.1145/2507157.2507181. URL: http://doi.acm.org/ 10.1145/2507157.2507181. (Accessed: 3 April 2022).

Pera, M.S. and Ng, Y.-K. (2014a) "How CanWe Help Our K-12 Teachers?: Using a Recommender to Make Personalized Book Suggestions". In: *Proceedings of the 2014 IEEE/WIC/ACM International Joint Conferenceson Web Intelligence (WI) and Intelligent Agent Technologies (IAT)* – Volume 02. WI-IAT '14. Washington, DC, USA: IEEE Computer Society, 2014a, 335–342. ISBN: 978-1-4799-4143-8. DOI: 10.1109/WIIAT. 2014.116. URL: http://dx.doi.org/ 10.1109/WIIAT.2014.116. (Accesse: 3 April 2022).

Pera, M.S. and Ng, Y.-K. (2014b) "Automating Readers' Advisory to Make Book Recommendations for K-12 Readers". In: *Proceedings of the 8th ACM Conference on Recommender Systems. RecSys '14*. Foster City, Silicon Valley, California, USA: ACM, 2014b, 9–16. ISBN: 978-1-4503-2668-1. DOI: 10.1145/2645710.2645721. URL: http://doi. Acm. org/10.1145/2645710.2645721. (Accessed: 3 April 2022).

Pera, M.S. and Ng, Y.-K. (2015) "Analyzing Book-Related Features to Recommend Books for Emergent Readers". In: *Proceedings of the 26th ACM Conference on Hypertext & Social Media*. HT '15. Guzelyurt, Northern Cyprus: ACM, 2015, 221–230. ISBN: 978-1-4503-3395-5. DOI: 10.1145/2700171.2791037. URL: http://doi.acm. org/10.1145/ 2700171.2791037. (Accessed: 3 April 2022).

Smith, W.B. (1988) "Curves of Pauline and Pseudo-Pauline Style I". In: *Unitarian Review*, 452–460.

Smith, S., Warburton, S. and Rutledge, J. (2016) *Connecting Patrons with Library Materials: A Readers' Advisory Crash Course Innovative Libraries Online Conference*. State Library of Iowa.

Solorio, T. et al. (2017) "Convolutional Neural Networks for Authorship Attribution of Short Texts". In: *Proceedings of the 15th Conference of the European Chapter of the Association for Computational Linguistics, EACL 2017*, Valencia, Spain, April 3–7, 2017, Volume 2: Short Papers. 2017, pp. 669–674.

Vaz, P. C., deMatos, D.M. and Martins, B. (2012a) "Stylometric Relevance-feedback Towards a Hybrid Book Recommendation Algorithm". In: *Proceedings of the Fifth ACM Workshop on Research Advances in Large Digital Book Repositories and Complementary Media*. BooksOnline '12. Maui, Hawaii, USA: ACM, 13–16. ISBN: 978-1-4503-1714-6. DOI: 10.1145/2390116.2390125. URL: http: //doi.acm. org/10.1145/2390116.2390125. (Accessed: 3 April 2022).

Vaz, P.C., Ribeiro, R. and deMatos, M.D. (2012b) "LitRec vs. Movielens – A Comparative Study". In: *KDIR 2012 – Proceedings of Natural Language Processing for Book Recommender Systems 11 the International Conference on Knowledge Discovery and Information Retrieval*, 370–373. Barcelona, Spain, 4–7 October, 2012.

Vladimir, V., Golowich, S.E., and Smola, A. (1996) "Support Vector Method for Function Approximation, Regression Estimation and Signal Processing". In: *Proc. 9th International Conference on Neural*

Information Processing Systems. NIPS'96, Denver, Colorado, 2–5 December. Denver, Colorado: MIT Press, 281–287. URL: http://dl.acm.org/citation.cfm?id=2998981.2999021. (Accessed: 3 April 2022).

Wang, C. and Blei, D.M. (2011) "Collaborative Topic Modeling for ecommending Scientific Articles". In: *Proc. 17th ACM SIGKDD International Conference on Knowledge Discovery and Data Mining*. KDD '11, 21–24 August, San Diego, California, USA: ACM, 2011, pp. 448–456. ISBN: 978-1-4503- 0813-7. DOI: 10.1145/2020408.2020480. URL: http://doi. acm.org/10.1145/2020408.2020480. (Accessed: 3 April 2022).

Zhang, H. and Chow, T.W.S. (2015) "Organizing Books and Authors by Multilayer SOM". In: *Neural Networks and Learning Systems, IEEE Transactions on PP.99*, 1–14. ISSN: 2162-237X. DOI: 10. 1109/TNNLS.2015.2496281.

Claudius-Marian Teodorescu

Chapter 7 Syntactic Tree Editor

Abstract: In this paper, the development of an editor for syntactic trees is presented. The editor can be used during the process of teaching grammar, according to the Government and Binding (GB) model, at the university level, and it can be extended in order to support various other grammar models. The paper comprises the analysis of a significant number of software products for editing or generating syntax trees, with the presentation of their functions and features. The description is the starting point for the elaboration of the list of functions and features of the self-developed syntax tree editor. The main functions and features are: a. the editor allows editing of syntax trees in a graphical mode, by drawing them on a surface, using the mouse (drag-and-drop the tree components), in a web navigator; b. after the syntax tree is edited, it can be exported as image (PNG or JPEG format) or as text (JSON format). The trees exported as images can be inserted in scientific papers or in grammar manuals, or they can be sent by the students to their teachers, as solutions for pieces of homework; c. if the editing of a tree has to be interrupted, the tree can be saved, in order for its editing to be continued afterwards; d. the editor is equipped with two node banks, both for the GB modes, one bank with the node names in the Romanian language, and the other bank with the node names in English; e. the editor's source-code is of open-source type. The technical documentation for using the editor can be found in the editor's website (see https://arin.solirom.ro). Finally, the paper presents some conclusions as to possible practical applications of the syntactic tree editor, such as: didactic instrument or scientific research instrument. Future directions of development are also discussed.

Keywords: editor, generative grammar, syntactic tree

1. Introduction

This chapter introduces a research project that aims at developing a software product for editing syntactic trees, irrespective of the language. There are many software products for producing syntactic trees, most of them being generators, which start from an annotated sentence that is transformed into a syntactic tree (jsSyntax Tree), (Syntax Tree Generator). The other type consists of editors, which start from unannotated texts.

The editor developed during our research project is freely available online (see https://arin.solirom.ro), thus overpassing the limitations of similar products, such as: the need to install the software product in one's computer (TreeForm Syntax); usage only with the Windows operating system (Syntax Tree Editor); usage as Java applet in web browsers (Visual Interactive Syntax Learning), a type of technology which is not accepted anymore by modern web browsers.

2. Methodology

2.1. Creating the bibliography

The bibliography was created considering the next criteria: providing the necessary and sufficient grammatical knowledge, apprehension of what was accomplished within the field, and establishing the set of programming languages (the technology stack). Thus, the bibliography comprises website addresses for similar software products, the technical specifications of the programming languages used HTML Living Standard, ECMA Script (2020), CSS Syntax Module Level 3, and, for some functions of the editor, software modules that were developed in academic institutions (Franz et al. 2015).

2.2. Initial documentation work

For each software product that was considered, a list with its functions and features was compiled. A list with the nodes that are specific for the GB (Government and Binding) grammar model (of university level) was also created, which also included the types of actions exerted over these nodes.

2.3. Designing the functions and sections of the editor's web interface

A synoptic table with the functions and features of the analysed software products was compiled, which facilitated the extraction of the general features and functions of the editor. To these, some specific features and functions were added, some of them new, while others allow the overpassing of the limitations of the analysed software products. The editor's web interface, namely its sections and layout, was also designed.

3. The theoretical framework

According to Bidu-Vrânceanu et al. (2005), the syntactic trees are "graphical representations used by the generative grammar for describing the structural hierarchy" of sentences. These representations codify "the dominance relations" (Gheorghe 2009) by using nodes for the syntactic categories and for the lexical constituents of the sentence, along with lines linking these nodes.

This editor, being for didactic use, currently contains only two node banks form GB grammar model: one bank with node names in the Romanian language, and the other bank with node names in English. Other node banks can be added quite easily, though, by codifying the nodes, edges, and actions in a special data format.

The editor's node banks contain the following classes of nodes (Gheorghe 2009):

- **Lexical heads and lexical projections.** These are represented by homonym buttons within the node bank: *V*, *V'*, *VP* (verb phrase); *N*, *N'*, *NP* (noun phrase); *Aj*, *Aj'*, *AjP* (adjective phrase); *Prep*, *Prep'*, *PrepP* (prepositional phrase); *Adv*, *Adv'*, *AdvP* (adverbial phrase); *Flex*, *Flex'*, *FlexP* (inflectional phrase); *C*, *C'*, *CP* (complementizer phrase); *Det*, *Det'*, *DetP* (determiner phrase).
- **Specifier.** This is represented by the button *Spec*.
- **Empty categories.** These are constituents without phonetic realization: *trace* is represented by the button *t*; little *pro* is represented by the button *pro*; big *PRO* is represented by the button *PRO*; *generic pronoun* is represented by the button *pro g.*; null determiner is represented by button *e*; null complementizer is represented by button θ.
- **Coordination.** This is represented by button *Coord*.
- The editor also has buttons for actions:
- **Marking of co-indexing.** This is done by using the buttons *i*, *j*, *k*, respectively.
- **Marking of co-indexing negation.** This is done by using the button * before using the button for indexing.
- **Movement.** This is done by using the button *d*.

4. The functions and features of the editors and generators that were studied

This section comprises the result of the analysis of similar software products. For the analysis, any relevant software product was considered, no matter the programming language or the languages used for developing it and no matter the operating system needed for it. This was done in order to take advantage of a large spectrum of possible functions and features from which to select the ones for the self-developed editor. Find below the synthesis of this analysis.

The analysis shows that the software products that output syntactic trees are of two types: *generators*, which generate syntactic trees starting from a sentence that is annotated by using the bracket notation, and *editors*, which allow obtaining trees by effectively editing them, staring from an unannotated sentence. One can also see that the number of generators is larger than the number of editors. A reason for this could be the fact that the development of an editor is more complex than the one of a generator.

By comparing the functions and features of existing software products, a set of functions and features for the self-developed editor was compiled. The new software should: be available for any operating system; be an editor, not a generator; allow resuming of editing; allow the export of the tree as image in an open-source format; allow the export of the tree as text in an open-source format; have a source-code of open-source type; be available online. The following table gives the main functions and features of the analysed software products.

Tab. 1. Functions and features of the analysed software products (each product has the starting year mentioned)

Function or feature	**Syntax Tree editor (2012)**	**TreeForm (2014)**	**JsSyntax Tree (2003)**	**Syntax Tree Generator (2012)**	**Rsyntax Tree (2009)**	**Tree Structure (1996)**	**Syntactic Tree Diagram (2018)**
Multiple operation systems	NO	**YES**	**YES**	**YES**	**YES**	**YES**	**YES**
Syntactic tree editor	**YES**	**YES**	NO	NO	NO	NO	**YES**
Resuming of editing	**YES**	**YES**	NO	NO	NO	NO	NO
Export tree as image	**YES**	**YES**	**YES**	**YES**	**YES**	**YES**	NO
Export tree as text	**YES**	**YES**	NO	NO	NO	**YES**	NO
Open-source code	**YES**	**YES**	**YES**	**YES**	**YES**	NO	NO
Available online	NO	NO	**YES**	NO	**YES**	**YES**	**YES**

5. The functions and features of the editor that was developed

The following table contains the functions and features retained after the previous analysis, as well as new functions and features, which are specific to the self-developed editor:

Tab. 2. Functions and features of the developed editor

Crt. No.	Function / feature	Methodology for development
1	The development has to be made by using modern programming languages, so that the available RAM memory to be used in an efficient manner.	I have chosen the Javascript, HTML, and CSS programming languages that, moreover, help to fulfill the second feature in this table.
2	The editor has to be available online.	The editor is available at the web address https://arin.solirom.ro being published as static website which, compared with dynamic websites, has the advantage of being faster and exposing a smaller attack surface. The hosting is completely free of charge, as offered by Gitlab (see line 3).
3	The source-code has to be of open-source type.	The source-code is available at the address https://gitlab.com/solirom-arin/site
4	The editor should have nodes grouped as node banks.	The editor's user interface has a section designated for the node bank. There is also the possibility to select between two node banks. In the future, other node banks can be added.
5	The editor has to allow export of the tree as image and text, respectively.	The editor allows export as image (PNG or JPEG format), and as text (JSON format).
6	The user has to be able to resume the editing of the tree.	The mechanism for resuming editing is to store the tree in the user's computer and to reload the tree when the user wants to continue the editing.

Tab. 2. Continued

Crt. No.	Function / feature	Methodology for development
7	When it is possible, the editor should use software components developed within academic research projects.	The editing surface consists of a software component called Cytoscape (Franz et al. 2015), which was developed at the Donnelly Centre of the Toronto University. Also, in order to improve this software component, I used some software modules, developed in an academic environment, too, as follows: for the nodes' layout (dagre), for drawing edges between nodes (Edge Creation UI Extension for Cytoscape.js), for double click event (cytoscape-dblclick). using the Cytoscape component for syntax tree editing is a premiere.
8	The sentence has to be modifiable by the user.	The editor's user interface has a text input for the sentence that is entered by the user. In order to edit the tree, the user selects words (or groups of words) and drags them onto the tree editing surface. As the words (or groups of words) are moved, they are inactivated within the sentence, becoming active again only when their copies on the editing surface are deleted. The editing allows adding of new words, even if the existing ones were already integrated within the tree.

An element of novelty of this editor is the fact that allows multiple node banks.

6. Description of the editor's user interface

The user interface of the editor comprises five sections, as follows: button toolbar, the selector for the grammar system, the text input, the node bank, and the editing surface.

6.1. Button toolbar

This section contains the buttons for the high-level functions of the editor:

Fig. 1. The button toolbar

The parts of this section are: 1 = the title of the web application, "Syntactic Tree Editor" (in Romanian language in the picture); 2 = button for importing of a syntactic tree that was previously exported from this web application; 3 = button for refreshing the layout of the syntactic tree during editing, any time is needed; 4 = button for entirely deleting the syntactic tree; 5 = button for saving the syntactic tree as text, in JSON format; 6 = button for saving the syntactic tree as image, in PNG format; 6 = button for saving the syntactic tree as image, in JPEG format.

6.2. Selector for the grammar system

This control provides a list of grammar systems that can be used for editing trees, as it can be seen in Fig. 2.

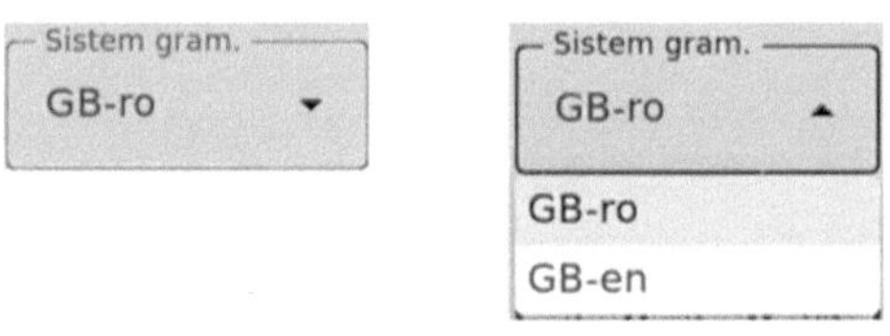

Fig. 2. The grammar system control

Currently, the editor allows selection of only one grammar system, namely the GB system, with the node names in Romanian language (value GB-ro above), respectively with the node names in English language (value GB-en above).

6.3. Text input control

This section contains only the control that will be used for entering the (multiline) text to be represented as a syntactic tree, as in Fig. 3.

Fig. 3. The text input control

6.4. Node bank

This section contains, along with nodes that can be used as internal nodes for the syntactic tree, two types of buttons that can be used to operate over the syntactic tree.

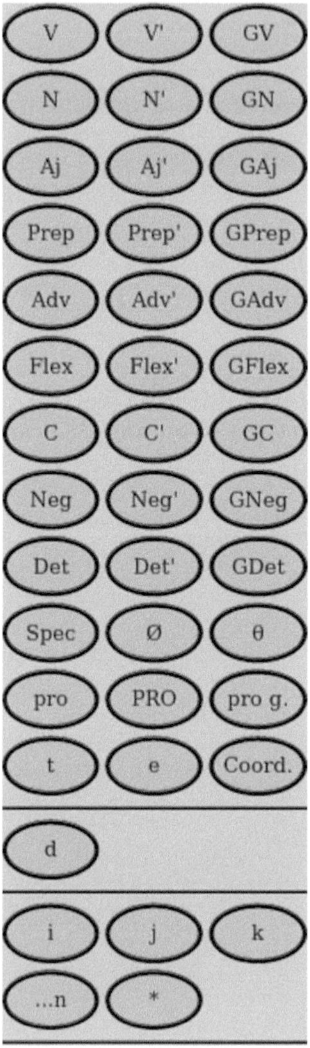

Fig. 4. The node bank control

There are three types of nodes, as follows: the top section contains all the internal and terminal nodes, according to the grammar system; the middle section contains the button *d* for representing the movement of a constituent; the bottom section contains indices that are used for marking the coindexing (i, j, k, ...n), as well as the button *, which is used for negating the coindexing.

6.5. Editing surface

This section consists of a rectangular surface on which the syntactic tree will be edited, as represented in Figs. 4 and 5.

Fig. 5. The editing surface control, at the beginning of editing

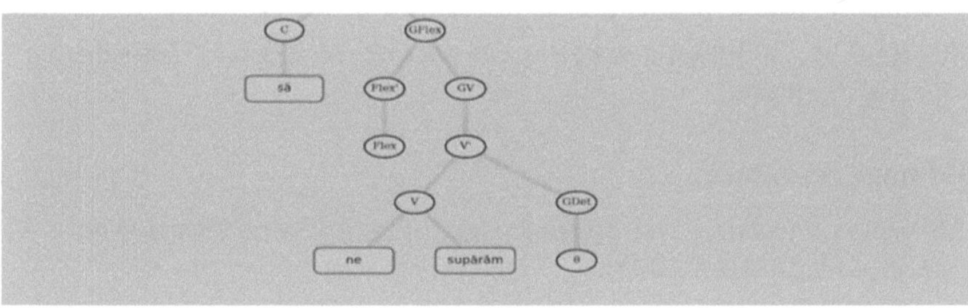

Fig. 6. The editing surface control, with an edited tree

7. Conclusions and future developments

This editor can be used for teaching students about generative syntax. The user documentation can be found in the editor's website (see https://arin.solirom.ro). The student has to edit the tree starting from the sentence received from the professor, and hand-over to the professor the tree, exported as image. The editor can also be used when a researcher needs to insert a syntactic tree in an academic paper.

There are some development directions for the future, of which a few should be mentioned: adding new node banks, adding *undo* and *redo* for editing, colour themes for the tree, and, for the user interface, export the sentence as text with bracket notation.

Acknowledgements

Developing the present editor was the theme of the dissertation for my Master's degree in Philology, under the supervision of Prof. Dr. Mihaela Gheorghe, with the Transylvania University of Braşov, Romania. I want to thank her for the encouragement to do such research.

References

Bidu-Vrânceanu, A., Călăraşu, C., Ionescu-Ruxăndoiu, L., Mancaş, M., Pană Dindelegan, M. (2005) *Dicţionar de ştiinţe ale limbii.* Bucureşti: Nemira.

Franz, M., Lopes, C.T., Huck G., Dong Y., Sume, O., Bader G.D. (2015) "Cytoscape.js: A graph theory library for visualisation and analysis". *Bioinformatics* 1–3, DOI:10.1093/bioinformatics/btv557.

Gheorghe, M. (2009) *Modele de descriere în sintaxă.* Braşov: "Transilvania" University Press.

Webpage resources

CSS Syntax Module Level 3 Homepage, https://w3.org/TR/css-syntax-3/. (Accessed: 25 April 2021).

cytoscape-dblclick Homepage, https://github.com/fixpoint/cytoscape-dblclick. (Accessed: 25 April 2021).

dagre – Graph layout for JavaScript Homepage, https://github.com/dagrejs/dagre (Accessed: 25 April 2021).

ECMAScript® 2020 Homepage, https://262.ecma-international.org/11.0/. (Accessed: 25 April 2021).

Edge creation UI extension for Cytoscape.js Homepage.https://github.com/cytoscape/cytoscape.js-edgehandles. (Accessed: 25 April 2021).

HTML Living Standard Homepage, https://html.spec.whatwg.org/. (Accessed: 25 April 2021).

jsSyntaxTree Homepage, http://ironcreek.net/syntaxtree/. (Accessed: 25 April 2021).

RSyntaxTree Homepage, https://yohasebe.com/rsyntaxtree/. (Accessed: 25 April 2021).

Syntax Tree Generator Homepage, http://mshang.ca/syntree/. (Accessed: 25 April 2021).

Syntax Tree Editor Homepage, https://github.com/jepst/Tree. (Accessed: 25 April 2021).

Syntactic Tree Diagram Homepage, https://elearning.cpp.edu/learning-objects/syntactic-tree-structures/?page=activity.html&level=1, (Accessed: 25 April 2021).

TreeForm Syntax Tree Drawing Software Homepage, https://sourceforge.net/projects/treeform/. (Accessed: 25 April 2021).

Visual Interactive Syntax Learning – Tree structure Homepage, https://visl.sdu.dk/visl/en/parsing/automatic/trees.php. (Accessed: 25 April 2021).

part of the *Principia* Descartes introduced the famous cosmological theory of the vortex.[8] According to his theory, the whole universe was composed of giant vortices formed around the fixed stars; the solar system being one such vortex. The analogy of the vortex also held for lesser systems, such as the system of the Earth, which kept the Moon in its orbit.

The engraved images of both sections of *Le monde* and the *Principia* were crucial explanatory devices of Descartes's cosmology. We included in the online platform all illustrations of *Le monde ou Traité de la lumière* and of the third part of the *Principia*. We did not, however, include images from the second and fourth parts of the *Principia*.[9] We decided (at least provisionally) to exclude these images because they are either connected to very general issues in physics (second part) or to particular earthly phenomena such as the formation of the Earth, magnetism, or meteorological problems (fourth part). In this respect, we followed Descartes's own structure of the *Principia*: I. The Principles of Human Knowledge; II. The Principles of Material Things; III. The Visible Universe; IV. The Earth. We have focused only on the third section, dealing with cosmology.

The initial release of the website included direct digital access to the cosmological illustrations printed in three editions of Descartes's works: (1) the original Latin edition of the *Principia philosophiae* of 1644; (2) the French translation of (1), *Les Principes de la philosophie* (1647); (3) the 1664 edition of *Le monde de Mr Descartes, ou Le traité de la lumière*. Upon collecting these images, we came across some notable changes – differences between the illustrations used in the *Principia* (1644) and *Les Principes* (1647) – see Fig. 2.

Whereas the first includes 44 illustrations – with some of them repeated often throughout the treatise – the latter only contains 10 illustrations. The quality of the print differs due to the type of engraving (woodcut vs. copper plate), but other changes in drawings are also noticeable.

---

8 It is not the place in this paper to discuss the details of Descartes's cosmology. For a detailed account of the theory of the vortex, including the reception of this theory in the early modern period, see (Aiton 1972). For a comparison between the cosmologies of *Le monde* and the *Principia*, see (Dobre 2021).

9 At least not until December 2020, when the work on the virtual collection presented in the current chapter was completed.

Since then, our team aimed at collecting and displaying *all* cosmological illustrations in the editions of the *Principia* and *Le monde* published between 1644 and 1677 (see Fig. 3). One main assumption to verify was the extent to which noteworthy variations of the cosmological images can be identified in the early modern editions of Descartes's works. Up to December 2020, our team managed to collect the cosmological illustrations of 12 editions of the *Principia*, and 2 editions of the *Le monde*. They are as follows[10]:

- *Renati Des Cartes Principia philosophiae* (Amsterdam: L. Elzevier, 1644); source: Gallica.
- *Les Principes de la philosophie, escrits en latin par René Descartes, et traduits en françois par un de ses amis* (Paris: H. Le Gras, 1647); source: Gallica.
- *Principia philosophiae* (Amsterdam: L. Elzevier, 1650); source: Archive.org.

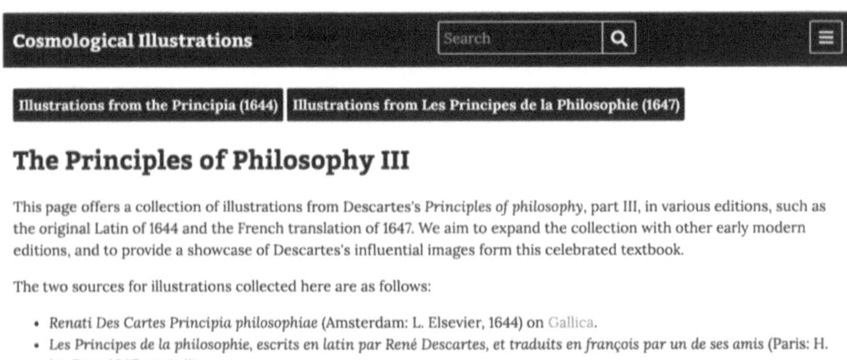

Fig. 2. The website including (at the date) the illustrations of the two editions of Descartes's *Principles*

10 The list follows (Otegem 2002). We include in this list links to the online repositories hosting each digital copy we used in the collection. We were unable to locate digital copies of two other early modern editions documented by Otegem: *Les Principes de la philosophie* (Paris: Henry Le Gras and Edme Pepingué, 1651) and the *Principia Philosophiae* (London: J. Hart, 1664).

- *Principia philosophiæ* (Amsterdam: Louis Elzevier; Daniel Elzevier, 1656); source: Archive.org.
- *Principia philosophiæ* (Amsterdam: Johannem Jansonium, 1656); source: Archive.org.
- *Principia philosophiæ of Beginselen der Wysbegeerte* (Amsterdam: Jan Rieuwertz, 1657); source: the library of the University of Ghent (via Google Books).
- *Les Principes de la Philosophie* (Paris: Henry and Nicolas Le Gras, 1659); source: La Bibliothèque numérique patrimoniale des universités Toulosianes.
- *Renati Des-Cartes Principia Philosophiae* (Amsterdam: Daniel Elzevier, 1664); source: Munich DigitiZation Center (MDZ).
- *Renati Des-Cartes opera philosophica. Principia Philosophiae* (Amsterdam: E. Weyerstraten and J. Janssonius van Waesberge, 1664); source: PLUME.
- *Le monde de Mr Descartes, ou Le traité de la lumière et des autres principaux objets des sens. Avec un discours de l'action des corps et un autre des fièvres, composez selon les principes du même auteur* (Paris: T. Girard, 1664); source: BIU Santé (Paris).
- *Les Principes de la philosophie* (Paris: Theodore Girard, 1668); source: Gallica.
- *Principia Philosophiae* (Amsterdam: Daniel Elzevier, 1672); source: Archive.org.
- *Principia Philosophiae* (Amsterdam: Daniel Elzevier, 1677); source: Archive.org.
- *L'Homme de René Descartes et la formation du foetus, Avec les Remarques de Louis de la Forge. A quoy l'on a ajouté Le Monde ou Traité de la Lumiere du mesme Autheur*. Edited by Claude Clerselier. 2nd ed. (Paris: Theodore Girard, 1677); source: Archive.org.

Aside from the 14 editions of the two treatises (12 of the *Principia* and 2 of *Le monde*), we decided to experiment and expand the collection with images from Descartes's *Correspondence*, as edited by Claude Clerselier. The images of all three volumes of the first early modern editions (*Lettres de M. Descartes*, ed. Claude Clerselier [Paris: Charles Angot, 1657–1667]) are also available on the platform (see Fig. 4).[11] Taken together, the attained results are encouraging, showing that an expansion of the platform, to include digital reproductions of all early modern Cartesian images, from all published works of Descartes between 1637 and 1677, should be pursued. We expect that in the near future we will be able to carry out this plan.

Fig. 3. The website's interface of image collections from the 12 editions of the *Principia* and 2 editions of *Le Monde*. Each thumbnail links to a collection of images from the respective edition

11 Unlike the images from *Le monde* and the *Principles* presented above, the set of illustrations from Descartes's correspondence needs further work on the metadata (only partly annotated by December 2020).

Fig. 4. The thumbnails of the Title pages of each volume of Clerselier's edition of Descartes's correspondence

It is important to highlight that a working principle we followed in our selection of sources was to restrict the use of resources only to those already available in the public domain. Leaving pragmatic reasons related to access aside, another intended aim was to encourage the use of open access sources and to offer a showcase of the exciting possibilities opened by a digital approach of the subject.

2.2. Description of the digital platform – sources, structure, tools

This section of the chapter describes the digital workflow. First, illustrations are selected from open sources – i.e., digital editions available in the public domain and accessible on Gallica (https://gallica.bnf.fr/) and other digital repositories (e.g., Munich DigitiZation Center, La Bibliothèque numérique patrimoniale des universités Toulosianes) – which are subsequently collected, catalogued, and annotated with metadata in a local database in Tropy (see Fig. 5). Metadata for items are annotated in the Dublin Core standard. The categories listed for each item are classified into three types, according to their purpose:

1. *descriptive metadata*: (a) factual and historical elements of identification such as Title, Creator (i.e., Descartes), Date (e.g., 1644, 1647, 1664), Language (French, Latin), Publisher (e.g., L. Elsevier), Coverage (e.g., Amsterdam, Paris), and Type (which refers to the engraving: woodcut or copper plate); (b) two elements generated in the project: Identifier (a unique number generated as a string which includes the year of the edition, abbreviated form of the publication title, section or chapter number, the order of the illustration inside the specific edition, and – in

some cases – a letter to designate a repeated illustration; for example, the string "44PP3.1" refers to the first illustration in the *Principia philosophia* of 1644, part III, while "44PP3.10" refers to the tenth unique image in the third part of the treatise, with repeated versions throughout the book: "44PP3.10a", "44PP3.10b" and so on; see Fig. 5) and Description (e.g., vortex, corpuscles, etc. – for the moment, the description field is rather limited and consists in keywords).

2. *structural metadata* that helps us create a relational database by the category "Relation" (cross-references to other resources on the platform). The advantages provided by this type of database are to be explained in the next pages of the current chapter.
3. *administrative metadata*, such as Source (this category includes both the title of the book and the external source of the image; e.g., to the original on Gallica, BIU, etc.), Format (for the moment, print, as all illustrations are from printed books).

Fig. 5. A screenshot with the list of illustrations from Descartes's *Principia* of 1644, as they are catalogued in Tropy

Once the local Tropy collection is complete, it is exported to the Omeka S platform. The metadata is verified again on the online platform and some relational content is added (e.g., link to the original source on Gallica; the "Relation" category, creating cross-references between items included in the exhibition). The information included in the metadata is thus curated twice in the process: first, when it is added to the local database, in Tropy, and the second time, when the item is already online, as part of the exhibition.

Furthermore, in order to build a shared team database, the data stored in Tropy is exported as multiple CSV files, organized by edition. These files are merged into a single worksheet which gathers the existing information about the collection of illustrations uploaded on the website and generates a detailed database. The resulting table provides a complete description of every item based on the categories of metadata mentioned previously; see Fig. 6.

With the expected growth of our collection in the future, careful attention must be ascribed to effectively organize the data. Hence, our workflow – described above – supplies a practical method to classify, catalogue, and offer descriptions of a visual archive which can be later used when testing digital tools. The general question arising at this point concerns the use and the benefits of creating a database of this kind. We regard this as a really important component for several reasons:

1. It allows the team to have remote access to a relational database;
2. It is a reliable way of backing-up the information in order to manage the platform in a secure way;
3. Processes such as tracking and checking the issues on the website can be done easily using the same document;
4. It represents a key-element for testing and implementing digitals tools (some of them being discussed below).

	A	B	C	D	E	F	G	H	I
1	Title	Creator	Date	Type	Source	Identifier	Rights	Subject	Language
2	PP III 23 (1644)	Descartes	1644	woodcut	Principia Philosophiae III	44PP3.1			Latin
3	PP III 70 (1644)	Descartes	1644	woodcut	Principia Philosophiae III	44PP3.10			Latin
4	PP III 71 (1644) rep. 70	Descartes	1644	woodcut	Principia Philosophiae III	44PP3.10a			Latin
5	PP III 72 (1644) rep. 70	Descartes	1644	woodcut	Principia Philosophiae III	44PP3.10b			Latin

	A	J	K	L	M	N	O	P
1	Title	Format	Contributor	Description	Publisher	Coverage	Relation	Tags (Tropy)
2	PP III 23 (1644)	Print		vortex	L. Elsevier	Amsterdam		
3	PP III 70 (1644)	Print		vortex	L. Elsevier	Amsterdam		
4	PP III 71 (1644) rep. 70	Print		vortex	L. Elsevier	Amsterdam	44PP3.10	
5	PP III 72 (1644) rep. 70	Print		vortex	L. Elsevier	Amsterdam	44PP3.10	

Fig. 6. The first items from the exported Tropy database with the information included in the metadata

A variety of uses can be derived from here and, depending on the research question, one can focus on forms of visualization, statistics about the number of images, networks of printers, etc. For example, in order to examine the relation between publishers and new editions of Descartes's works, we used Palladio, a web-based digital humanities tool for creating visualizations. We introduced the spreadsheet with sources in Palladio and generated a simple graph, which offers a convenient visualization of Theodore Girard's role in the publication of both *Le monde* and the *Principia* (see Fig. 7). For a historian interested in the microhistories around the publication of a work, such approach can lead to interesting outcomes.

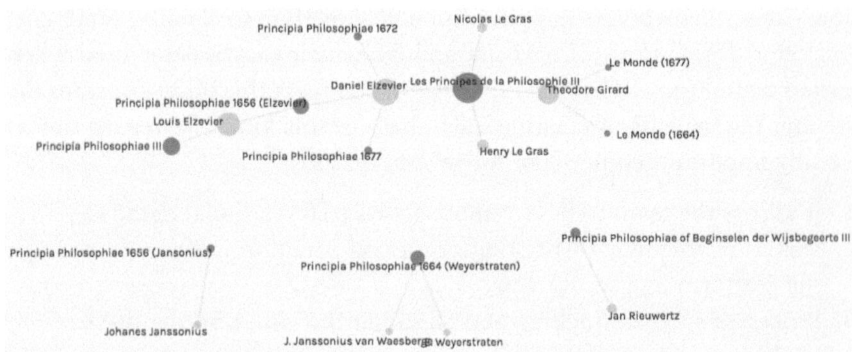

Fig. 7. A network generated in Palladio, showing relations between publishers and editions of Descartes's works

Such and similar findings are supported by the database we are currently constructing as the groundwork of the online exhibition.

Another use of the virtual collection is to conduct an in-depth analysis to identify invariances, correlations, and fluctuations: (a) within the same edition (e.g., can we identify similar illustrations? What are the ways in which they differ?), (b) between two or more editions, and (c) between Descartes's cosmological writings and other authors from the early modern period. To study differences between editions or even similar sets of illustrations repeated throughout one publication, we added the module Mirador Viewer for Omeka (see Fig. 8).[12] Mirador is a useful open-source

12 On Mirador, see (Sanderson et al. 2015; Zundert 2018). Initially, we started our tests with an alternative module, Universal Viewer for Omeka S.

image comparison tool, which is often used by scholars in medieval studies with the aim of digitally comparing and analysing manuscripts exhibited in different libraries. Originally developed by a team at Stanford, it was soon recognized that Mirador's usage can be extended to many academic fields and even cultural institutions can benefit from it (e.g., museums, archives, cultural organizations).

One main advantage of Mirador is its configurability. Thus, it allows the user to add multiple illustrations (up to 25) which are displayed in the same case (so there is no need to open multiple tabs). The additional slots can be configurated in various vertical or horizontal grid views (by selecting "Change Layout" option, see Fig. 8). Each image can be examined in terms of several options: zoom in/out, rotate left/right, contrast of colours (adjustments of brightness/contrast/saturation); in addition, the user can view information regarding the metadata of the added object(s). The viewer is designed for any 2D object and does not provide 3D features, which fits well within the general use of our collection.

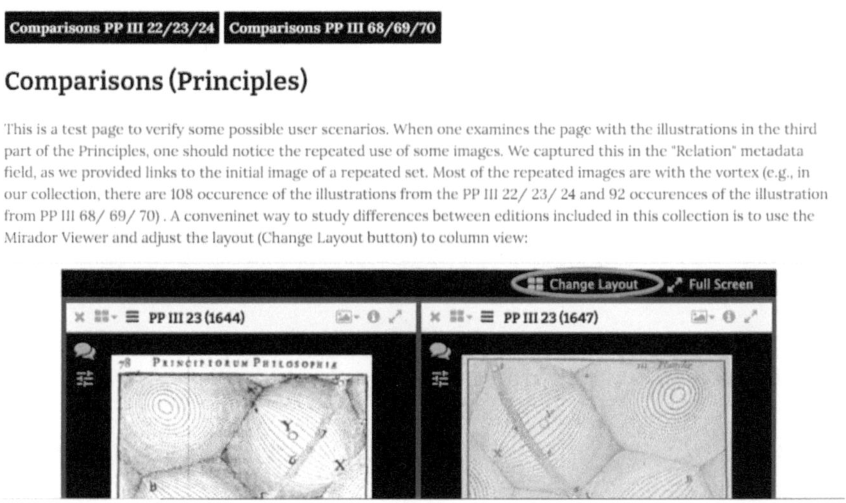

Fig. 8. The image presents one possible user scenario: to perform comparisons with the use of the Mirador Viewer

However, there is one drawback we identified while testing Mirador on our platform. Counterintuitively, the user is unable to choose and to add new objects (even from those uploaded on the website) to generate her own showcases of comparisons. Hence, one can only analyse the repeated use of images from the possible user scenarios that were already provided on the website. At the moment, we offer two cases for comparisons, both of them comprising in the famous illustrations of Descartes's vortices. Our choice is motivated by the prevalence of the vortex images in the third part of the *Principia*. The two sets of comparisons currently available on the platform – illustrations usually printed as part of the PP III 22/23/24 and PP III 68/69/70 – include images depicting the Cartesian vortex. The selection of these images is grounded in their significance, which makes them the most repeated cosmological illustrations in the early modern editions of Descartes's *Principia*, as can be seen in Fig. 9. The diagram shows another interesting development in the evolution of Descartes's cosmological imagery: while the text of the *Principia* stayed the same, the image of the vortex as part of the PP III 22/23/24 was becoming more prominent, although the first editions featured more repeated images of the illustration for PP III 68/69/70.[13]

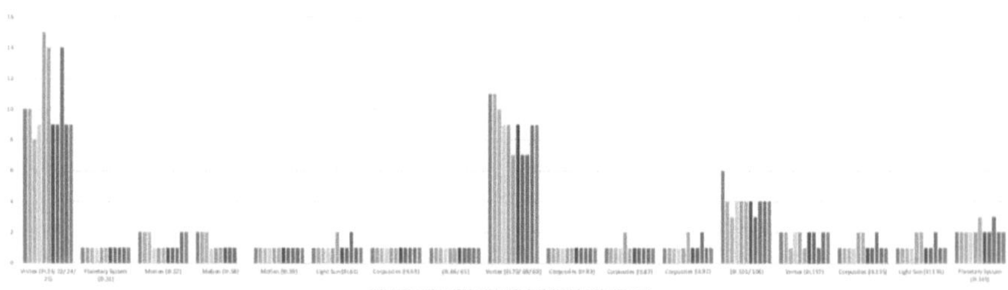

Fig. 9. Sample images from *Principia* III (horizontal) related to the number of repetitions of each of them (vertical)

Another visualization tool included is a timeline, which was generated with an open-source tool: TimelineJS, developed by a team of developers from The Northwestern University Knight Lab. It allows us to produce a

13 A discussion of this finding is in (Dobre forthcoming).

timeline with the sources included in the collection and make it available on the website. The result was posted on our "About" page (https://cartesian.unibuc.ro/s/cosmologicalillustrations/page/about).

This is, in brief, an overview of how digital tools can enhance research in the history of philosophy and science, and how we applied these tools in order to benefit from the virtual collection of Cartesian cosmological images. However, the platform can be used in multiple ways by scholars of early modern cosmological imagery. The planned development of the collection to include more images from the early modern period is expected to reveal new open possibilities for the use of the digital collection.

Acknowledgements

This work was supported by two grants of Ministery of Research and Innovation, CNCS-UEFISCDI, projects number PN-III-P1-1.1-TE-2016-0710 and PN-III-P1-1.1-TE-2019-0841, within PNCDI III. Several prior drafts have been circulating as preprints, and presentations have been made in Bucharest and in online conferences. We would like to thank the audience and the readers of previous versions of the paper for comments and discussions

References

Aiton, E.J. (1972) *The Vortex Theory of Planetary Motions*. London: MacDonald.

Berger, S. (2017) *The Art of Philosophy. Visual Thinking in Europe from the Late Renaissance to the Early Enlightenment*. Princeton: Princeton University Press.

Descartes, R. (1974–1986) *Œuvres de Descartes* (11 vol). Paris: Vrin.

Descartes, R. (1984–1991) *The Philosophical Writings* (3 vol). Translated by J. Cottingham et al. Cambridge: Cambridge University Press.

Dobre, M. (2021) *Cosmologia carteziană*. Bucharest: Editura Universității din Bucureşti.

Dobre, M. (forthcoming) "Depicting Cartesian Cosmology in the Seventeenth Century", in Mantovani, M. and Cellamare, D. (eds) *Cartesian Images. Depicting Natural Philosophy in the Seventeenth Century*. Leiden: Brill (Medieval and Early Modern Philosophy and Science).

Dobre, M., Babeş, O. and Bujor, I. (2020) "Cartesian Cosmological Illustrations: A Digital Approach". Zenodo. Available at: http://doi.org/10.5281/zenodo.3878937 (Accessed: 5 June 2020).

Lo, M.M.-H. (2014) *Between Figure and Line: Visual Transformations of Cartesian Physics, 1620–1690*. Ph.D. Harvard: Harvard University.

Lüthy, C. (2006) "Where Logical Necessity Becomes Visual Persuasion: Descartes's Clear and Distinct Illustrations". In Maclean, I. and Kusukawa, S. (eds) *Transmitting Knowledge: Words, Images and Instruments in Early Modern Europe*. Oxford/New York: Oxford University Press, pp. 97–133.

Mantovani, M. and Cellamare, D. (eds) (forthcoming) *Cartesian Images. Depicting Natural Philosophy in the Seventeenth Century*. Leiden: Brill (Medieval and Early Modern Philosophy and Science).

Nadler, S. (2016) "The Art of Cartesianism: The Illustrations of Clerselier's Edition of Descartes's 'Traité de L'Homme' (1664)". In Antoine-Mahut, D. and Gaukroger, S. (eds) *Descartes' Treatise on Man and its Reception*. Dordrecht: Springer, pp. 193–223.

Otegem, M.V. (2002) *A Bibliography of the Works of Descartes (1637–1704)*. Zeno: The Leiden-Utrecht Research Institute of Philosophy.

Sanderson, R. et al. (2015) "Mirador: A Cross-Repository Image Comparison and Annotation Platform", in *OR2015|10th International Conference on Open Repositories. OR2015|10th International Conference on Open Repositories*, 8-11 June, Indianapolis, IN. Available at: http://program.or2015.net/sanderson-mirador-226.pdf. (Accessed: 5 June 2022).

Schuster, J. (2012) *Descartes-Agonistes: Physico-mathematics, Method & Corpuscular-Mechanism 1618–33*. Dordrecht: Springer.

Sepper, D. (2000) "Figuring Things Out: Figurate Problem-solving in the Early Descartes". In Gaukroger, S., Schuster, J. and Sutton, J. (eds) *Descartes' Natural Philosophy*. London: Routledge, pp. 228–248.

Strazzoni, A. (2015) "The Didactic, Persuasive and Scientific Uses of Illustrations after Descartes", *Noctua*, 2(1–2), pp. 432–480.

Wilkin, R.M. (2003) "Figuring the Dead Descartes: Claude Clerselier's 'L'Homme' de René Descartes" (1664)", *Representations*, 83, pp. 38–66.

Zittel, C. (2011) "Conflicting Pictures: Illustrating Descartes's 'Traité de l'homme'". In Dupré, S. and Lüthy, C. (eds) *Silent Messengers. The Circulation of Material Objects of Knowledge in the Early Modern Low Countries*. Münster: Lit Verlag, pp. 217–260.

Zundert, J. van (2018) "On Not Writing a Review about Mirador: Mirador, IIIF, and the Epistemological Gains of Distributed Digital Scholarly Resources", *Digital Medievalist*, 11(1), 5 p. doi:http://doi.org/10.16995/dm.78. (Accessed: 5 June 2022).

Digital tools

Mirador Viewer [online] available from https://projectmirador.org/ (Accessed: 5 June 2022).

MIT Libraries [online] available from <https://libraries.mit.edu/music/sequentiary/using-the-iiif-mirador-viewer/>(Accessed: 5 June 2022).

Omeka S [online] available from https://omeka.org/s/. (Accessed: 5 June 2022).

Palladio [online] available from http://hdlab.stanford.edu/palladio/. (Accessed: 5 June 2022).

TimelineJS (Knight Lab) [online] available from <https://timeline.knightlab.com/> (Accessed: 5 June 2022).

Tropy [online] available from <https://tropy.org/> (Accessed: 5 June 2022).

Universal Viewer [online] available from <https://omeka.org/s/modules/UniversalViewer/>(Accessed: 5 June 2022).

Alexandra Lițu and Valentin Bottez

Chapter 9 An Evaluation of the *Ithaca* Tool Performance for Restoring Lost Texts (Ancient Greek)

Abstract: Recently, a digital tool for restoring ancient lost texts written in Ancient Greek and for their geographical and chronological attributions has been proposed to Antiquity specialists. *Ithaca*, as the tool is called, was trained to restore fragmentary texts that were put forward in Antiquity as inscriptions (i.e., texts engraved on stone and other materials, and meant to be exposed in a public place). Many of these texts have a formulaic quality in the sense that their structure, lexical choices, turns of phrase or syntactic organization can potentially be inferred from other texts belonging to the same category, and accordingly, lost portions of text can be restored by the specialists. Our aim is to check its performance against a series of examples belonging to a funerary inscription from Callatis that we recently published, a text positing its own challenges in order to make it usable for *Ithaca*.

Keywords: automatic restoration, Black Sea, Callatis, epitaph, Greek inscriptions, *Ithaca* tool

1. Introduction

Last year, at the first international conference in Digital Humanities organized at the University of Bucharest, we presented a series of exercises meant to test the performance of Pythia, the first digital tool meant for restoring Greek inscriptions. In the meantime (this year, in March), a newer and more interesting tool was presented to scholars by the team that developed Pythia plus additional members. In the following pages, we aim rather to illustrate our first contact with the *Ithaca* tool than to perform a full set of tests of its performance. Our first contact with *Ithaca* will be mediated by an inscription we published recently and that will serve as ground truth for our exercises.

Short description of *Ithaca*

We chose to highlight in this short presentation of the *Ithaca* tool its most relevant features we retained as archaeologists and people working professionally with inscriptions.

As the authors present it (Assael et al. 2022;), *Ithaca* is an assisting tool meant to aid epigraphists in their inductive work through providing highly interpretable outputs – predictions ranked by probability for restoring ancient Greek inscriptions, for attributing them to a specific region and for establishing its chronology. *Ithaca* is trained on 78.608 inscriptions, basically all inscriptions in the Packard Humanities Institute (PHI) dataset minus the inscriptions under 50 characters, dating from the 7th c BC to the 5th c AD. Text augmentation measures were taken in order to aggrandize the data available, but not to distort the content of the corpus.

All three tasks are accomplished through proposing to specialists hypotheses ranked according to probability. For restoring texts, top-20 hypotheses are presented to the specialist, with probabilities attached. The geographical attribution is realized through a set of regional hypotheses according to the regional distribution taken into account by PHI. The predicted chronology is delivered according to decades. Especially important is the tool's sensitivity to character, word and positioning, briefly meaning sensitivity to context in terms of character, words and distinctive features for classifying inscriptions and for chronological and geographical distribution. Greek personal names (as compiled in the Lexicon of Greek Personal Names), and their distribution, were deemed important for chronological and geographical attributions. What's more, *Ithaca* uses visualization of the predictions ranked by probability in order to lend more interpretability to the outputs, and most important it provides saliency maps that make explicit those features in the input that were more influential in reaching and ranking the predictions. Basically, *Ithaca* presents the epigraphist with a range of most probable choices. All in all, a joint effort from the specialists and *Ithaca* lead to a significant improvement in performance on all three accounts, surpassing the previous state-of-the-art digital tool Pythia (+human work) presented by Assael, Sommerschield and Prag in 2019.

2. Case study

Our first case study deals with an inscription we published two years ago (Bottez and Lițu 2019). It is a funerary inscription coming most probably from Callatis, a Greek colony on the Western shore of the Black Sea. Callatis belongs to the Megarian network of colonies, and thus its inscriptions exhibit traits of the Greek Doric dialect. The inscriptions from Callatis were gathered and published by A. Avram in 1999 in the dedicated corpus *Inscriptiones Scythiae Minoris* (ISM) III and they were entered in the PHI dataset.

The structure of the short text of the funerary inscription has good analogies in other funerary inscriptions also, but not exclusively, from Callatis[1]: the name of the deceased woman in the nominative case + the name of her father in the genitive case + the name of her husband in the genitive + the noun *gunā* ("wife") in the nominative, with the expected *alpha* for Doric dialects.[2]

The text of the inscription was conserved in full and its interest lies in the Greek personal names that appear in it (see our article for the full discussion). One of these names is *Khoiros*, a name attested only eleven times (different individuals) in the *Lexicon of Greek Personal Names* (LGPN) online, only for males, and not once in the Scythia Minor area (to which Callatis belongs).[3] What's more, the time span it is attested in lies from the 6th c BC to the first quarter of the 4th c BC. In our inscription, *Khoiros* is clearly applied to a woman. One other thing must be kept in mind with respect to *Khoiros* (since it might influence automatic restoration proposals), namely the existence of the common name *khoiros*, "pig", fairly present especially in inscriptions pertaining to religion. Although it is not listed as a female name in the LGPN, Khoiros appears once as such in the PHI dataset.[4]

---

1 For example, ISM III 159 or 172.

2 See del Barrio Vega 2018, for linguistic features in the Black Sea area, and for the particularities of the Megarian dialect.

3 http://clas-lgpn2.classics.ox.ac.uk/cgi-bin/lgpn_search.cgi?name=%CE%A7%CE%BF%E1%BF%96%CF%81%CE%BF%CF%82 . All digital resources were consulted on 05.04.2022.

4 https://inscriptions.packhum.org/text/237390?hs=95-104 (for the implications of this occurrence, see Bottez and Lițu 2019: 238–239).

The other most interesting name belongs to Khoiros' father, *Simoleōn*.[5] Following a pattern long attested in the practices of Greek naming (for example, *Timoleōn*), *Simoleōn* is a compound personal name with the largely recognizable *–leōn* in second position. However, it is in our inscription that the name *Simoleōn* as such is attested for the first time ever. In contrast, the name of Khoiros' husband, *Aristōn* is a rather unremarkable one.[6] On the basis of its lettering and the existence of very close analogies in Callatis with respect to its structure we proposed the 3rd c. BC as its probable date. The full text of our inscription reads as such:

Χοῖρος Σιμολέοντος Ἀρίστωνος γυνά

"Khoiros, daughter of Simoleon, wife of Ariston"

We were interested to see how *Ithaca* would perform in the case of such difficult personal names (in terms of their limited presence/nonexistence in the training dataset), although we kept in mind the fact that texts under 50 characters (which are most probably short funerary inscriptions, dedications and the like) were eliminated from the dataset. Thus, the most direct analogies for our inscription in terms of structure were eliminated since there were usually fewer than 50 characters. One should also note that the vocabulary retained for I.PHI contains the words that appear more than 10 times in the dataset (Methods).

We decided to use for our tests the public interface of *Ithaca*, available online (https://ithaca.deepmind.com). In order to overcome the fact that our inscription counted itself under 50 characters, we artificially augmented the preserved text, adding words that did not change the meaning, nor the character of the inscription, and are otherwise attested in inscriptions of the same kind in Callatis. The words we added are an unknown patronymic, *tou deinos*, after the name of Khoiros' father, as if it were "*Simoleōn*, son of…". Immediately after we added the word *thugatēr*,

5 With the name *Khoiros* ("sow") for a daughter and with her father name finishing in *–leōn* ("lion"), this family displays interesting naming choices in terms of affinity for the animal world. As we highlighted in our article, the daughter's name does not have demeaning connotations *per se*. Her father's name is an expressive compound since *simos*, the adjective that gives the first part of the name means "flat-nosed" (Bottez and Lițu 2019: 239).

6 With 1232 occurrences of different individuals in the LGPN online (http://clas-lgpn5.classics.ox.ac.uk:8080/exist/apps/lgpn1-search/index.html?name=%CE%B1%CF%81%CE%B9%CF%83%CF%84%CF%89%CE%BD).

"daughter", and at the end we added the word *khaire*.[7] All these words are attested in inscriptions of the same kind in the same area (they are in fact common words and phrases all over the Greek world) and were proposed as restorations, when necessary, by the editor of the ISM III. We felt that we could augment our input text this way since the *Ithaca*'s authors (Methods) accepted in the I.PHI dataset both the restorations advanced by specialists, present in the PHI dataset, and the possible texts obtained by a series of data augmentation methods. The artificially enhanced text we obtained (our ground truth) is the following:

> Χοῖρος Σιμολέοντος τοῦ δεῖνος θυγάτηρ Ἀρίστωνος γυνά. Χαῖρε
> "Khoiros, daughter of Simoleon, son of…., wife of Ariston. Greetings!"

We decided to mask parts of the personal names in different tests while leaving the rest of the enhanced inscription unchanged. First, we hid the last three characters in the name *Khoiros* and designate them as characters to be predicted (noted with "?"). Thus, we obtained the following input text:

> χοι??? Σιμολεοντος του δεινος θυγατηρ αριστωνος γυνα. Χαιρε[8]
> "Khoi-, daughter of Simoleon, son of…, wife of Ariston. Greetings!"

The context provided was admittedly very limited. Among the top-20 predictions for restoration, there was no *Khoiros*, which is perhaps understandable in the sense that our example was only the second attested use of *Khoiros* as personal name for a female and both are not included as of yet in the LGPN.[9] The difficulty implied by the restoration task was also visible in the very small percentages of probability attached to the predictions. The first position was occupied by *Khoinix*, a proper noun only once attested as a masculine name and not at all as a female name (Figs. 1, 2). It might be a case of conflation with the common feminine noun *khoinix*, a measure unit, a more popular noun in inscriptions.

7 *Tou deinos* is restored as such in ISM III 168, 170, two other funerary inscriptions from Callatis. ISM III 168 also has *thugatēr* clearly attested. *Thugatēr* is restored in ISM III 170 once again after the deceased's father's patronymic. The order of the words is the same. *Khaire* is a not unusual word placed at the end of funerary inscriptions, preserved, for example, in ISM III 175.

8 We used minuscule letters in order not to provide hints with respect to the existence of proper nouns in the text.

9 According to the LGPN online (http://clas-lgpn2.classics.ox.ac.uk/cgi-bin/lgpn_search.cgi?name=%CE%A7%CE%BF%E1%BF%96%CE%BD%CE%B9%CE%BE).

Input text: χοι??? σιμολεοντος του δεινος θυγατηρ αριστωνος γυνα. χαιρε

1.	4%	χοινιξ σιμολεοντος του δεινος θυγατηρ αριστωνος γυνα. χαιρε
2.	2%	χοισκα σιμολεοντος του δεινος θυγατηρ αριστωνος γυνα. χαιρε
3.	2%	χοι οι σιμολεοντος του δεινος θυγατηρ αριστωνος γυνα. χαιρε
4.	2%	χοιρει σιμολεοντος του δεινος θυγατηρ αριστωνος γυνα. χαιρε
5.	2%	χοιρεα σιμολεοντος του δεινος θυγατηρ αριστωνος γυνα. χαιρε
6.	2%	χοι δε σιμολεοντος του δεινος θυγατηρ αριστωνος γυνα. χαιρε
7.	2%	χοιρις σιμολεοντος του δεινος θυγατηρ αριστωνος γυνα. χαιρε
8.	1%	χοιριν σιμολεοντος του δεινος θυγατηρ αριστωνος γυνα. χαιρε
9.	1%	χοισια σιμολεοντος του δεινος θυγατηρ αριστωνος γυνα. χαιρε
10.	1%	χοι τω σιμολεοντος του δεινος θυγατηρ αριστωνος γυνα. χαιρε
11.	1%	χοινηι σιμολεοντος του δεινος θυγατηρ αριστωνος γυνα. χαιρε
12.	1%	χοιται σιμολεοντος του δεινος θυγατηρ αριστωνος γυνα. χαιρε
13.	1%	χοισκω σιμολεοντος του δεινος θυγατηρ αριστωνος γυνα. χαιρε
14.	1%	χοιλια σιμολεοντος του δεινος θυγατηρ αριστωνος γυνα. χαιρε
15.	1%	χοισιω σιμολεοντος του δεινος θυγατηρ αριστωνος γυνα. χαιρε
16.	1%	χοινωι σιμολεοντος του δεινος θυγατηρ αριστωνος γυνα. χαιρε
17.	0%	χοιτις σιμολεοντος του δεινος θυγατηρ αριστωνος γυνα. χαιρε
18.	0%	χοιτηι σιμολεοντος του δεινος θυγατηρ αριστωνος γυνα. χαιρε
19.	0%	χοιρτω σιμολεοντος του δεινος θυγατηρ αριστωνος γυνα. χαιρε
20.	0%	χοιστω σιμολεοντος του δεινος θυγατηρ αριστωνος γυνα. χαιρε

Fig. 1, 2. Top-20 restoration predictions for χοι???

The saliency map for restorations (Fig. 3) shows however that Ithaca focused correctly on the word *gunā*, wife, and with less intensity on the word *thugatēr*, both important for gendering the proper noun. However, the name highlighted by the saliency map for restorations is *Khoiris* (in the 7th position in the top-20 restorations) which is indeed a feminine personal name, and one of the two possibilities for restoration when referring to the LGPN online.[10] Ithaca also seems to have focused on the closest proper name after *Khoi-*, which might show its sensitivity to the syntactical connexion between the two. *Aristōn*, in the genitive, was also taken into consideration in the saliency map, which seems to show that it was identified as a meaningful factor in proposing restorations. On the whole, both common names denoting family relationships and both genitives of the personal names indicating potential relationships of belonging were considered significant.

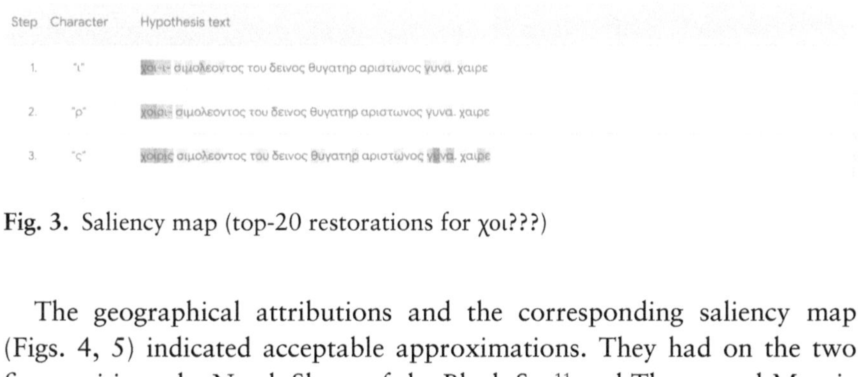

Fig. 3. Saliency map (top-20 restorations for χοι???)

The geographical attributions and the corresponding saliency map (Figs. 4, 5) indicated acceptable approximations. They had on the two first positions the North Shore of the Black Sea[11] and Thrace and Moesia Inferior which place the inscription in areas compatible with Scythia Minor

10 Meaning that from the set of all personal names beginning with *Khoi-* listed in the LGPN online, it satisfies all conditions – the number of missing characters (3), being in the nominative case, and being a feminine personal name (http://clas-lgpn5.classics.ox.ac.uk:8080/exist/apps/lgpn1-search/index.html?name=%CF%87%CE%BF%CE%B9*#top).

11 This prediction might be influenced by the important number of similar inscriptions from the Tauric Chersonese (https://inscriptions.packhum.org/search?patt=%CE%B3%CF%85%CE%BD%CE%B1+) which exhibit traits similar/identical to those from Callatis.

even if the latter one was not explicitly specified in the Top-10 predictions. The saliency map shows that *Ithaca* tried to take into consideration the characteristics of the personal names, most of all, *Simoleōn* (highlighting the *lambda* in the middle and apparently sensing it as a compound personal name- both *Simos* and *Leōn* are well represented personal names) and the Doric form *gunā*. From a chronological point of view (Figs. 6, 7), Ithaca's predictions were a bit at odds with our estimation. We estimated the 3rd c BC as a potential date for the inscription (not having a more precise criterion), while *Ithaca* proposes a mean of 108 BC seeming to concentrate strongly, but not uniquely, on *Simoleōn*. It is perhaps to be taken *cum grano salis* since the name is first attested in our inscription.[12]

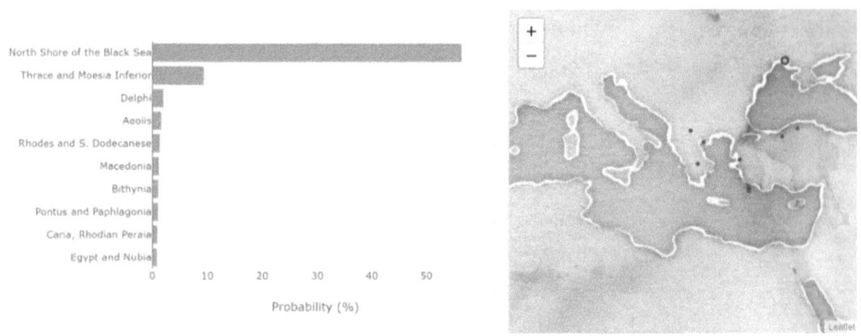

Fig. 4. Geographical attributions (χοι???)

Fig. 5. Saliency map (geographical attributions χοι???)

12 A quick look in the ISM III shows that inscriptions which are, from a structural point of view, identical to our inscription (as it was in fact attested), are dated to the 3rd c BC (ISM III 158, 159), respectively to the 1st c BC (ISM III 172). Inscriptions that also have *thugatēr* and/ or the patronymic of the father and/ or *khaire* (ISM III 168, 170, 173) are dated to the 2nd or 1st c BC. This aspect might factor in the chronological predictions offered by Ithaca.

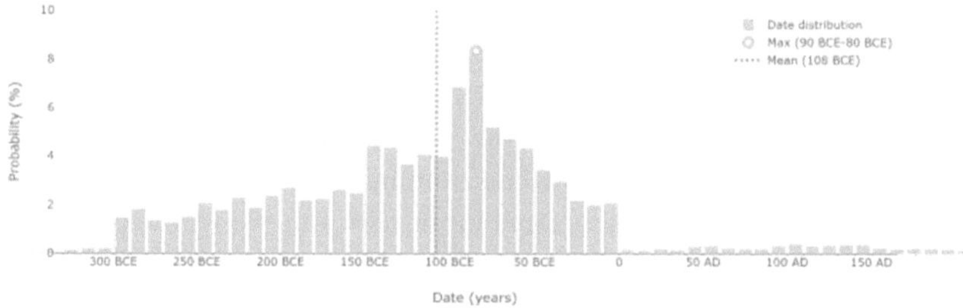

Fig. 6. Chronological attributions (χοι???)

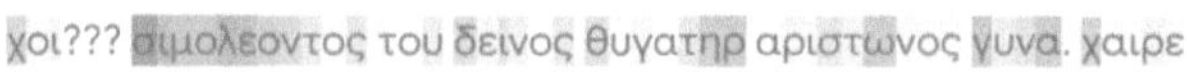

Fig. 7. Saliency map (chronological attributions χοι???)

One of the questions for us was the non-appearance of the feminine personal name *Khoidra* in the predictions given by the *Ithaca* public interface. Together with *Khoiris*, this was one of two names listed in the LGPN online, and present in the PHI dataset (and presumably in the I.PHI dataset) that was a feminine personal name and had three other characters after *Khoi-* compatible with the nominative case.[13] According to these datasets, *Khoidra* has a very specific distribution, being attested only in Pantikapaion (on the North Shore of the Black Sea, in the 1st and 2nd c AD).

We tried to further work on our input text, and we added another full stop in front of *thugatēr*, thus insulating the phrase "daughter of Ariston", an option that had the advantage of further clarifying at least one of the three genitives. Accordingly, the input text became

χοι??? Σιμολεοντος του δεινος θυγατηρ. Αριστωνος γυνα. Χαιρε

"Khoi-, daughter of Simoleon, son of.... Wife of Ariston. Greetings!"

Running once again the *Ithaca* public interface, we were able to "catch" this time *Khoidra* in the fourth place in the top-10 restorations (Fig. 8).

---

13 https://inscriptions.packhum.org/search?patt=%CE%A7%CE%BF%CE%B9%CE%B4%CF%81%CE%B1;http://clas-lgpn2.classics.ox.ac.uk/cgi-bin/lgpn_search.cgi?name=%CE%A7%CE%BF%CE%AF%CE%B4%CF%81%CE%B1.

Running the same input text in the Ithaca collaborative notebook (Fig. 9), we obtained a top-20 restorations, that had in the first four places three personal names (all minus *khoirea*), two of them being the two feminine personal names, *Khoidra* and *Khoiris*. There seem to be slight discrepancies among the results obtained when running the public interface and the collaborative notebook on the same input text, but we will not try to go further into the subject since this is our first experience with *Ithaca* and it is a first contact evaluation. In the public interface exercise, the appearance of the additional full stop also meant slight modifications in terms of geographical (Thrace and Moesia Inferior got down on third place) and chronological attribution (the mean became 146 BC).

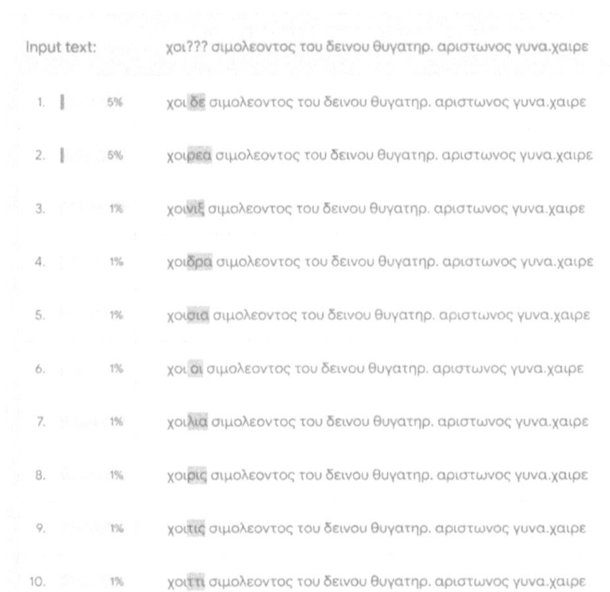

Fig. 8. Top-10 restoration predictions for χοι??? + full stop (public interface)

Input text:		χοι??? σιμολεοντος του δεινος θυγατηρ. αριστωνος γυνα. χαιρε
Hypothesis 1:	6.3%	χοινιξ σιμολεοντος του δεινος θυγατηρ. αριστωνος γυνα. χαιρε
Hypothesis 2:	3.3%	χοιδρα σιμολεοντος του δεινος θυγατηρ. αριστωνος γυνα. χαιρε
Hypothesis 3:	3.0%	χοιρεα σιμολεοντος του δεινος θυγατηρ. αριστωνος γυνα. χαιρε
Hypothesis 4:	2.5%	χοιρις σιμολεοντος του δεινος θυγατηρ. αριστωνος γυνα. χαιρε
Hypothesis 5:	1.3%	χοιρων σιμολεοντος του δεινος θυγατηρ. αριστωνος γυνα. χαιρε
Hypothesis 6:	1.1%	χοι δε σιμολεοντος του δεινος θυγατηρ. αριστωνος γυνα. χαιρε
Hypothesis 7:	1.0%	χοιδια σιμολεοντος του δεινος θυγατηρ. αριστωνος γυνα. χαιρε
Hypothesis 8:	1.0%	χοιλια σιμολεοντος του δεινος θυγατηρ. αριστωνος γυνα. χαιρε
Hypothesis 9:	0.8%	χοισια σιμολεοντος του δεινος θυγατηρ. αριστωνος γυνα. χαιρε
Hypothesis 10:	0.6%	χοιρου σιμολεοντος του δεινος θυγατηρ. αριστωνος γυνα. χαιρε
Hypothesis 11:	0.4%	χοικου σιμολεοντος του δεινος θυγατηρ. αριστωνος γυνα. χαιρε
Hypothesis 12:	0.2%	χοινια σιμολεοντος του δεινος θυγατηρ. αριστωνος γυνα. χαιρε
Hypothesis 13:	0.1%	χοιεια σιμολεοντος του δεινος θυγατηρ. αριστωνος γυνα. χαιρε
Hypothesis 14:	0.1%	χοισκα σιμολεοντος του δεινος θυγατηρ. αριστωνος γυνα. χαιρε
Hypothesis 15:	0.1%	χοιρια σιμολεοντος του δεινος θυγατηρ. αριστωνος γυνα. χαιρε
Hypothesis 16:	0.1%	χοιτια σιμολεοντος του δεινος θυγατηρ. αριστωνος γυνα. χαιρε
Hypothesis 17:	0.1%	χοιοια σιμολεοντος του δεινος θυγατηρ. αριστωνος γυνα. χαιρε

Fig. 9. Top-17 restoration predictions for χοι??? + full stop (collaborative notebook)

Overall, *Ithaca* seems to provide valuable hints even when provided with reduced means in terms of context and potential occurrences in the dataset for the words in the input text. It also seems very sensitive to the provided context[14]; the introduction of a single full stop brought changes in results. It remains to be determined if additional insulation of phrases inside the input text (other than indicating the end of sentence through full stop) might introduce in the system useful information for restorations.

In a new exercise, we rearranged the artificially enhanced input text by conserving the whole name *Khoiros* and hid the last five characters of the personal name *Simoleōn*, in the genitive in our ground truth text. The input text looked as follows:

χοιρος σιμολε????? Του δεινος θυγατηρ αριστωνος γυνα. Χαιρε

"Khoiros, daughter of Simole-, son of…, wife of Ariston. Greetings!"

14 Saliency maps also show that the similarities in terms of characters between *khoi-* and *khaire* seemed relevant features for making predictions. It might be interesting to inquire how stylistic features of texts (repetitions, alliterations etc.) might or might not influence predictions.

Although *Simoleōn* is a personal name first attested in our input text, its common pattern (see above) made the predictions for restoring the word very straightforward. The correct genitive *Simoleontos* is in the second position in top-20 restorations if the last five characters are marked for restorations (Fig. 10), and in the first position if only the last 4 characters are to be restored (but with a quite small probability, Fig. 11). When the number of characters to be predicted goes down to the last three, the restoration *Simoleontos* is in the first position with an overwhelming probability (85 %) for morphological reasons – the very obvious singular genitive ending (Fig. 12); it is rather a case of a foregone conclusion. The saliency maps for predicting restorations show (Figs. 13, 14, 15) demonstrate clearly how *Ithaca* mostly attends to the internal features of the personal name to be restored in order to establish the predictions and pays attention to the characters immediately preceding the missing characters (which is to be expected for languages with inflexion-that is also why we chose to delete those characters in particular). It also seems to have recognized that the sequence *leo* as well as *simo* can also exist as part of an independent word.

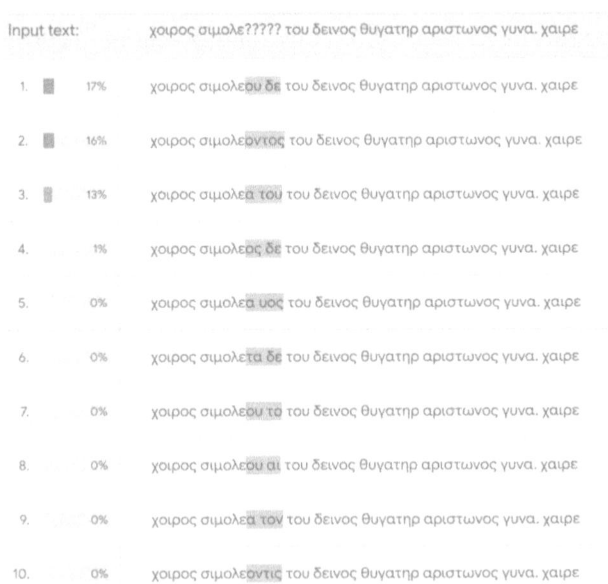

Fig. 10. Top-10 restoration predictions for σιμολε?????

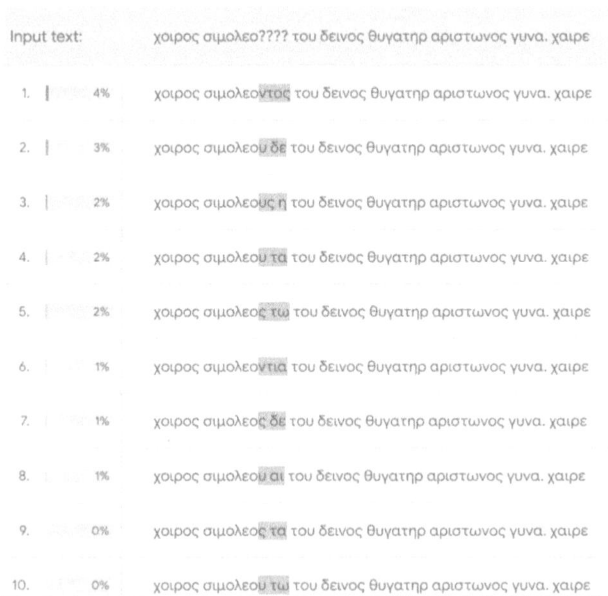

Fig. 11. Top-10 restoration predictions for σιμολεο????

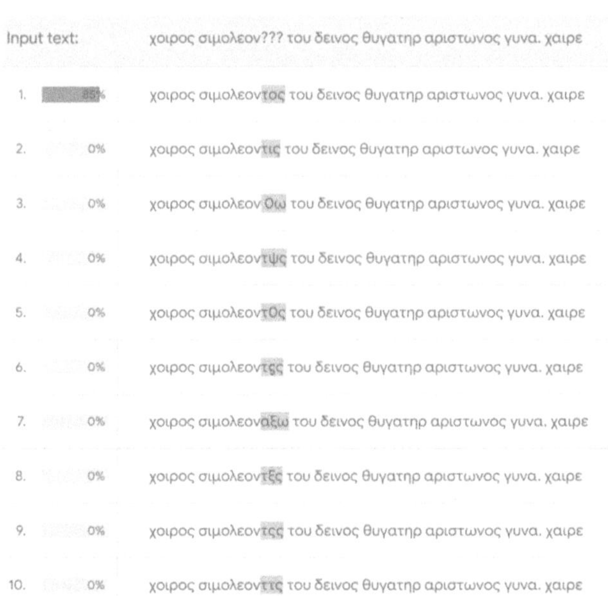

Fig. 12. Top-10 restoration predictions for σιμολεον???

Fig. 13. Saliency map restoration (σιμολε?????)

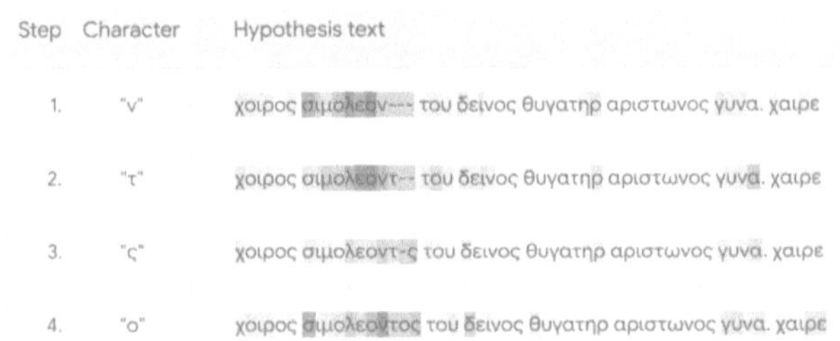

Fig. 14. Saliency map restoration (σιμολεο????)

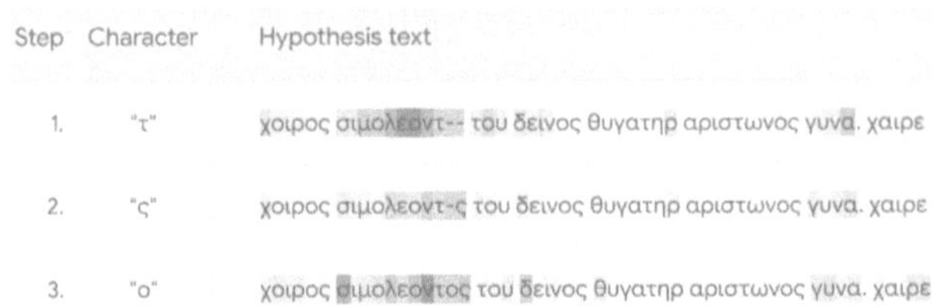

Fig. 15. Saliency map restoration (σιμολεον???)

The geographical attribution is once again straightforward, overwhelmingly proposing in all three cases the North Shore of the Black Sea as first prediction (Figs. 16, 17, 18). The saliency maps (we only show the saliency map for the five missing characters, Fig. 19, since the maps are similar enough in the three cases), show that the first two personal names were looked at (apparently meaning that Ithaca sensed their peculiarities) plus the word *gunā* which has, as we said before, an ending characteristic to the Doric dialects. It is a fact that will be confirmed in the following exercise.

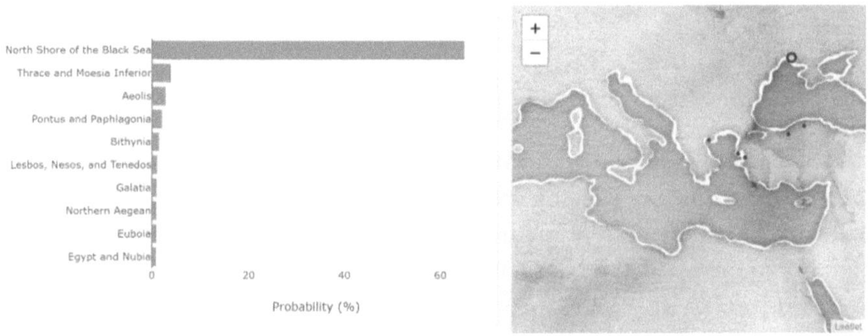

Fig. 16. Geographical attributions (σιμολε?????)

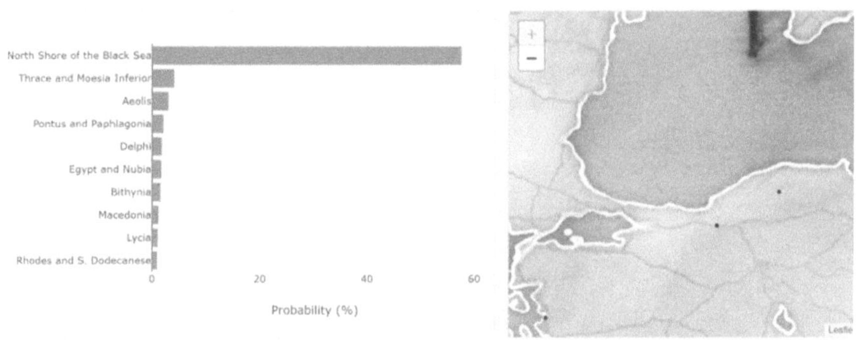

Fig. 17. Geographical attributions (σιμολεο????)

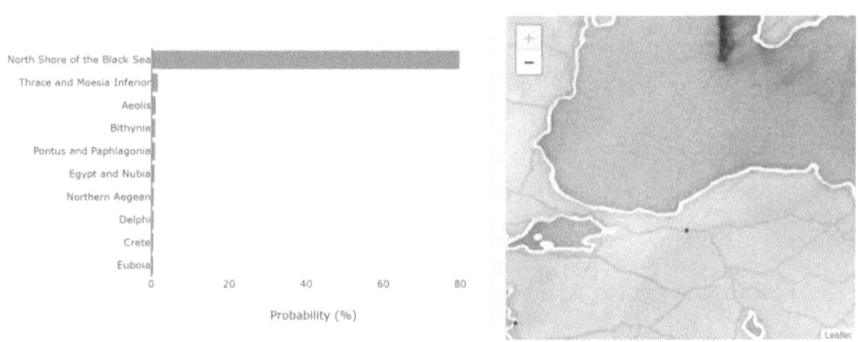

Fig. 18. Geographical attributions (σιμολεον???)

Fig. 19. Saliency map (geographical attributions Figs. 15, 16, 17)

The chronological attribution is instead a little bit diverging (Figs. 20, 21, 22), with means ranging from the 22 BC (five characters missing) to 108 BC (three characters missing). The 108 BC mean is identical to the one obtained when the characters to be predicted belonged to the name *Khoiros* (see above). The saliency maps showed once again attention paid mostly to the same three words as in the case of geographical attribution, and mainly for the same reasons.

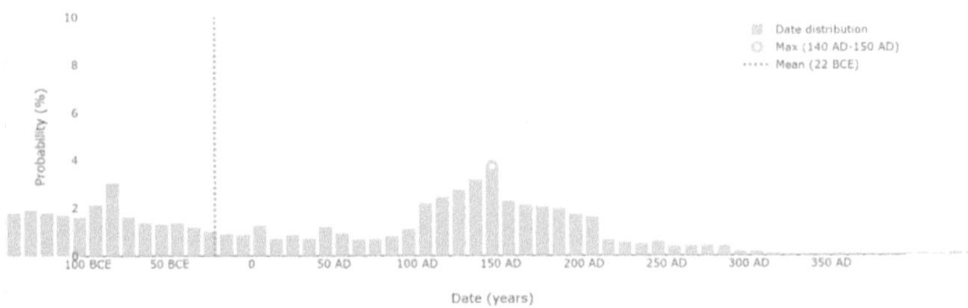

Fig. 20. Chronological attributions (σιμολε?????)

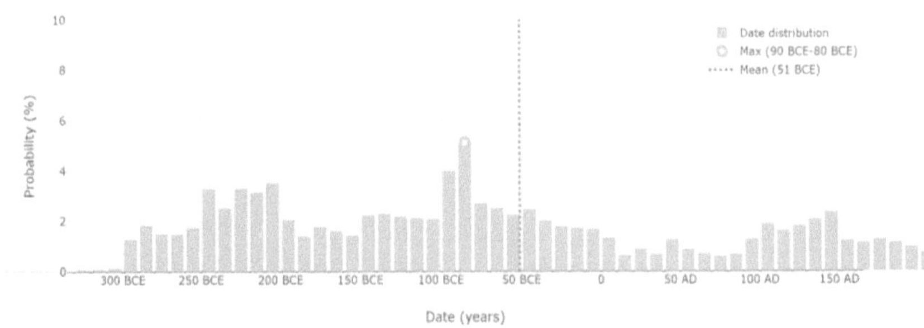

Fig. 21. Chronological attributions (σιμολεο????)

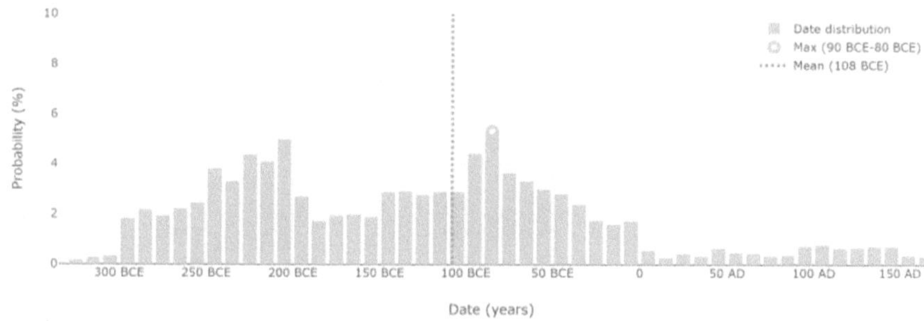

Fig. 22. Chronological attributions (σιμολεον???)

The last exercise on this inscription was performed in order to check on the importance of the Doric *gunā*. We erased the last two characters of *gunā* and asked for them to be predicted. Our input text became:

χοιρος σιμολεοντος του δεινος θυγατηρ αριστωνος γυ??. Χαιρε

"Khoiros, daughter of Simoleon, son of…, ?? of Ariston. Greetings!"

As expected, *Ithaca* overwhelmingly proposed the word for "wife" to be restored. Nevertheless, the word restored was not the Doric *gunā*, but the rather unmarked *gunē* (Figs. 23, 24). Attention was paid to the immediate vicinity of the word in order to get the restoration, to the masculine personal name in the genitive, Ariston, and to the preceding word "daughter", but the most important influencing factors were the preserved parts of the word.

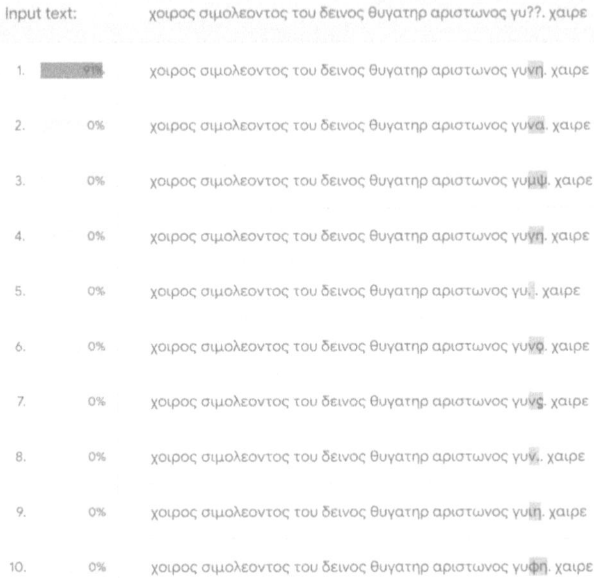

Fig. 23. Top-10 restoration predictions (γυ??)

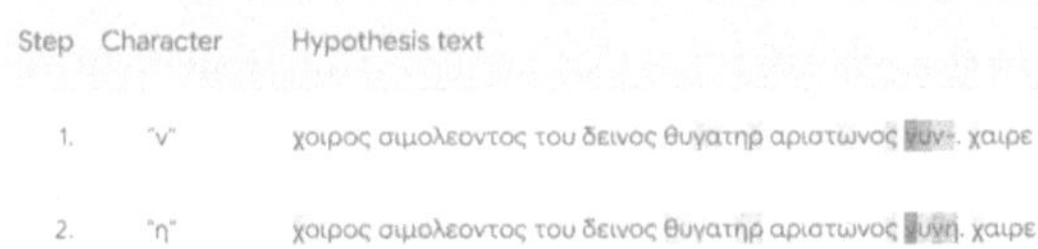

Fig. 24. Saliency map restoration (γυ??)

Even in the absence of *gunā*, the top dominant prediction for geographical attribution was the North Shore of the Black Sea with *Ithaca* attending to basically all the words in the input text (Figs. 25, 26), but once again, most of all, to the first two personal names (precisely those that could not furnish information). Perhaps, this might imply sensitivity to the whole syntactic structure of the text that might send to the North Shore of the Black Sea as place of origin.[15] The chronological attribution to a mean of 76 BC keeps in line with the other attributions around the 1st c BC or immediately before (Figs. 27, 28).

15 There are several examples with the same/similar structure, as in CIRB (= Corpus Inscriptionum Regni Bosporani) 582, 583, 634, 649, 658 etc. as shown by the

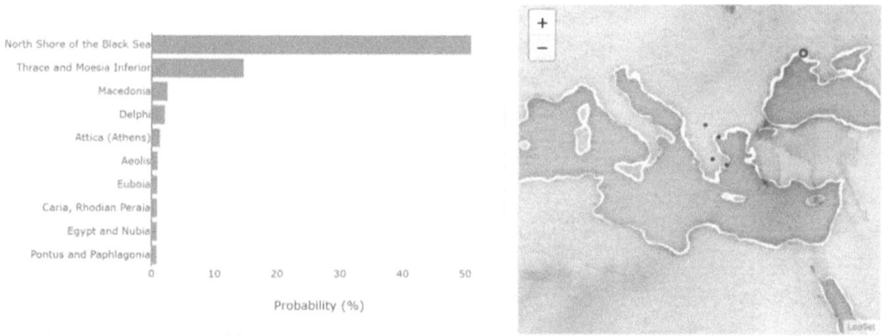

Fig. 25 Geographical attributions (γυ??)

Fig. 26. Saliency map for geographical attributions (γυ??)

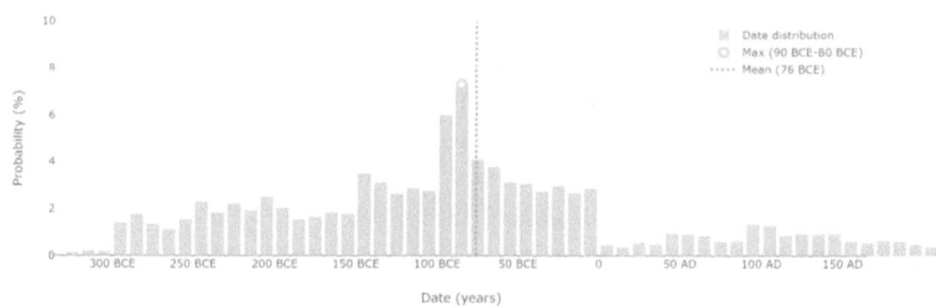

Fig. 27. Chronological attributions (γυ??)

Fig. 28. Saliency map (chronological attributions γυ??)

PHI dataset (https://inscriptions.packhum.org/search?patt=%CE%B8%CF%85%CE%B3%CE%B1%CF%84%CE%B7%CF%81).

3. Conclusion

We proposed a series of exercises conducted with the aid of the *Ithaca* tool. As a basis for these exercises, we used an inscription we published recently and that was fully preserved (it also seems to be a less straightforward material that the input texts published by the authors of Ithaca as test cases). In order to overcome the requirement of having at least 50 characters in order to use *Ithaca* (and with the understanding that *Ithaca* was built with larger and more complex patterns to identify in mind), we proposed some text augmentation ways that we initially considered non-intrusive with respect to the category the inscription belonged to and to its content.

However, these augmentations might have proved influential for geographical and chronological attribution. The fact is that, as we explained when we published the inscription, its place of origin was not known (it was found built in a wall in Bucharest) and we inferred that it should have come from Callatis according to content characteristics. *Ithaca*'s predictions might inspire us to further thought.

One of the salient features of *Ithaca* proved to be its receptiveness to context. It performed less interestingly in the case of *Khoiros*, but identified patterns in the case of *Simoleōn.* It also proved itself very sensitive to slight changes in the input text, even on the level of basic punctuation.

One can be hopeful that in future developments, texts of less than 50 characters might be included in the training dataset since, as we said in the beginning, there are large numbers of inscriptions belonging to important categories with less than 50 characters. Sometimes, these kinds of inscriptions posit interesting problems as it was the case with the epitaph we used for exercises.

References

Assael, Y., Sommerschield, T. and Prag, J. (2019) "Restoring Ancient Text Using Deep Learning: A Case Study on Greek Epigraphy". *Proceedings of the 2019 Conference on Empirical Methods in Natural Language Processing and the 9th International Joint Conference on Natural Language* Processing (EMNLP-IJCNLP), 3–7 November, Hong Kong, 6269–6376. Hong Kong: Association for Computational Linguistics).

Assael, Y., Sommerschield, T., Shillingford, B., Bordbar, M., Pavlopoulos, J., Chatzipanagiotou, M., Androutsopoulos, I., Prag, J. and de Freitas, N. (2022). "Restoring and Attributing Ancient Texts Using Deep Neural Networks". *Nature* 603, 280–283.

Bottez, V. and Lițu, A. (2019) "A Travelling Stone from Callatis". *Pontica 52 Suppl.* VI, 237–241.

Del Barrio Vega, M.L. (2018) "The Greek Language in the Black Sea". In Giannakis, G.K., Crespo, E. and Filos, P. (eds.), *Studies in Ancient Greek Dialects. From Central Greece to the Black Sea*, 511–530. Walter de Gruyter: Berlin/Boston.

ISM III. Avram, A. (1999) *Inscriptions grecques et latines de Scythie Mineure, III. Callatis et son territoire*. Bucarest-Paris: Editura Encicplopedia.

LGPN online. *Lexicon of Greek Personal Names* (https://www.lgpn.ox.ac.uk/). (Accessed: 23 March 2022).

Section 3: Computational Methods: Analysis, Classification, Clustering

Andrea Sgarro

Chapter 10 At the Boundaries of Syntactic Prehistory: Metric and Non-Metric Distances

Abstract: Language relatedness was established in Ceolin et al. (2021) without resorting to cognate words, following instead a new way to tackle the issue which is based on the Parametric Comparison Method PCM, combined with a theory of possible language and the use of dedicated statistical tools; languages are represented through ternary strings of logical values. Controversial language clusters, object of long-standing debates, are supported, e.g., Altaic and Uralo-Altaic, while others test negatively, e.g., Indo-Uralic or Basque-Northeast Caucasian. The mathematics involved is quite engaging and gives the chance of discussing what a string distance between languages should be and which metric properties it should have.

Keywords: language relatedness, linguistic philogeny, syntactic similarity, string distances

1. Introduction

The existence of an Indo-European linguistic *family* is something which even a non-linguist is ready to accept, due to the similarity of *words* in Indo-European languages: take e.g., the Italian *padre* and the Persian (Farsi) *pedar*, or the Persian *barādar* and *dohtar* and the German *Bruder* and *Tochter* or the English *brother* and *daughter*. Even more striking is the similarity of words within a *subfamily*, say Romance languages derived directly from Latin, as are French, Spanish, Portuguese, Italian and Romanian, to quote only those with a larger number of speakers. However, the approach of linguists to word similarity (and diachronic sound change) is all but I and they will convince you that words like the English *bad* and the Farsi *bad*, though having the very same meaning, are totally unrelated, precisely as happens with the Spanish *mucho* and the English *much*: in both cases one is facing mere random coincidence. Be as it may, words are no doubt a precious instrument to study linguistic families, their diachronic evolution in time with the divergences that this evolution brings about: *lexical cognates* are indispensable to study *linguistic phylogeny*.

Let us consider the case of Romanian, a Romance language which is definitely the most remarkable member of the eastern sub-family[1] of the grouping comprising neo-Latin languages. Latin was brought to what is now Romania by Trajan's army and this feels, indeed. Let us take into account a basic element of Romanian life even nowadays, the *village*, *sat* in Romanian from the Latin *fossatum*, i.e., the *ditch* surrounding a camp. In a *sat* you can talk to a *bătrân*, an *old* man, so as to learn village customs: *bătrân* from the Latin *veteranus*, why *old* referring to things is *vechi*, another unmistakably Latin word very similar to the Italian *vecchio*, which however refers also to persons and so translates both *bătrân* and *vechi*. The basic elements of a village are equally Latin, *casă* = house, in Italian *casa*, *fereastră* = window, in Italian *finestra*, *masă* = *table* from the Latin *mensa* and *scaun* = *chair*, similar to the Italian *scagno* = *stool* (an Italian chair is instead *sedia*). Another remarkable cognate: the word *wall*, *perete (Romanian)* and *parete (Italian)*; *acoperiş* = *roof* has nothing to do with Italian *tetto*, but is obviously related to the Italian verb *coprire*, *to cover*. All the objects we are mentioning are compatible with a wooden building as in a Roman camp: going to stone *perete* becomes a solid *wall* = *zid*, a Slav word. Do you want to be even more sophisticated and get further away from the uncouth Roman soldiers? A window has a *geam* = *pane* and a *pervaz* = *windowsill* and is protected by a *perdea* = *curtain*, all Turkish words that the Turks, soldiers themselves, have borrowed from the Persians.

As soon as you become more modern-oriented you find French words, starting e.g., with *electricitate*, one of the very many "recent" borrowings going back to the re-latinization of the language which took place starting from the 19th century. To say nothing of contemporary English borrowings (rather: American), but in this case all our languages seem to be more or less equally affected, save English, of course. Basic Romanian vocabulary

---

1 Beside Romanian, the Eastern group comprises three languages, Aromanian (spoken by a few hundreds of thousand persons mainly in Greece, Albania and North Macedonia), Meglenoromanian (a few thousand mostly in Greek Macedonia) and Istroromanian (spoken in Istria and nowadays virtually extinct: it used to be spoken in an area that nowadays intersects Croatia, Slovenia and Italy around Trieste).

is mostly and largely Latin, but Slav words have entered even into this sanctuary: take e.g., *a iubi* = *to love*, *prieten* = *friend*, *bogat* = *rich*, *bolnav* = *ill* (while *healthy* is *sănătos*, an obvious Latin word). A fascinating language, indeed!

Let us change the point of view; if one takes Romanian as a second language starting from a Romance language like Italian or French, apart from a lot of friendly words, one will be even more surprised by the Romanian grammar, which, if he knows some Latin, will often appear to him rather archaic, beginning with the fact that Romanian nouns still have a declension, although a limited one, compared with Russian or with Latin, but, all the same, the Romanian noun, unlike what happens with western Romance languages, is declined: *o fată* = *a girl*, *unei fete* = *of a girl* (the word derives from the Latin *phoetum*, definitely less poetic than the Italian *fata* which means *fairy*). Slav influences on the Romanian syntax are almost nil: one of the rare examples is negation through *ne*, cfr. e.g., the older form *cu neputintă* = *with non-possibility* = *impossible, unachievable* (but *putinta* is of course a Latin word), with the newer French- or Italian-derived *imposibil*. Actually, there are some odd features in the Romanian grammar, those belonging to the so-called Balkan languages,[2] features which are shared basically by Romanian, Bulgarian, Albanian and modern Greek; an example is the explicitation after modal verbs: you say *he can that he goes*, or *he wants that he goes* for *he can* or *wants to go* (in Romanian resorting to the subjunctive tense for *he goes*).

The fact that languages which are all Indo-European but are not so closely related should share many important features (Bulgarian is Slavic and the other two are isolated) has been a hot subject of discussion for linguists. One of the competing explanations is that these features might be derived from the *substratum*, i.e., from old Geto-Dacic languages. A remarkable fact is that the Slav *adstratum*, which chronologically came *after* Latin, is almost inoperative on Romanian syntax, while it is the old

2 The common features of Balkan languages which a priori are not so tightly related was first recognized in 1829 by the Slovenian linguist Jernej (Bartholomeus) Kopitar (1780–1844); the expression "Balkan linguistic union or league" (*uniunea lingvistică balcanică*) was first used in 1958 by the Romanian linguist Alexandru Rosetti (1895–1990).

Geto-Dacic *substratum* which might instead be active, even if linguists have put forward also other explanations. Concluding and using a term of which communications engineers are fond: *the **lexical signal** evolves comparatively quickly, while the **syntactic signal** is slower and so delves deeper into the past.*

2. Linguistic phylogeny based on syntax

A question arises: why are we not using syntax rather than lexica to classify languages and to construct a reliable linguistic phylo geny? The traditional argument was: unfortunately, the syntactic signal cannot be used in practice, it is too difficult or even *cu neputintă* to be managed. It is an Italian linguist now based in York, UK, Giuseppe Longobardi and his school which were so bold as to subvert this attitude and, by so doing, they opened new and exciting paths in linguistic phylogeny; we refer in particular to paper Ceolin et al. (2021), but the road has been long and not devoid of stumbling blocks. This approach, the Parametric Comparison Method or PCM, inspired also by the success obtained by bioinformaticians in DNA phylogeny, involves a lot of mathematics, statistics, and computer science.

2.1. Methodology

In Ceolin et al. (2021), 58 languages from the Old World are selected and a dataset of 94 syntactic parameters (syntactic features relative to the nominal syntax) is used. Each feature can be either present or absent and so one would expect that to each language a *binary* string is associated. Unfortunately, there is a snag: a complex network of *logical* (not simply statistical) dependences constrains the structure of the sequence; we shall give an over-simplified example, just to understand the situation. Say feature number 10 is a *no* to the question *Are the nouns of the language declined*? While feature number 20 asks for the existence of the ergative case. Clearly, question number 20 cannot even be posed once the answer to question 10 has been given the negative logical value. Thus, the language in question, in position 20, will have a third logical value meaning *logically inconsistent*. Sequences, therefore, are *ternary* rather than binary, and to evaluate the dissimilarity of two sequences (the dissimilarity of the two corresponding languages) one cannot simply resort to Hamming distance which counts the number of positions where the two sequences differ, in case dividing by the length of the sequences, which in the case of Ceolin et al. (2021) is 94, and so passing from the *absolute* Hamming distance to the *normalized Hamming distance* (from the number of differences to the percentage).

The maximum value in the latter case is of course 1, or rather 100 %: the two strings differ in *all* positions. With ternary strings, the following option was adopted: one deletes positions where at least one of the two languages has the third logical values (one deletes *inconsistent positions*). In a way, strings are shortened and then one computes the normalized Hamming distance between the shortened strings. For this distance or dissimilarity measure we find it convenient to use the name *Longobardi distance*; mathematicians, after observing that the distance would be undefined if all positions are inconsistent, a case never happening with couples of our real languages, actually, will be curious to know which are the "technical" properties of this new normalized distance: not even the *triangle inequality* necessarily holds, which implies that one is dealing with a rather unruly mathematical object.

The 58 languages of Ceolin et al. (2021) belong to 15 traditionally recognized families (Indo-European, Finno-Ugric, Altaic and so on). Some macro-families have been proposed by linguists, but the traditional tools of linguistic are at a loss to decide whether these kinships are or are not tenable. A famous example: are Japanese and Korean related, is there a common ancestor lurking back in their remote past? The idea is based on statistics and consists in sampling significant similarities against random similarities. To achieve this, one should be able, using a computer, to generate a huge number of *random* strings, random but of course obeying the logical constraints. With the (over-simplified) example above, if a string is extracted which has a *no* in position 10 and a *yes* in position 20, that string should be discarded and thrown into the garbage bin: only strings obeying the constraints should be retained to construct a random set of *possible language*, numerous enough so as to be used in statistics. Now, the logical network is extremely complicated (cfr. Bortolussi et al. 2011: to have an idea take a look at Fig. 1, which shows only a small subgraph of dependences), so complicated that in practice almost all the generated strings would have to be thrown into the bin, and years of computations would be necessary to find a reasonable number of random strings which are so kind as to obey the constraints. The technical problems were solved, (cfr. Bortolussi et al. 2011): one can build a generator where a reasonable percentage of dependences are built in (not all of them, unfortunately), and the number of discarded sequences becomes tolerable so as to allow a tolerable computing time. In Ceolin et al. (2021), 5000 *possible* languages randomly generated are used (a possible language being a ternary string which obeys all the constraints, independently whether this string represents a real language or not) and allow one to avail oneself of statistical methods to decide which similarities between families are statistically significant and which are not. We will not enter here into the technical details of statistics for which the reader is referred directly to Ceolin et al. (2021), but we will stress some of the results which are obtained, a few of which are of paramount interest in comparative linguistics and linguistic phylogeny.

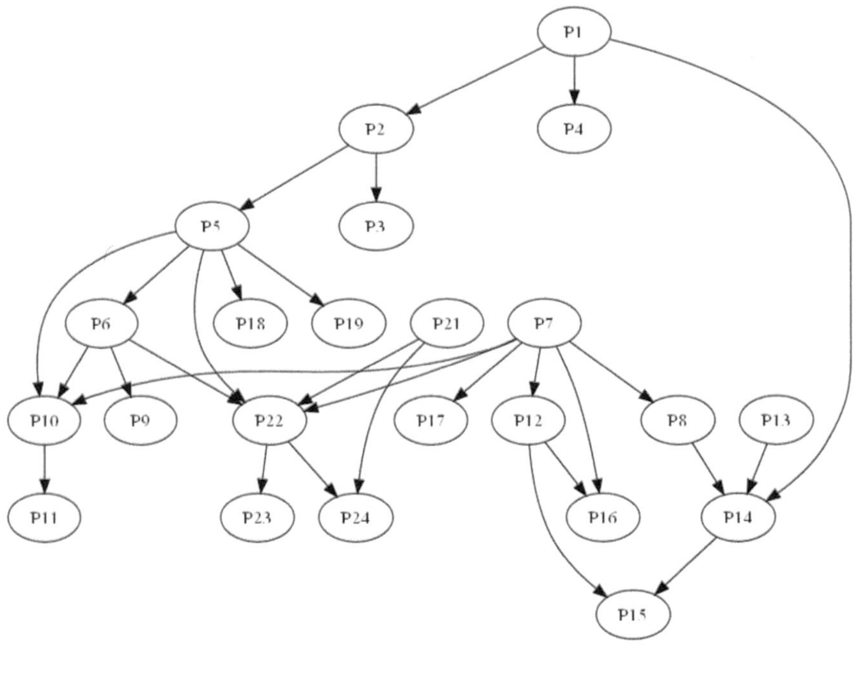

Fig. 1. Logical dependences among 24 parameters (Bortolussi et al. 2011)

2.2. Results

Thus, let us move to the subject of greater interest to linguists (of course the exacting reader is once more referred to Ceolin et al. (2021) where all needed information is provided and extensively discussed): are certain conjectured or established macrofamilies validated by the syntactic approach (by the parametric method PCM), while others are not? We stress once more that one is assessing relatedness between linguistic families against chance in situations when *etymological evidence is missing*.

The results, in short, are:

- The Indo-European and the Finno-Ugric unity (Balto-Finnic, Ugric, Volgaic, Pernic) are fully recognized.
- A controversial cluster such as Altaic and Uralo-Altaic is significantly supported, while other possible macro-grouping, as are Indo-Uralic or Basque-Northeast Caucasian are not.
- The overall unity of the five well-established groups, Turkic, Mongolian, Tungusic, Korean and Japanese which make up the macro-Altaic stock remains controversial. Supported by Ceolin et al. (2021) is the connection between Japanese and Korean (a remarkable result, indeed); supported is also the less controversial micro-Altaic group (Tungusic, Turkic, and Mongolian).
- Instead, a possible kinship between Basque and Japanese-Korean, though suggested by the classification tree and conjectured by some linguists, tests negatively.

2.3. Experimenting with well-behaved distances

Let us go back to distances and, for the moment being, let us consider only binary strings; after coding *yes* (feature present) to 1 and *no* (feature absent) to 0, we are left with numeric strings of bits zero-one. Assume one is not interested in positions where both strings have a zero, because these positions seem totally irrelevant. Then one might proceed as follows, moving from the (possibly normalized) Hamming distance to so-called Jaccard or Matsumoto distance (which is always normalized and assumes maximum value 1 = 100 %, when all positions are different): in Jaccard's case, one deletes positions where both strings have a zero and normalizes with respect to the reduced length. So, the Hamming distance between the two binary strings 0100 and 0010 is 2, the normalized Hamming distance is 2 divided by 4 = 0.5 and the Jaccard distance is as high as 1 i.e., 2 divided by 2 = 100 %, since the first and the last positions are irrelevant (in a way they do not exist) which implies that the two sequences differ in *all* the valid surviving positions.

There is a mathematical transformation called the *Steinhaus transform,* extensively described in (Franzoi et al. 2019; 2020) which is quite a general tool which in particular can be used to obtain the Jaccard distance starting from the Hamming distance (normalized or not). With Steinhaus transforms, one has to specify one or more *pivots*; if the pivot chosen is the all-0 sequence and the Steinhaus transform is applied to the Hamming distance (normalized or un-normalized) one obtains precisely the Jaccard distance. A precious property, which a well-behaved mathematical distance should have, is that it should verify the *triangle inequality*:

$$\text{dist}(x,z) + \text{dist}(z,y) \geq \text{dist}(x,y)$$

i.e., if you go from x to y and you have the constraint of first passing through z, then the distance can only increase with respect to the situation when you have no constraint whatsoever and can choose the shortest (unconstrained, direct) way. A very natural requirement indeed, but quite many of the distances listed in the *Dictionary of Distances* (Reza and Deza 2006) do *not* verify triangularity and are not *metric distances,* as mathematicians define them. Recall that Longobardi's distance is *not* triangular, a fact which might displease many mathematicians. Before proceeding, we quote a theorem: the Steinhaus transform, whatever the pivots, preserves triangularity (as a corollary, the Jaccard distance verifies the triangle inequality); moreover, it is a normalized distance, its maximum possible value being 1, even if the distance to be transformed was not normalized.

In Franzoi et al. (2019) and Franzoi et al. (2020), we tried to understand what happens if one replaces Longobardi's distance by a new well-behaved triangular distance obtained by means of a Steinhaus transform, whose pivot, rather than the all-0 sequence, as in the Jaccard case, is the sequence made up only of stars *. Since our strings are ternary rather than binary, first of all we have to generalize the Hamming distance: in the binary zero-one case, positions with different symbols contribute one, while positions with the same symbol contribute zero; the generalization we need is that if a star appears in one of the string, while in the other one has a *crisp* logical value, be it 0 or 1, then the additive contribution of that position is only 1\2. If one numerizes the star symbol as 1\2, rather in the spirit of *fuzzy logic*, which admits of logical values intermediate between 0 = false and 1 = true (in a way fuzzy logic, beside white and black, knows also the colour grey in all its shades, including the one we need, *totally ambiguous* between false and true), mathematicians will soon recognize the so-called *taxicab* or *Minkowski distance*, a very well-known generalization of the Hamming distance which verifies the triangle property. In Franzoi et al. (2019) and Franzoi et al. (2020), we decided to use the Steinhaus transform of the taxicab distance by choosing the all-star string (the totally ambiguous string) as pivot. The distance one obtains, referred simply as the Steinhaus distance in the following, is triangular and of course has 1 as its maximum value. Technical comments and critical observations are to be found in Franzoi et al. (2019) and Franzoi et al. (2020), here we shall only discuss the impact on linguistics.

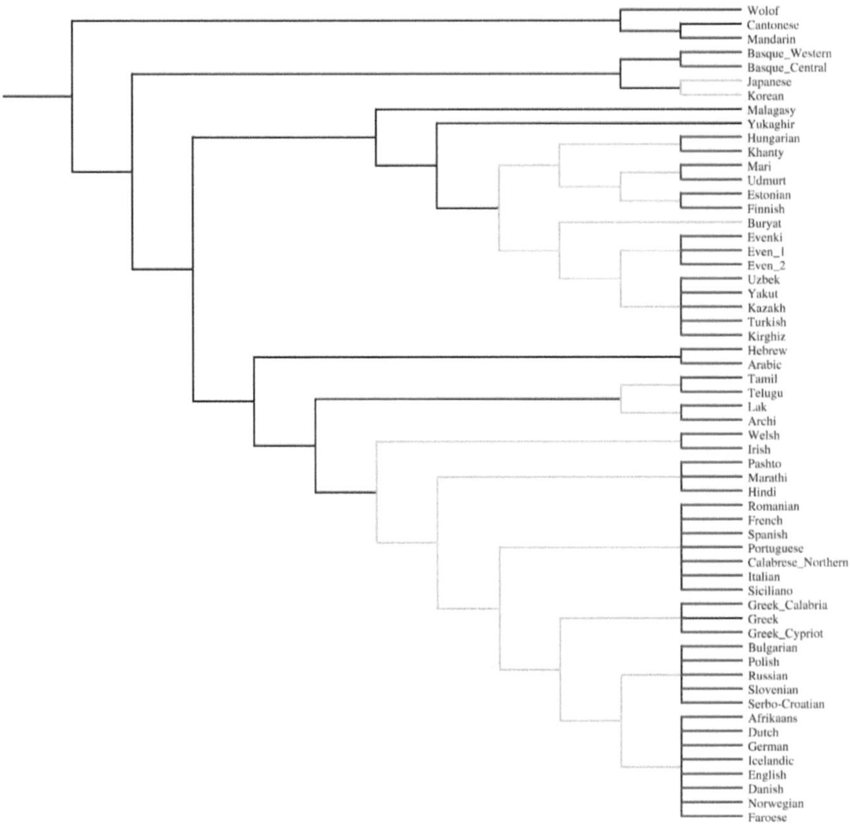

Fig. 2. A classification tree

Visible at first glance, the tree we obtained in Franzoi et al. (2019) and Franzoi et al. (2020) is very similar to the tree depicted in Fig. 2, with the same languages and the same parameters as obtained by Longobardi's school in research slightly prior to Ceolin et al. (2021). In Franzoi et al. (2019) and Franzoi et al. (2020) and in current research we are trying to make more precise this "feeling" by using a well-known ad well-behaved distance between trees, namely the Robinson-Fould tree distance. The feeling, as to be expected, is largely validated. Steinhaus and Longobardi's trees are quite similar and have nearly the same distance from what can be considered a benchmark tree for language classification, the one due to

D. Gray and Q.D. Atkinson (2003); actually, the Steinhaus tree performs slightly better.

3. Conclusions and open ends

Rather than assessing which is the winner in a competition between string distances and classification trees, Steinhaus vs. Longobardi, the relevant argument appears to be another, cf. also Franzoi et al. (2019) and Franzoi et al. (2020). The distances used are quite different, but the results obtained are practically the same, which strongly pledges in favour of the robustness of the linguistic data and of their structure. Statistical methods exported from bioinformatics and DNA phylogeny, starting with the so-called *bootstrapping*, had not been so friendly, however. Why this discrepancy? Why perturbing the distance, as we did in Franzoi et al. (2019) and Franzoi et al. (2020), pledges for robustness, while perturbing the data, as done by using bootstrapping, gives weaker results? The reason, in the opinion of this writer, is the strong and complex network of logical (and not simply statistical) dependences constraining the linguistic parameters, beside the "shortness" of linguistic ternary linguistic strings with respect to quaternary DNA strings (from a magnitude of one hundred to hundreds of thousands).

Exporting tools from bioinformatics to linguistic phylogeny should not overlook these paramount oppositions and requires much care. Actually, we are convinced that linguistics needs *new specific tools*: perturbing the distance and leaving data as they are follow precisely this line of thought. The Parametric Comparison Method PCM of Longobardi and his school of linguists opens fascinating domains of research also to mathematicians, statisticians, and computer scientists.

References

Ceolin, A., Guardiano, C., Longobardi, G., Irimia, M.A., Bortolussi, L. and Sgarro, A. (2021) "At the boundaries of syntactic prehistory". *Philosophical Transactions of the Royal Society* B 376 (1824). Royal Society Publishing. doi.org/ 10.1098/rstb.2020.019797.

Bortolussi, L., Sgarro, A., Guardiano, C. and Longobardi, G. (2011) "How many possible languages are there?". *Biology, Computation and*

Linguistics (Frontiers in Artificial Intelligence and Applications) 228, 168–179 (eds). Bel-Enguix, G., Dahl, V., Jiménez-López, M.D. IOS Press. doi: 10.3233/978-1-60750-762-8-168.

Franzoi, L., Sgarro, A., Dinu, A. and Dinu, L.P. (2019) "Linguistic classification: Dealing jointly with irrelevance and inconsistency". *Proceedings of Recent Advances in Natural Language Processing RANLP*, 345–352. doi: 10.26615/978-954-452-056-4040.

Franzoi, L., Sgarro, A. and Dinu, A. and Dinu, L.P. (2020) "Random Steinhaus distances for robust classification of partially inconsistent linguistic data". *IPMU, International Processing and Management of Uncertainty in Knowledge – Based Systems* 1239, 17–26. doi:10.1007/978-3-030-50153-2_2. (Accessed: 23 March 2022).

Gray, D. and Atkinson, Q. D. (2003) "Language-tree divergence times support the Anatolian theory of Indo-european origin". *Nature* 426, 435–439. https://doi.org/10.1038/nature02029. (Accessed: 23 March 2022).

Reza, E. and Deza, M.-M. (2006) *Dictionary of Distances*. Elsevier. doi.org/10.1016/B978-0-444-52087-6.X5000-8. (Accessed: 23 March 2022).

Miguel Cavadas Docampo and Pablo Gamallo Otero

Chapter 11 Automatic Authorship Attribution in the Work of Tirso de Molina

Abstract: Automatic Authorship Attribution (AAA) is the result of applying tools and techniques from Digital Humanities to authorship attribution studies. Through a quantitative and statistical approach this discipline can draw further conclusions about renowned authorship issues which traditional critics have been dealing with for centuries, opening a new door to style comparison. The aim of this paper is to prove the potential of these tools and techniques by testing the authorship of five comedies traditionally attributed to Spanish playwright Tirso de Molina (1579–1648): *La ninfa del cielo*, *El burlador de Sevilla*, *Tan largo me lo fiáis*, *La mujer por fuerza* and *El condenado por desconfiado*. To accomplish this purpose some experiments concerning clustering analysis by Stylo package from R and four distance measures are carried out on a corpus built with plays by Tirso, Andrés de Claramonte (c. 1560–1626), Antonio Mira de Amescua (1577–1644) and Luis Vélez de Guevara (1579–1644). The results obtained point to the denial of all the attributions to Tirso except for the case of *La mujer por fuerza.*

Keywords: authorship attribution, Spanish literature, clustering

1. Introduction

The objective of this article is to highlight the role that certain tools coming from computational linguistics may have in an authorship study and, consequently, to point out the value of AAA as a profitable convergence between disciplines. In order to illustrate this, we will focus specifically on the Tirsian debate with the aim to draw conclusions that may serve as relevant arguments in order to reinforce some of the most supported critical positions. More in particular, we aim to find the most probable authors of five plays from the Golden Age that were traditionally attributed to Tirso de Molina, including the two that introduce the character that will initiate the Don Juan myth. All these plays have been surrounded, especially in the last decades, by great controversy regarding their alleged authorship. Tab. 1 depicts their current situation.

Tab. 1. Texts under discussion and their corresponding possible authors

Text	Possible Authors
El burlador de Sevilla	Claramonte / Tirso
El condenado por desconfiado	Claramonte / Guevara / Mira / Tirso / Collaboration
La mujer por fuerza	Tirso / Other (no name proposed)
La ninfa del Cielo	Guevara / Tirso
Tan largo me lo fiáis	Claramonte / Tirso

Therefore, the authors involved in this study are, apart from Tirso: Andrés de Claramonte, Mira de Amescua and Luis Vélez de Guevara. We have collected and pre-processed several *comedias* by all of them from both the Miguel de Cervantes Virtual Library and the online library of the Association for Hispanic Classical Theater.

2. Method

AAA relies on different statistical measures that take into account the distribution of function words. The selection of the most appropriate measure depends on the available corpus and the objective of the study. However, according to Grieve (2005), the best approach to quantitative authorship attribution is one that is based on the values of as many textual measurements as possible. This is because, in general, small variations in the configurations can produce very large changes in the results. For this reason, five different strategies are used in this work. The five strategies are divided in two opposing approaches: instance and profile-based.

2.1. Instance-based approach

Individual texts are the basic items of the procedure. Following this approach, we use clustering analysis on individual texts so as to group them on the basis of stylistic similarities, which is equivalent, if the adjustments are correct, to group the texts by author. The resulting grouping of individual texts is displayed in a dendogram. The clustering process is based on the Delta measure, created by John Burrows in 2002 specifically for stylometric purposes. This method was implemented by Stylo, a flexible

R package for the high-level stylistic analysis of text collections (Eder, Rybicki and Kestemont 2016). The Delta measure normalizes frequencies by means of z-score to reduce the influence of very frequent words. For fi(D) being the frequency of n-grami in document D, μi the mean frequency of the n-gram in the corpus, and σi its standard deviation, then z-score is defined as follows:

$$z(fi(D))=(fi(D)-\mu i)\,/\,\sigma i \qquad (1)$$

The difference between a set of training texts written by the same author and an unknown text is the mean of the absolute differences between the z-scores (Stamatos 2009). Given the normalized document vectors, the Burrows's Delta is just the Manhattan distance by using normalized frequencies with z-scores. Given documents D1 and D2, distance Delta Δ is computed as follows:

$$\Delta=\sum_{i=}^{n} 1\,|(fi(D1))-z(fi(D2))| \qquad (2)$$

The lower the Delta value the higher the similarity between the texts studied.

2.2. Profile-based approach

In this approach, the known texts belonging to one author are merged into one single document (profile of the author) and then, a distance measure is computed between the profile of the author and the profile of an unknown text. Four different distance measures were designed and implemented: Kullback-Leibler divergence, Perplexity, Ranking-based distance, and Distributional similarity. These measures represent four different corpus-based strategies to compare texts. They were not originally designed to serve the purposes of AAA, but are commonly employed in other computational tasks such as language identification, language distance, information retrieval and data mining.

Kullback-Leibler. Kullback-Leibler divergence compares two distributions, more precisely, is a measure of how one probability distribution (for instance, the profile of an unseen document) is different from a second, reference probability distribution (the profile of the author). In

Iriarte et al. (2018) it was used to measure the distance between texts written by different social groups of individuals: men / women, university / non-university people, and so on. Given a test or unknown text (T) and the known texts of an author (A), the Kullback–Leibler divergence KL of the distributions T and A is defined as follows:

$$\mathrm{KL}(\mathrm{A,T}) = \sum A(\mathrm{ngr}_i)\log\frac{A(\mathrm{ngr}_i)}{T(\mathrm{ngr}_i)} \quad (3)$$

Equation 3 allows computing how far the T distribution is from the A distribution, taking into account the probabilities of the n-grams (of words or characters) in each compared text corpus, either T or A. The divergence (which is an asymmetric measure) was converted into a symmetric one (i.e., into a distance) by computing the mean of the two complementary comparisons: divergence of X from Y, and divergence of Y from X. In our experiment, we applied Kullback-Leibler divergence on distributions of the most frequent word unigrams.

Perplexity. Perplexity is frequently used as a quality measure for language models built with n-grams extracted from text corpora, and can be used to measure how well a model (for instance, the profile of an author) fits the test data (the profile of an unseen document). More formally, perplexity is the normalized inverse probability of an input test. It can be used to compare a test text (T) with the author model (A). The perplexity PP of T given the author model A is defined by the following equation:

$$\mathrm{PP}(\mathrm{A,T}) = 2 - \sum T\,(\mathrm{ngr}i)\log 2M\,(\mathrm{ngr}i) \quad (4)$$

where ngri is a n-gram shared by both T and A. Equation 4 can be used to set the divergence between a test set and the author model. The lower is the perplexity of T given A, the lower is the distance between the two compared objects. Texts may be modelledwith n-grams of either words or characters. In our experiments, we applied PP distance to texts lwith 7-grams of characters. In other pieces of work, PP was also used to compare the linguistic distance between 40 European languages (Gamallo, Pichel and Alegria 2017), as well as to compute the distance between diachronic varieties of the same language (Pichel, Gamallo and Simões 2018).

Rank-Based. The rank-based distance between two languages is obtained by comparing the ranked lists of the two languages. It takes two-word profiles (the author and the unseen document) and calculates a simple rank-order statistic based on an "out-of-place" measure. This measure determines how far out of place an n-gram in one profile is from its place in the other profile (Cavnar and Trenkle 1994). This measure is often used to compute language identification (Gamallo et al. 2014). More formally, given the ranked lists RankT and RankA of the test text (T) and the texts of a given author (A), respectively, the rank-based distance, R, is computed as follows:

$$R(\mathrm{A,T}) = \sum_{\mathrm{i=1}}^{K} \left|\mathrm{Rank}_A(\mathrm{ngr}_i) - \mathrm{Rank}_T(\mathrm{ngram}_i)\right| \tag{5}$$

where K stands for the number of the most frequent n-grams, RankA(ngri) is the rank of a specific n-gram, ngri, in A, and RankT(ngri) is the rank of the same n-gram in T. In our experiments, we applied this distance on lists of word unigrams.

Distributional similarity. As a fourth measure, we use vector space models, which is one of the most popular representations of document vocabulary, to compute distributional similarity between documents. In particular, this strategy compares the word vectors extracted from the author's profile with those extracted from the unseen document. Given that it is a measure of similarity, the higher its value, the higher will be the similarity between the texts, being the maximum value 1. As it works in an inverse way to the other three, which are distance measures, we turn it into a distance by subtracting the values from 1. In our experiments, we used Distributional similarity by considering the comparative study made by Afzali and Kumar (2017) on different metrics, namely Cosine, Jaccard and Dice, to evaluate their performance in finding the similarity of two text documents. Cosine outperformed the other metrics in a significant way. Given A and T, Cosine (as a distance) is defined in this way

$$\mathrm{Cosine}(\mathrm{A,T}) = 1 - \frac{\Sigma A(\mathrm{ngr}_i) T(\mathrm{ngr}_i)}{\sqrt{\Sigma A(\mathrm{ngr}_i)^2} \sqrt{\Sigma T(\mathrm{ngr}_i)^2}} \tag{6}$$

Mean of measures. Finally, the four measures defined above were merged by averaging their values. In order to compute the mean of the values obtained by the four distance measures, their final scores were normalized. The four measures and its mean combination have been implemented by the authors into an executable written in PERL language (see *Autoria*, Gamallo and Cavadas n.d.).

It must be stressed that the use of four different profile-based strategies, in addition to the instance-based one defined above, allows us to reach more solid and reliable conclusions about authorship. These are not different configurations of a single strategy, as is usually done in most Stylo-based work, but five complementary methods of covering diverse aspects of the same problem.

3. Experiments

3.1. Clustering analysis

To configure the Stylo tool (version 0.6.9) properly we carried out a set of preliminary tests with a reduced version of the corpus (eliminating works of unknown authorship). This way we checked which values offered the most consistent results. We concluded that the most appropriate value for the MFW parameter (most frequent words) was 250 for both maximum and minimum, in order to build one single dendogram. This is the essential point of the experiment, as variations on that figure may alter the results substantially. The features we decided to extract from the texts were unigrams of words, that is, tokens, and we did not consider necessary to perform any culling. The dendogram resulting from the experiment is depicted in Fig. 1.

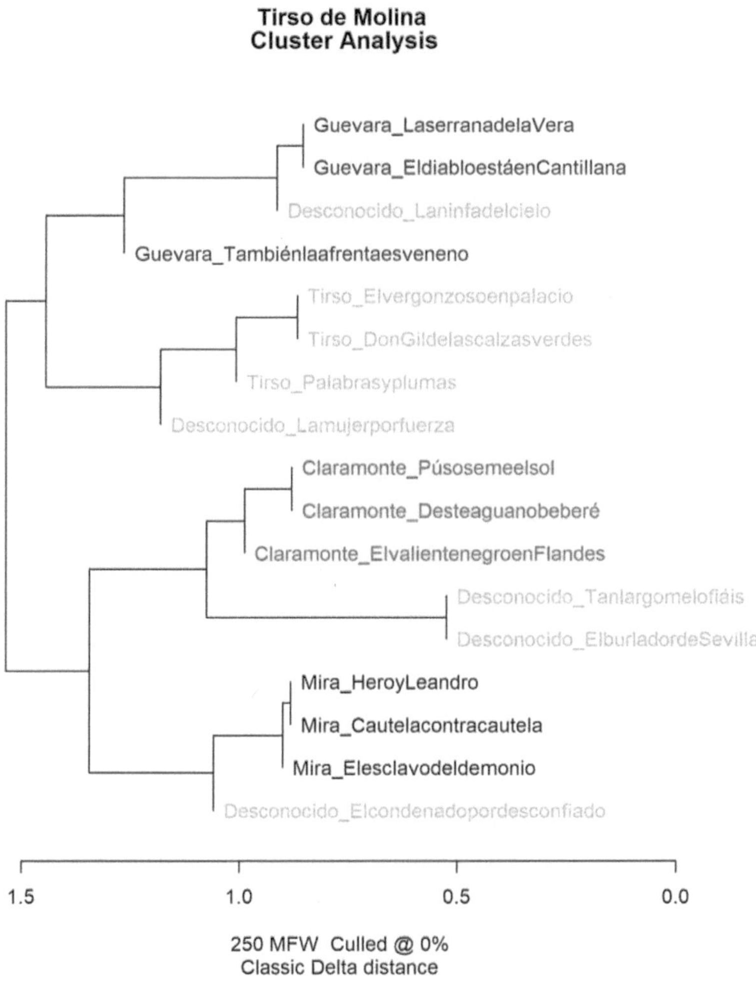

Fig. 1. Dendrogram of the clustering analysis using Delta Burrows distance

As was to be expected, the smallest distance is that which separates *El burlador de Sevilla* and *Tan largo me lo fiáis*, since they are, in a high percentage, the same text. They are undoubtedly grouped together with Claramonte's production. Mira seems to be the author with the most homogenous style by virtue of the small distance between his three comedies of assured authorship, while Guevara presents the most unstable style. The pairs Guevara-Tirso and Claramonte-Mira are the ones that share the most stylistic similarities. As for the attributions of the plays of unknown authorship, the results obtained are categorical: *el condenado por desconfiado* is associated with the plays of Mira, *La mujer por fuerza* is agglutinated with the plays of Tirso, and *La ninfa del cielo* joins Guevara, the latter being the most categorical attribution of all.

3.2. Distance measures

We implemented an AAA free software tool to use the four distance measures defined in the previous section: Perplexity, Kullback-Leibler divergence, Ranking-based measure, and Distributional similarity. Tab. 2 shows the normalized average scores of the four measures.

Tab. 2. Mean of the results obtained comparing doubtful authorship plays with authors under discussion. Authors abbreviations: Mira = Mira de Amescua, Guev = Luis Vélez de Guevara, Tirso = Tirso de Molina, Clar = Andrés de Claramonte

La ninfa del Cielo	*El burlador de Sevilla*	*Tan largo me lo fiáis*	*La mujer por Fuerza*	*El condenado por desconfiado*
0.000 Mira	*0.000 Clar*	*0.000 Clar*	*0.043 Tirso*	*0.123 Mira*
0.596 Guev	*0.571 Tirso*	*0.575 Tirso*	*0.193 Mira*	*0.192 Clar*
0.631 Tirso	*0.685 Mira*	*0.620 Mira*	*0.546 Clar*	*0.587 Tirso*
0.720 Clar	*0.830 Guev*	*0.718 Guev*	*0.911 Guev*	*0.961 Guev*

La ninfa del cielo, whose authorship for Guevara was established as quite sure by experts, does not seem to come so close to the style of this author, but rather presents more confluences with Mira de Amescua. The results for *El burlador de Sevilla* and *Tan largo me lo fiáis* are sufficiently categorical and similar across all measures to reject Tirso de Molina's supposed authorship. All the measures aim to support the position of critics who defend the authorship of Claramonte. *La mujer por fuerza* and *El condenado por desconfiado* are the plays that leave more room for doubt and alternative hypotheses, since the four distances differ in small values from each other. In fact, the distance between the first and second authors is less than or equal to 0.15 in all cases. Mira and Tirso, respectively, are the most likely authors of these two comedies.

4. Conclusions

It is now up to us to carry out a joint comparison of the various results obtained by all the strategies. This will allow us to draw conclusions in order to confirm or not the authorship of the texts. Authorships proposed by the different methods, including traditional philological studies, are illustrated in Tab. 3.

Tab. 3. Authorship attributions of the plays under discussion proposed by the strategies

	Philological studies	Clustering Analysis	Distance Measures
La ninfa del Cielo	Tirso / Guevara	Guevara	Mira
El burlador de Sevilla	Tirso / Claramonte	Claramonte	Claramonte
Tan largo me lo fiáis	Tirso / Claramonte	Claramonte	Claramonte
La mujer por fuerza	Tirso / Other	Tirso	Tirso
El condenado por des- confiado	Tirso / Claramonte / Guevara / Mira / Collaboration	Mira	Mira

In short, Tirso has been attributed a considerable number of works based on conjectures and critical arguments lacking in solidity and documentary proof. So far, a high percentage of the production plays traditionally assigned to Tirso do not actually belong to this author. In the 17th century comedies were published under the name of famous authors in order to increase sales; it seems that subsequent literary critics have been carried away by this personalist tendency by favoring attributions to renowned authors. The curious thing about Tirso de Molina's case is that these false attributions have been elaborated one on top of the other, in such a way that questioning one implies questioning them all. It is important to point out that the controversial plays are precisely those on which the fame of Tirso among the public and his excellent critical appraisal are based. So perhaps the place occupied by this playwright in the history of Spanish literature should begin to be reconsidered. It is more urgent, however, to draw attention to the traditional studies of authorship attribution, which on many occasions have not respected the basic principles of scientific rigor that should govern any kind of humanistic research.

The rotundity of the results from the non-traditional studies, along with the most popular philological hypothesis, force us to position ourselves in favour of those theories that propose less famous authors who have been relegated to a second place in the panorama of Golden Age theatre. Among these less-famous authors, Mira de Amescua, Vélez de Guevara and, especially, Andrés de Claramonte should be pointed out. The conclusive proof that Claramonte was the author of the first don Juan seems to be closer than ever. An act of justice would be to vindicate his work, starting by editing it. Yet, in spite of the evidence shown by our study, in order to be even more certain of the results, it will be still necessary to approach this problem with new studies that use more texts, more authors and more advanced NLP strategies such as those based on distributional semantics and contextualized word embeddings (Gamallo et al. 2019).

In future work, the comedy *El condenado por desconfiado* would deserve a separate study, as its authorship hypotheses are too varied and confusing to fit into our current work. For this purpose, it will be necessary to employ tools that study pieces of texts separately so as to determine if it is a work composed in collaboration or if one of the proposed authors is indeed the authentic one. The development and improvement of the AAA tools is, in fact, another step to follow in order to continue deepening the AAA studies. This is the most promising point of our work, since we explored computational strategies that are useful and efficient in this task, even though their original functionality was not the quantification of style for authorship attribution. We think that, in the future, it will be possible to find other techniques and strategies that fit well within the AAA studies. In any case, the most urgent initiative that should be encouraged is the edition and digitization of Golden Age plays, so that it is possible to replicate our experiment on the work of Tirso on a large scale.

References

Azfali, M. and Kumar, S. (2017) "Comparative Analysis of Various Similarity Measures for Finding Similarity of Two Documents". *International Journal of Database Theory and Application* 10(2), 23–30.

Cavnar, W.B. and Trenkle, J.M. (1994) "N-gram-based Text Categorization". *Proceedings of the Third Symposium on Document Analysis and Information Retrieval.* 11–13 April, Las Vegas. Las Vegas: University of Nevada.

Eder, M., Rybicki, J. and Kestemont, M. (2016) "Stylometry with R: A Package for Computational Text Analysis". *R Journal* 8(1), 107–121.

Gamallo, P. and Cavadas, M. (n.d.) *Autoria: Authorship Attribution* [online] available from https://github.com/gamallo/Autoria. (Accessed: 23 March 2022).

Gamallo, P., Garcia, M., Sotelo, S. and Pichel, J.R. (2014) "Comparing Ranking-based and I Bayes Approaches to Language Detection on Tweets". *Proceedings of XXX Congreso de la Sociedad Española de Procesamiento de lenguaje natural*, 18–20 September, Girona. Girona: SEPLN.

Gamallo, P., Pichel, J.R. and Alegria, I. (2017) "From Language Identification to Language Distance". *Physica A* 484, 162–172.

Gamallo, P., Sotelo, S., Pichel, J.R. and Artexte, M. (2019) "Contextualized Translations of Phrasal Verbs with Distributional Compositional Semantics and Monolingual Corpora". *Journal of Computational Linguistics* 45(3), 395–421.

Grieve, J. (2005) *Quantitative Authorship Attribution: A History and an Evaluation of Techniques*. Burnaby: Simon Fraser University.

Iriarte, Á., Gamallo, P. and Simões, A. (2018) "Estratégias Lexicométricas para Detetar Especificidades Textuais". *Linguamática* 10(1), 19–26.

Pichel, J., Gamallo, P. and Alegría, I. (2019) "Measuring Diachronic Language Distance Using Perplexity: Application to English, Portuguese, and Spanish". *Natural Language Engineering*, 1(1), 1–22 (2019).

Stamatos, E. (2009) "A Survey of Modern Authorship Attribution Methods". *Journal of the American Society for Information Science and Technology* 60(3), 538–556.

Anca Dinu, Dan Ioan Dobre, Andreea-Codrina Moldovan and Elena-Daniela Nicolescu

Chapter 12 Computational Analysis and Author Detection for Political Discourses of Romanian Presidents

Abstract: The application of Natural Language Processing methods in the context of political sciences leads to augmented analysis of political texts which makes possible a broader view and understanding of political systems across decades. The political discourse in the space of post-communist Romania posits the existence of strong divergent views: from the old communist discourse now turned democratic, to focusing on the fight against corruption, all the way to the neoliberal 2000s. Our contribution consists of a computational analysis of Romanian political speeches and of assembling for this task a novel corpus of the last four Romanian Presidents, which will be freely available for the research community. We perform a quantitative analysis by obtaining and interpreting features such as part of speech frequencies, vocabulary density, keywords, language complexity and average sentence length. We also experiment with topic modelling to reveal the prevalent topics for each president. Finally, we automatically classify the presidential speeches by author, using the relatively newly created BERT implementation for Romanian, along with other three machine learning techniques: SVMs, Bernoulli Naïve Bayes and K-Nearest Neighbours. We obtained accuracies over 95 %, confirming that the quantitative features and the speech topics are very specific for each president, making them highly distinguishable.

Keywords: corpus, digital humanities, document classification, less-recourced language, text mining

1. Introduction

There are several significant events that mark the apparition of ruptures in the political climate, which are difficult to understand by looking at individual speeches. Romania has been through difficult times: from the fall of a totalitarian regime to the installation of capitalism, the EU accession and the 2007–2008 financial crisis.

Analysing how political discourse evolves in a country undergoing such changes is a task most suitable for natural language processing techniques. Such analysis can help us discover how the political climate evolved in Romania. These major changes emerge from the discourse of the political leaders who were each working towards different goals in fundamentally different contexts. Political texts have been used for a wide range of tasks (Glavaš, Nanni and Ponzetto 2017): stance detection (Thomas et al. 2006), ideology detection (Hirst et al. 2010), argument mining (Haddadan et al. 2019). Therefore, through computational discourse analysis we can derive important insight about how political discourse is shaped by an individual's background, political orientation and the events of the time.

Our main goal is to computationally analyse the political speeches of the last four Romanian presidents, in an attempt to find significant patterns and compare them. This is amongst the first computational analyses of Romanian political speeches, the only one we are aware of being (Biro 2020). To this end, we first compiled a corpus containing the political speeches, collected from the official presidency site of the four leaders: Ion Iliescu, Emil Constantinescu, Traian Băsescu and Klaus Iohannis.

To perform the quantitative and qualitative analysis of the corpus, we used text analysis tools like AntConc and Voyant for extracting word frequencies, stop words, keywords, parts of speech, and relevant features such as vocabulary density and average words per sentence. We also use Topic ModellingTool from MALET to discover prominent topics for each president.

As for the qualitative interpretation, we draw the background of each leader in the context of the political party they are affiliated with, along with the defining components of these parties. Then, we trace the informative features (words and topics) to the ideology they embrace, and we observe any particularities or modifications of the core values that ideology is based on. Additionally, we map the affinities for certain subjects in the presidential speeches (EU accession, NATO, Schengen, UN etc.) to the events in each president's mandate, in order to see how the state goals have changed over time.

The quantitative and qualitative analysis supplied the evidence that we have the proper environment for a classification task, namely, clear differences between the four presidents' speeches. We train several classification algorithms to see which one is more fitted for the task.

We first resort to BERT, which is known to achieve state-of- the-art performance for a wide range of tasks (question answering, machine translation, language generation). We use the Romanian BERT implementation, the first transformer model for Romanian, introduced by Dumitrescu et al. (2020). Then, we use other established machine learning classifiers as well: BernoINaive Bayes, Mulmial Naive Bayes, Linear Support Vector Machine and K-Nearest Neighbours with uniform weight and K-Nearest Neighbours with distant neighbours. Most of these algorithms performed fairly well. We obtained accuracies over 90 %, confirming that the quantitative features and the speech topics are very specific for each president, making them highly distinguishable.

We discovered that some of the machine learning algorithms, which do not take into account as many features as a Transformer based approach, reach a surprising performance for this task and, in some cases, outperform BERT.

Thus, we establish a baseline for future research at the intersection of political sciences and machine learning which is still unexplored when it comes to Roman politics.

2. Literature review

There is no similar research performed in the Romanian research field. However, related work has been done for other languages. Biro (2020) performed a sentiment analysis on a corpus of presidential speeches from 1922 to 2004 and discovered that the presidents use many expressions of trust. The dataset used by Biro has not been made available for further use. Ovádek (2020) has a topic modelling approach for Slovak presidents in order to retrieve their agendas and how they have changed over time. In their study, Hansen et al. (2019) addressed the semi-automatic topic annotation of the Danish Parliament Corpus 2009–2017 to construct a "gold standard corpus" for automatic classification. They mainly used subject categories proposed by Danish scholars in political sciences in their annotation work. In addition, they manually annotated the relevant subject areas of the speeches using the titles of the agendas items for the parliamentary meetings and then the subject areas have been assigned to the corresponding speeches. Further, they described automatic classification experiments on a subset of the corpus. The best results (96 % F-score) were obtained using features extracted from the agenda items. The results indicate that the gold standard corpus and agenda items can be used to automatically classify parliamentary debates with high accuracy.

Another relevant article is by Eitan Sapiro-Gheiler (2018), an article in which the author explores the value of word-level statistical data from the US Congressional Record, which contains the full text of all speeches made in the US Congress, for studying the ideological positions and behaviour of senators. By applying machine learning techniques, he used the data to automatically classify senators according to party, obtaining an accuracy ranging between 70–95 %. Furthermore, he argues that text-based predictions are less accurate than those based on voting behaviour, which supports the theory that roll-call votes represent greater commitment on the part of politicians, therefore are a more "accurate reflection of their ideological preferences".

3. Data

This investigation employs its own linguistic data formed by transcripts of speeches in Romanian. The data consists of discourses given by the presidents of Romania after 1990 which were selected during their term as President: Ion Iliescu (1992–1996; 2001–2004); Emil Constantinescu (1996–2000); Traian Băsescu (2004–2009; 2009–2014) and Klaus Iohannis (2014–2019; 2019–present). The texts were collected from three separate websites: the Official Website of the Romanian presidency,[1] the Archive of Romanian presidency,[2] and the personal website of Emil Constantinescu.[3]

The corpus contains 1592 for Iliescu, 6909 speeches for Emil Constantinescu, 1373 for Băsescu and 9101 for Iohannis.

1 https://www.presidency.ro/.
2 http://old.presidency.ro/?_RID=arh.
3 http://constantinescu.ro/ .

We have balance at the level of number of words. The corpus contains 1 389 818 words in total: Ion Iliescu's speeches have 347 625 words; Emil Constantinescu's speeches have 347 597 words, while Traian Băsescu's have 347 397 words and Klaus Iohannis' 347 199 words. We aimed for balanced corpus that contains a close number of words per president.

The dataset is in .txt format and it has been pre-processed and cleaned from any html artifacts. The dataset will be made available for researchers to further explore it.[4] The code is made available at the same link.

Tab. 1. Vocabulary density, average sentence length

Presidents	Density	Avg sent Length
Emil Constantinescu	0.080	24.2
Ion Iliescu	0.072	**31.2**
Traian Băsescu	0.063	22.6
Klaus Iohannis	0.057	23.8

4. Quantitative analysis

This section will provide insightful findings about how each president builds his speeches and about the connections between the speeches and presidents' background and political orientation. We start by stating the political stance of each Romanian president. Ion Iliescu, Romania's first president after the fall of the socialist dictatorship, was a social democrat and a left-wing populist. Following, Emil Constantinescu was a conservative Christian Democrat. After him, Traian Băsescu was a right-wing populist. Finally, Klaus Iohannis is a centre-right liberal. For an easier understanding, we provide Tab. 3 with each president, the political party they were affiliates with, and the political stance.

4 See Dinu et al. (2020): https://github.com/grrrrah/RomanianPresidentialDiscourses.

Tab. 2. POS with their means and the p-value of Welch's t-test

POS Tags	Iliescu	Constantinescu	Băsescu	Iohannis	P-value
ADJ	**10.77**	9.20	**6.98**	9.32	<0.0
ADV	5.81	**6.01**	6.99	**5.33**	0.0001451
CCONJ	2.61	**1.97**	2.08	**5.32**	<0.0
NOUN	28.92	29.02	**25.65**	**31.09**	<0.0
PART	**2.69**	3.08	**4.07**	3.20	<0.0
SCONJ	0.91	**0.71**	**1.61**	0.98	<0.0
VERB	**6.79**	7.14	**8.00**	6.81	< 2.2e-16

Tab. 3. Timeline of the Romanian presidents together with the year they took office respectively left political party and political stance

Presidents	Years in rule	Political party	Political stance
Ion Iliescu	1992–1996	PDSR (*Social Democratic Party*)	Syncretic towards left
Emil Constantinescu	1996–2000	PNŢ-CD (*Christian Democratic National Peasants' Party*)	Centre-right
Ion Iliescu	2000–2004	PSD (*Social Democratic Party*)	Syncretic towards left
Traian Băsescu	2004–2007 (impeached)	PD (*Democratic Party*)	Centre-right
Traian Băsescu	2007–2012 (impeached)	PDL (*Democratic Liberal Party*)	Centre-right
Traian Băsescu	2012–2014	PDL (*Democratic Liberal Party*)	Centre-right
Klaus Iohannis	2014–incumbent	PNL (*National Liberal Party*)	Centre to Centre-right

Tab. 4. Most common topics and the frequency with which they occur in the presidential speeches

Topics	Iliescu	Constantinescu	Băsescu	Iohannis
Romania/ Romanians (terms: *Romania, oameni, romani, noastra, societate, tara, national, stat, unit)*	2.6 %	1.4 %	3.6 %	2.4 %
Europe/ E.U. (terms: *uniune, europeana, ue, dezvoltare, intram, pregatire)*	0.5 %	0.4 %	0.7 %	1.4 %
Time (terms: *viitor, ani, trecut, plan, 2005)*	0.3 %	0.3 %	0.3 %	0.4 %
NATO (terms: *NATO, alianta, Marea Neagra,armament)*	0 %	0 %	0.1 %	0.1 %
External politics (terms: *kosovo, transnistria, balcani, ungaria, conflicte, georgia, moldova)*	0.9 %	1 %	0.8 %	0.6 %

There are conflicting views about the way in which right wing and left-wing politicians use language. There is research supporting that conservatives and right-wing populists use less complex language, so that they appeal to the masses of people, while liberals display a higher language complexity in order to gain the support of the elites (Mudde 2007; Moffitt 2016; Schoonvelde et al. 2019). However, there are studies that contest not only the surety of stating that conservative discourse is rather facile, but they also show that the readability scores using the Flesch-Kincaid test yield similar results, both in the case of conservatives and liberals (McDonnell et al. 2020). McDonnell et al. accuse the majority of research in this area of looking at party manifestos rather than discourses by individuals and concentrating on a single country. It is not obvious whether linguistic simplicity is a trait of conservatives and right-wing populists.

Most readability tests take into consideration the number of syllables and are adapted for English, reason for which we will not use any. However, we wish to discuss the complexity of the presidential discourses based on vocabulary density, average sentence length and the distribution of the parts of speech. Before calculating the frequencies, we lemmatised and lowercased the speeches. We calculate the vocabulary density by dividing the total number of words to the number of unique words as seen in Tab. 1.

Tab. 5. Most frequent words with semantic content

Iliescu		**Constantinescu**		**Basescu**		**Iohannis**	
Lemma	**Freq**	**Lemma**	**Freq**	**Lemma**	**Freq**	**Lemma**	**Freq**
românia/ *Romania*	0.0055	românia/ Romania	0.0037	românia/ Romania	0.0072	românia/ Romania	0.0088
țară/*country*	0.0052	stat/state	0.0033	stat/state	0.0047	European/ European	0.0047
economic/ *economic*	0.0041	țară/country	0.0031	European/ European	0.0042	stat/state	0.0037
stat/*state*	0.0039	om/man	0.0027	an/year	0.0026	an/year	0.0036
European/ *European*	0.0034	an/year	0.0027	uniune/ union	0.0026	uniune/ Union	0.0023
process/ *process*	0.0030	Europa/ Europe	0.0025	om/man	0.0025	politică/ politics	0.0021
an/*year*	0.0026	economic/ economic	0.0024	politică/ politics	0.0024	proiect/ project	0.0021
social/*social*	0.0026	lume/world	0.0021	țară/country	0.0023	om/man	0.0018
dezvoltare/ *development*	0.0026	politică/ politics	0.0018	guvern/ government	0.0020	viitor/future	0.0016
politic/ *political*	0.0025	mare/big	0.0017	zonă/area	0.0017	dezvoltare/ development	0.0014
societate/ *society*	0.0024	viitor/future	0.0015	mare/big	0.0016	puternic/ powerful	0.0013
economie/ *economy*	0.0023	democratic/ democratic	0.0015	negru/black	0.0016	Securitate/ Security	0.0013
românesc/ *Romanian*	0.0021	reformă/ reform	0.0014	Securitate/ Security	0.0015	cadru/ framework	0.0013
națională/ *national*	0.0020	est/East	0.0012	politic/ politica;	0.0013	societate/ society	0.0013
politică/ *politics*	0.0020	zonă/area	0.0012	ue/EU	0.0012	nato/NATO	0.0011
plan/*plan*	0.0018	cooperare/ cooperation	0.0012	nato/NATO	0.0011	împreună/ together	0.0011

By looking at the results of our analysis, we can observe that Ion Iliescu, a left-wing populist, has a moderately complex discourse, judging by the density of the vocabulary, contrasting Traian Băsescu's speech, which is simpler. Emil Constantinescu, who is known to have appealed to the more educated stratum of the society, exhibits the densest discourse, but shorter sentences than his predecessor does. Klaus Iohannis, whose mother tongue is German, exhibits the least dense vocabulary and the shortest sentences out of the four presidents. A comparison with the evolution of political discourse in other post-communist countries in Eastern Europe would be useful in order to be able to understand the broader context into which political discourse changes in order to cater for the passage to democracy and it represents a plan for future research. There is little research done in this area (Dryzek et al. 2002).

Thus, the idea that right-wing leaning politicians like Traian Băsescu and Klaus Iohannis express themselves in a simpler manner in order to appeal to the majority of the population is backed up by our findings. The only left-wing politician, who is himself a populist as well, had a more complex discourse. Even though our findings seem to be in line with the literature, looking at only four presidents (three right wing and one left wing) is not enough to conclude that political discourse in Romania has the same particularities as in the political climates of Western Europe and North America, on which most of the literature concentrates (Schumacher et al. 2016; Schoonvelde 2019).

We also looked at parts-of-speech where we observed some notable differences which are given in Tab. 2. For each president and for each part of speech, we measured the pos frequency per each document (normalising by the number of words in the document) in our dataset and found the mean. We have a high usage of verbs on Traian Băsescu's side and a higher frequency of nouns and adjectives for Ion Iliescu. Băsescu also displays the lowest frequency for adjectives with 6.98. We also found a high usage of coordinating conjunctions on Iohannis' side and the lowest frequency on Constantinescu's side.

To check whether these differences are statistically significant or not, we conducted Welch's test for each part of speech, only for the pair of presidents with the highest difference in mean of the part of speech (in bold in Tab. 2). We found out that in each case, the p-values are significant, therefore, we can reject the null hypothesis that the difference in mean is due to chance.

We could speculate that these differences are based upon the personal background (studies, occupation, mother tongue, etc.) and the political orientation. However, research in this area is scarce and inconsistent. We find out from Cichocka et al. (2016) that conservatives prefer to use nouns instead of verbal phrases or adjectival phrases, as they denote more stability and clarity. Complexity can also be attested by a greater use of conjunctions (Cichocka et al. 2016). This is not in line with our findings as both right-wing politicians and left-wing ones use varying percentages of subordinating and coordinating conjunctions.

Another variable that contributes to changes in the area of political rhetoric is the one of digitalisation and the internet era. The importance of public image raises the implication of PR specialists and speechwriters, which can strongly affect the character of a discourse (Lim 2008). Therefore, cataloguing the discourse of a president, as being in a certain way can be misleading, as it often is the product of several professional advisors and is meant to create a certain effect.

We also obtained the keywords for each president that do not occur at all or at least not so often in the presidential speeches. Thus, these terms are expected to best distinguish between the presidents' speeches. Some of the most typical words for Ion Iliescu are *process* /proces, *plan* /plan, *economie* /economie; for Emil Constantinescu words like *democratic* /democratic, *reformă* / reform, *sud* /south, *est /east*; for Traian Băsescu *guvern* / government, *Moldova, negru* /black; and lastly, some characteristic words for Klaus Iohannis used terms are words like *proiect* /project, *împreună* / together, *cadru* /frame, *tot* /all.

We also performed an analysis using the MALLET topic modelling package. We arbitrarily chose to have 5 topics because a higher number of topics lead to major overlaps. Tab. 4 displays the five topics and their occurrence in the presidents' discourses. This table is based on Tab. 5, which means the ratio is between the number of lemma words, which are the thirty most frequent words, and the number of words per corpus. In Băsescu's speeches the topic of *Romania and Romanians* occurred the most, i.e., 3.6 %. In Constantinescu's discourses this topic occurred the least, with 1.4 %. In Iohannis' speeches, the topic *Europe and the European Union* occurred the most, i.e., 1.4 %. The topic *Time* had a similar percentage in all corpora. The topic *NATO* only occurred in the speeches of Traian Băsescu and Klaus Iohannis. Ultimately, in Constantinescu's discourses, the topic *External politics* occurred the most by 1 %. In Iohannis' speeches, this topic occurred the least, i.e., 0.6 %.

Ion Iliescu was the first president of post-socialist Romania. He was an ex-member of the PCR (Romanian Communist Party). His presidency coincided with the kick-start of a hard transition process for the country, both economically (from socialism to capitalism) and politically (from dictatorship to democracy). This context explains the higher frequency of words like *economic, proces, dezvoltare* /development/ and *plan*. On the other hand, his higher use of words referring to society - *social* /social/ *and societate* /society/ - is a reflection of his left-wing ideology. The usage of words related to Europe coincides with the moment Romania submitted its official application for membership in the EU.

Emil Constantinescu was elected with hope for Romania to move away from its communist past, represented by Iliescu. The shift towards European values made Constantinescu the only president that presented a high frequency for the term *democratic,* mostly referring to democracy as opposed to communism. The term *reformă* is linked to the major changes planned for the economic, law and administrative sectors. His strong focus on words that refer to external politics: *Europa, European, lume* /world/, *est* /East/, *zonă* /area/ and *cooperare* /cooperation/ can be explained in the context of Romania's interest to enhance the relationship with other countries in order to join the European Union and NATO. In February 1997, he meets the members of the North Atlantic Council and NATO Secretary General Javier Solana in Brussels. On this occasion, he reasserts Romania's firm desire to join NATO. On 11 December 1999, takes place an event related to Romania's desire to enter the EU. The European Council decided to begin negotiations with Romania on the conditions for its entry into the Union.

The first term of Traian Băsescu's presidency was marked by Romania's acceptance in NATO (in 2004) and European Union (in 2007) as it can be seen in frequent use of terms related to these events: *europa, european, UE, NATO* and *Securitate* /security/. One of the other characteristics of his presidency was Băsescu's strong focus on anti-corruption, seen as a historic heritage from the communist era. The fight against corruption and the black market explain his frequency of the word *negru* /black/, referring to black market and tax evasion. His term was also marked by his suspension due to overstepping his presidential attributes in 2012.

Klaus Iohannis was seen a as a more democratic leader, compared to Băsescu who tended to overstep his constitutional attributions, therefore he was the only president who had a high usage of terms like *împreună* /together/. Not going beyond the constitutional role of the president is reflected in the frequency of the term *cadru* /frame/, which, in his view, should be ensured by a president. Iohannis also had a strong focus on international cooperation reflected in the frequency of terms like *European* /european/, *uniune* /union/, *Securitate* /security/ and *NATO*.

To conclude, the quantitative analysis reveals fundamental differences between the political leaders and the politics in Romania during each presidency. These particularities include: orientation, political strategies, plans and the events of the time. The idiosyncrasies of each leader and their distinct political discourse led to a successful authorship identification task, which is detailed in the following section.

5. Autorship identification task

We aim to apply a series of deep learning and machine learning algorithms in order to see how idiosyncratic each president's political expression is. We perform Multi class classification by using both deep learning and machine learning algorithms. We use the Hugging Face BERT Implementation and the Scikit-learn implementations for: Bernoulli naïve Bayes, Gaussian NB, Multinomial NB, Linear Support Vector Machine, K-nearest Neighbours with Uniform Weight and KNN with Distant Neighbours. We use the default implementations of each algorithm and present the results in Tab. 6.

The data for these experiments is split as such: 9100 texts for training and 4973 for testing. For each president, we have the following numbers of texts: 4800 for Constantinescu, 6849 for Iohannis, 1153 for Băsescu and 1271 for Iliescu.

We use the Romanian BERT, which, as its authors point out: "is the first purely Romanian transformer-based language model, pretrained on a large text corpus" (Dumitrescu et al. 2020). This model is pretrained on 15.2GB of data. The data comes from Wikipedia, OPUS (a collection of translated texts from the web) and OSCAR (the Romanian section of the Common Crawl corpus). This BERT model, specifically built for Romanian, outperforms the only other model, a multilingual one, which works on Romanian too. For BERT, we use only the texts shorter than 512 tokens; we use a batch size of three and train the model for 3 epochs as it plateaus after more than three. We use the AdamW optimiser and a learning rate of 1e-5. The results for each algorithm are detailed in Tab. 6.

Tab. 6. Experiments performed together with the best accuracy

Algorithm	Constantinescu acc %	Iohannis acc %	Băsescu acc %	Iliescu acc %	Average acc %
BERT with Romanian Embeddings	0.89	0.92	0.89	0.90	0.90
Bernoulli naïve Bayes	0.89	0.92	0.81	0.87	0.9
Multinomial naïve Bayes	0.84	0.81	0.01	0.01	0.75
Linear Support Vector Machine	**0.96**	**0.97**	**0.9**	**0.91**	**0.96**
K-Nearest Neighbours with Uniform Weight	0.74	0.94	0.54	0.72	0.81
K-Nearest Neighbours with Distant Neighbours	0.75	0.94	0.55	0.7	0.81

The first experiment we have conducted uses the Romanian BERT. We expected good results, but in the end, a Support Vector Machine managed to outperform the advanced Transformer model by 0.06 %. We obtained the best results using a SVM with an accuracy of 0.96 %. In the third place comes a Bernoulli Naïve Bayes, an algorithm perfectly fitting for this task as it works best with shorter documents. Nevertheless, we obtained over 0.90 % accuracy with 3 methods, which is encouraging.

We also depict in Figs. 1 and 2 the confusion matrices for the two algorithms which performed best, the Bernoulli Naïve Bayes and the Support Vector Machine.

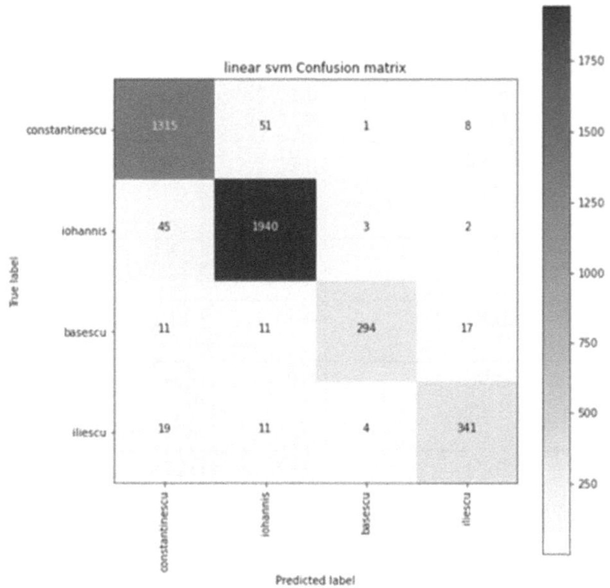

Fig. 1. Confusion matrix for the Linear Support Vector Machine

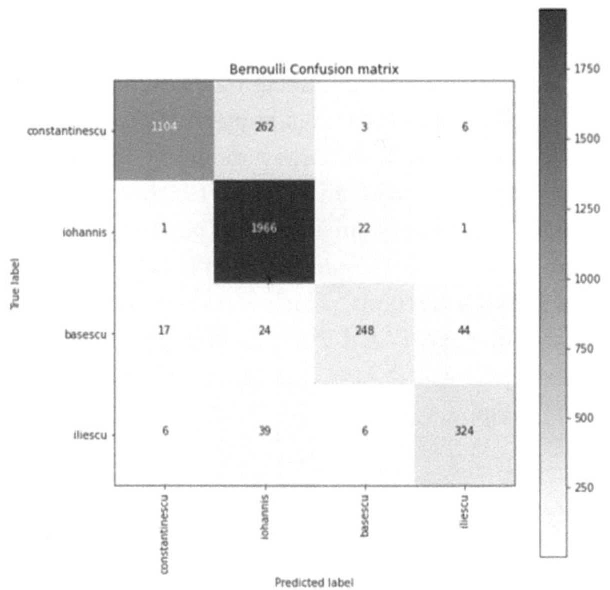

Fig. 2. Confusion matrix for the Bernoulli naïve Bayes

To conclude, we enumerate the contributions this article brings. First, we build the first corpus of political discourses in Romanian, which encompasses presidential discourses from all post-communist four Romanian presidents. Second, we perform a quantitative analysis from where we find out that the right-wing Romanian presidents align with the general idea that right-wing discourse is simpler and straightforward. Finally, yet importantly, we perform a quantitative analysis based on the topic extraction task from which we observe how the interests of the politicians changed and how the state has evolved in the post-communist era. Further research could include a comparative approach regarding how the political climate evolved in the post-socialist countries from Eastern Europe. We want to underline the importance of building corpora for such studies and finding interested collaborators in the NLP and Political Science fields. Such comparison could shed light on Romania's and the other ex-communist states political evolution and reveal patterns in their development towards democracy.

Acknowledgements

This work was supported by a grant of the Ministry of Research, Innovation and Digitization, CNCS/CCCDI UEFISCDI, project number 108, COTOHILI, within PNCDI III.

References

Biro, D. (2020) "Emotions in the political discourse of Romania. A corpus-driven analysis of multiword expressions". *Bulletin of the Transilvania University of Brașov, Series IV: Philology. Cultural Studies*, 13 (62), nr. 1, September 2020, 17–38. DOI.org (Crossref), https://doi.org/10.31926/but.pcs.2020.62.13.1.2. (Accessed: 5 March 2022).

Cichocka, A., Bilewicz, M., Jost, J.T., Marrouch, N. and Witkowska, M. (2016) "On the grammar of politics-or why conservatives prefer nouns: On the grammar of politics". *Political Psychology*, 37(6),799–815. https://doi.org/10.1111/pops.12327. (Accessed: 5 March 2022).

Devlin, J., Chang, M.-W., Lee, K. and Toutanova, K. (2019) Bert: Pre-training of deep bidirectional transformers for language understanding. arXiv:1810.04805 [cs]. http://arxiv.org/abs/1810.04805. (Accessed: 5 March 2022).

Dinu et al. (2020) Romanian presidential discourses. https://github.com/grrrrah/RomanianPresidentialDiscourses. (Accessed: 5 March 2022).

Dryzek, J.S. and Holmes, L. (2002) *Postcommunist democratization: Political discourses across thirteen countries*. Cambridge: Cambridge University Press.

Dumitrescu, S.D., Avram, A.-M. and Pyysalo, S. (2020) The birth of Romanian bert. arXiv:2009.08712 [cs]. http://arxiv.org/abs/2009.08712. (Accessed: 5 March 2022).

Glavaš, G., Nanni, F. and Ponzetto, S.P. (2017) "Cross-lingual classification of topics in political texts". *Proceedings of the Second Workshop on NLP and Computational Social Science*, 42–46. https://doi.org/10.18653/v1/W17-2906. (Accessed: 5 March 2022).

Haddadan, S., Cabrio, E. and Villata, S. (2019) "Yes, we can! Mining arguments in 50 years of us presidential campaign debates". *Proceedings of the 57th Annual Meeting of the Association for Computational Linguistics*, Florence, Italy, 28 July- 2 August, 4684–4690. https://doi.org/10.18653/v1/P19-1463. (Accessed: 5 March 2022).

Hirst, G. et al. (2010) "Party status as a confound in the automatic classification of political speech by ideology". *Proceedings, 10th International Conference on Statistical Analysis of Textual Data,* Rome, 9–11 June. *JADT*, 2, 731–742. Rome: Sapienza University of Rome.

Hansen, D.H., Navarretta, C., Offersgaard, L. and Wedekind, J. (2019) "Towards the Automatic Classification of Speech Subjects in the Danish Parliament Corpus". *CEUR Workshop Proceedings*, Copenhagen, Denmark, 6–8 March, 2364, 166–174, http://ceur-ws.org/Vol-2364/15_paper.pdf. (Accessed: 17 March 2002).

Lim, E.T. (2008) *The anti-intellectual presidency: The decline of presidential rhetoric from George Washington to George W. Bush*. Oxford University Press.

Liu, D. and Lei, L. (2018) "The appeal to political sentiment: An analysis of Donald Trump's and Hillary Clinton's speech themes and discourse strategies in the 2016 US presidential election". *Discourse, Context & Media*, 25, 143–152. https://doi.org/10.1016/j.dcm.2018.05.001. (Accessed: 5 March 2022).

McDonnell, D. and Ondelli, S. (2020) "The language of right-wing populist leaders: Not so simple". *Perspectives on Politics*, 1–14.

Cambridge: Cambridge University Press. https://doi.org/10.1017/S1537592720002418. (Accessed: 5 March 2022).

Moffitt, B. (2016) *The global rise of populism: Performance, political style, and representation.* Stanford: Stanford University Press.

Mudde, C. (2007) *Populist radical right parties in Europe.* Cambridge: Cambridge University Press.

Ovádek, M. (2020)" 'Popular tribunes' and their agendas: Topic modelling Slovak presidents' speeches 1993–2020". *East European Politics.* DOI: 10.1080/21599165.2020.1756785. (Accessed: 5 March 2022).

Sapiro-Gheiler, E. (2018)'Read my lips': Using automatic text analysis to classify politicians by party and ideology.arXiv:1809.00741 [cs, econ, q-fin]. http://arxiv.org/abs/1809.00741. (Accessed: 5 March 2022).

Schoonvelde, M., Brosius, A., Schumacher, G. and Bakker, B.N. (2019) "Liberals lecture, conservatives communicate: Analyzing complexity and ideology in 381,609 political speeches". *PLOS ONE*, 14(2), e0208450. https://doi.org/10.1371/journal.pone.0208450. (Accessed: 5 March 2022).

Schumacher, E. and Eskenazi, M. (2016) A readability analysis of campaign speeches from the 2016 us presidential campaign (Report). arXiv:1603.05739 [cs]. Language Technologies Institute/School of Computer Science, Pittsburgh. http://arxiv.org/abs/1603.05739. (Accessed: 5 March 2022).

Thomas, M., Pang, B. and Lee, L. (2006) "Get out the vote: Determining support or opposition from congressional floor-debate transcripts". *Proceedings of the 2006 Conference on Empirical Methods in Natural Language Processing – EMNLP* '06, 327. https://doi.org/10.3115/1610075.1610122. (Accessed: 5 March 2022).

Arya Rahgozar, Mehran Rahgozar and Diana Inkpen

Chapter 13 Contemporary Chronological Classifications of Hafez Poetry and Influences on French Literature

Abstract: Semantic analysis is an important literary endeavour, especially in poetic texts. Analysing latent semantics is more challenging in poetry than in prose for evident reasons, such as conciseness, imaginary concepts and metaphors. Hafez's poetry is cryptic and complex because of his era's restricting social properties and impediments, and it's also sophisticated because of his encapsulation of high-caliber worldviews, mystical and philosophical attributes, artistically knitted within majestic decorations. We show that Natural Language Processing (NLP) techniques, such as classification and topic modelling, can facilitate and automatic semantic analysis of Hafez's poetry, and enhance the quality of the analytics efforts, by defining and applying rigorous and repeatable procedures. This will also inform our deeper understanding of Hafez's influence on French poets such as Gide, Hugo. We prepared a new set of chronological scholarly labels of Hafez's poetry, based on the two annotators. We measured the inter-agreement between two scholars from different time periods, Houman and Raad, before and after automatic classification. We present and compare two independent chronological labelling of Hafez ghazals and their semantic properties. We also show that the elimination of inconsistent labels enhances the accuracy.

Keywords: chronological classification, Hafez poetry, latent semantics

1. Introduction

Khwaja Shams-ud-Din Muhammad Hafez-e Shirazi, known by his pen name Hafez (1325–1389) wrote ghazal poems. His ghazals reflected deep philosophical viewpoints and have been the subject of many interpretations, but mostly the contextual question becomes whether he is criticizing the social settings of his time or he is referring to mystic ideas. Chronological classification of some of Hafez's ghazals were manually done by the scholar Houman (see Houman 1938) about a century ago, and the work (Rahgozar and Inkpen 2016a) used as training data to predict the time period of the rest of ghazals. The 6 classes are Youth, After Youth, Maturity, Middle Age, Before Elderly, and Elderly.

In this paper, we used the class coherence and labelling inconsistencies as a guide to improve the same classification. Topic coherence was used in (Herbelot 2014) to compare poetic texts and to show that poetry maintains distributional and latent semantics. This inspired us to apply topic modelling on the Hafez's ghazals.

We used a digital version of the Hafez corpus[1] that applied all the necessary Persian linguistic properties in a consistent manner to support NLP tasks (Rahgozar and Inkpen 2016a). In this paper, we further validate the chronological classification of Hafez's ghazals from our previous work (Rahgozar and Inkpen 2016a; Rahgozar and Inkpen 2016b) based on Houman's labels as training data by using the new labels from Raad. Houman labelled Hafez chronologically about 80 years ago and Raad, as a contemporary Hafez scholar, did the same recently. The level of their labelling differences was insightful and helped to better classify and decipher the monumental poetry of Hafez. We isolated the inconsistent instances between the two labels, to measure and to compare their class coherences with and without such instances, then we used the insights to guide, inform and improve the automatic chronological classifications and predictions. We show that removing inconsistency can in some cases drastically improve classification performance. This showed which segments of Hafez poetry influenced French literature since the 19th century.

1.1. Related work

There is significant evidence that Hafez influenced the French literature. For example, André Gide (1869–1951) copied a line of Hafez poem in the preface of his book *Les Nourritures Terrestres* (1897). Another evidence of impact on French literature is the Hafez references in *Les Orientales* (1825) by Victor Hugo (1802–1885) to inspire resolution in religious divide and to praise love instead (Moussa 2011; Tavakoli 2018). Hafez

1 We developed the digital corpus of Hafez in 2016 (Rahgozar and Inkpen 2016a), with the help of Mehran Rahgozar. Alternative data source can be obtained from https://ganjoor.net/hafez.

also influenced Armand Renaud referenced in his book (Renaud 1870) and Jean Lahore regarding gender implications of "*Beloved*" (De Souza 2021).

Lustrek (2007) performed genre detection in text classification, and Simonton (1990) ran experiments in authorship attribution, poetry analysis, and lyric classification, using shallow features such as part-of-speech (POS) and function word distribution. Simonton (1990) also analysed the 154 sonnets attributed to William Shakespeare. Each sonnet consists of four consecutive units (three quatrains and a couplet). A computer gauged how the number of words, different words, unique words, primary process imagery and secondary process imagery changed within each sonnet unit and noticed a common vocabulary change in the couplet. Kim S., Kim. H., Weninger and Han (2010) used deeper features, such as the distribution of syntactic constructs in prose to analyse authorship and writing style. While meter may sacrifice the syntax, rhyme and meter can form effective features to classify lyrics.

Scott and Matwin (1998) used synonymy and hyponymy, while Mayer, Neumayer and Rauber (2008) applied the POS proportion of hapax legomena per document and end-of-line rhyme as features. Hirjee and Brown (2010) developed statistical rhyme detection to extract in-line and slant rhymes while analysing Rap lyrics. Fell (2014) classified by approximately when the lyrics were published, and detected the genre using features such as vocabulary, style, semantics and world orientation toward world and song structure.

2. Scholarly chronological classifications

In this paper, we used the inter-annotator agreement to examine the validity of Houman classifications against a contemporary scholarly chronological classification of Hafez, by Raad in 2019.[2] According to Barthes (2001) each scholarly perspective or interpretation of Hafez, almost 100 years apart, has its own independent unique stance and value. Regardless of the invaluable independence of the two scholarly perspectives of Hafez, not only did we want to compare the inter-annotator agreement between them

2 Mehran Raad labelled Hafez's ghazals in 2019 as part of this research project.

to generate insights, but in the reverse direction and as a side benefit, we also wanted to see whether their labelling inconsistencies could guide us to go back and improve the automatic classification. In the end, we realized that the two perspectives need not necessarily be perceived as contradictory but overlaid to deepen our semantic analysis.

2.1. Houman's perspective of Hafez

Dr. Mahmoud Houman (1938) presented Hafez as a very special poet whose poetry includes mysticism, resentment against pretentious clergies, demeaning towards dialectic philosophy, while praising love and Rend aspects. Dr. Houman strongly sees and encourages the deep interrelation of the ghazal lines and, as many others claim, the first line often carries the main semantic topic. Houman believed that the common contexts of *Love*, *Wine* and *Rend* have different mystical and philosophical meanings as the poet matured. He explains that understanding Hafez is in fact possible; and although there is not any supporting document available to us other than his poems, one can still understand them by setting aside personal tastes and presumptions and then only using scholarly analysis. His chronological classification in Houman (1938) is based on Hafez's evolutionary maturity in his worldviews.

2.2. Raad's perspective of Hafez

Raad[3] viewed and analysed Hafez from four figurative dimensions or elemental perspectives: Virtue; Politics; Technique; Time periods. In terms of *Virtue*, Hafez elaborates on ideas from philosophy, sophism, religion, and anthropology. When it came to *Politics*, Hafez was sensitive to the improvements of social affairs, security, he discussed and cared for political figures and their effects on social classes. Technically, his poetry was full of linguistic innovations, cerebral imagery, and discerning characterizations, meanwhile coming across as apt and ingenious. Raad, similarly to Houman, believed in the effects of Time-Periods as an evolutionary or temporal dimension in the pursuit of dissecting Hafez's poetry. However, Raad distinguished and divided Hafez's chronological life-periods only into four

3 Interviews and lecture notes, *Ghalmro-Adab* 2019.

classes, as opposed to the six mentioned above, named by their association to two leading political figures: (1) Youth, before *Amir Mobarezzeddin*; (2) *Amir Mobarezzeddin*; (3) *Shah Shoja*; (4) After *Shah Shoja*.

3. Experiments

Cohen's Kappa (Fleiss, Cohen and Everitt 1978) can be used to measure the agreement between two sets of labels, generated by classification or clustering. Hubert (1978) later refined this measure and used the weighted Kappa as a bilinear permutation assuming marginal frequencies of responses were fixed. Below, Po and Pe are probabilities of the relative observed and chance agreements among raters, respectively:

$$\kappa = \frac{(P_o - P_e)}{(1 - P_e)} = 1 - \frac{(1 - P_o)}{(1 - P_e)} \tag{1}$$

In our case of comparing the Raad and Houman annotations, we computed the Spearman correlation between them (it is 0.897, p value= 6.18e-178), in addition to the kappa values with linear weights (it is 0.68, which is considered substantial, see McHugh 2012). In linear weights vs. quadratic, the distance between classes and the number of categories is not squared. We also used several other coherence measures based on pointwise mutual information and probabilistic measures Röder, Both and Hinneburg (2015) and Mimno et al. (2011) had used log (PMI) in the definition of coherence, which drew from the smoothed conditional probability of asymmetric confirmation measure of top words per topic. Rehurek and Sojka (2010) implemented them in Gensim Python library. Inspired by PMI, Newmann et al. (2010) developed the UCI measure and Mimno et al. (2011) developed the UMass measure of coherence. P(w) is the probability of word tokens. The coherence closer to 1 would be the better.

$$C_{UCI} = \frac{2}{N.(N-1)} \sum_{i=1}^{n-1} \sum_{j=i+1}^{N} \frac{P(w_i, w_j) + \varepsilon}{P(w_j)} \tag{2}$$

$$C_{UMass} = \frac{2}{N.(N-1)} \sum_{i=2}^{n} \sum_{j=1}^{i-1} log \frac{P(w_i, w_j) + \varepsilon}{P(w_j)}. \quad (3)$$

For the Houman labels, we used the 6 labels, but we also grouped the first two, the next two, and the last two, to have coarser-grained labels. As shown in Tab. 1,[4] the Houman labels with 6 classes have higher coherence than those with 3 classes.

To have a homogeneous comparison between the two independent scholars' annotations, we also merged the Houman's 6-period chronological classifications into 4 classes (class 1 includes classes Youth and Post-Youth, class 2 = Maturity, class 3 = Middle Age, and class 4 includes classes Before Elderly and Elderly). The LDA-driven coherence (Hoffman, Bach, and Blei 2010) (Coh_{uci}) of Houman (0.51) is still higher than that of Raad (0.49), as shown in Tab. 2.

The objective of this section was to measure the impact of inconsistent or disagreed upon instances on the change in coherence for each class, which can guide labelling to refine the performance in classifications.

Tab. 1. Houman Labels of Three and Six Classes: Coherence

Class	Coh_{umass}	Coh_{uci}	**Log Perplexity**
3 Class Avg	-10.37	**0.52**	-10.12
6 Class Avg	-7.61	**0.55**	-8.67

Tab. 2. Raad (R.) and Houman (H.) Labels of Four Classes: Coherence

Class	Coh_{umass}	Coh_{uci}	**Log Perplexity**
H. Class Avg	-8.56	0.51	-9.18
R. Class Avg	-8.87	0.49	-7.72

4 We used LDA-driven Coherence and Log Perplexity from the Gensim Python library.

3.1. Preprocessing

In our preprocessing, we removed the stop words and the tokens that occurred only once. We built the dictionary of documents, every document being a poem (ghazal). Then using the bag-of-words, we set up and transformed the corpus into vector representations. We then built the TF-IDF vectors accordingly. We initialized LSI, LDA,[5] Log-Entropy (Le and Mikolov 2014) and Doc2Vec objects using the Persian section of our corpus as training data (Mikolov et al. 2011). Doc2Vec is based on Word2Vec which are word embeddings or distributed representations of words using neural network models (Mikolov et al. 2011); both are extended to build Continuous Bag-of-Words (CBOW) and the Skip-Grams. We used the Gensim library and the HAZM[6] Python library for Persian preprocessing tasks such as tokenization, normalization and lemmatization.

3.2. Classifications

The inter-annotator agreement has been used before to refine classifications. For example, Wiebe, Bruce and O`Hara (1999) used kappa results to inform annotations in an iterative manner and were able to both improve the classifier's accuracy and the agreements among the annotators. If multiple classifiers predicted, classified, labelled, or voted differently for an instance or a unit of training data, then the question becomes how we can decide its class in better ways. If we wanted to reannotate such instances as training data, naturally we consider the effects of such items on the quality of training material for machine learning and predictions. We also used coherence as an index of within-class relatedness. Hence, we considered the semantic effects of either changing the label of an instance poem or excluding it from the training material when conclusive, or otherwise disregarded it to enforce any changes in the label if the improvement in coherence was very small. We show that the isolated inconsistencies between the two independent labelling systems of Houman and Raad

---

5 A high number of topics were pointless given our small corpus size, but we chose (5 < number_of_topics < 20), based on Silhouette convergence, in each experiment setting.

6 https://pypi.org/project/hazm/.

could provide us with clues to improve and produce a third, but refined training material for classification. A similar concept is used in a bottom-up clustering in which maximizing the mutual information between adjacent classes guides the algorithm (Manning, Raghavan and Schütze 2009); during the iterations, the algorithm only merges the two clusters that produced a minimum loss in mutual information.

$$\left(c_{n1},c_{n2}\right)=argmin_{c_i,c_j}MILoss\left(c_i,c_j\right). \tag{4}$$

We extended the notion of loss in mutual information in Equation 5 and used LDA- driven coherence change per class to measure the impact of inconsistent labels. We calculate the difference in coherence among the union of the inconsistent poems with their corresponding two classes that our scholars had labelled differently. We then measure and anticipate the semantic impact of the inconsistent segment accordingly, by numerical analysis of the rate of change in coherence among the segment's memberships (see Equation 5). The interplay of coherence measurements guided and informed the training-data decisions and their make-up. For example, when we added the inconsistent segment to either class voted by classifiers, and it deteriorated the coherence in both cases, then using the *DeltaSem* index defined in Equation 5 we compared the rate of change in both cases to measure the difference. In other words, the index informed the direction of change. If both ΔCoh were positive, it meant that the inconsistent segment impaired both classes. Further, if the *DeltaSem* was small ($\delta \rightarrow 0$), it meant that the inconsistent segment almost equally impaired both classes; therefore, it was better to exclude the inconsistent segment from adjacent training classes altogether.

$$DeltaSem: |\Delta Coh\ (Cincons., Cyouth) - \Delta Coh\ (Cincons., CMid\text{-}age)| \rightarrow \delta. \tag{5}$$

For example, to demonstrate that this procedure of identification of culprit poems can refine the quality of the training data and hence improve classifications, we took the items out of the multiple categories of inconsistencies for which Houman and Raad had labelled Youth and Middle Age, respectively, and compared their change in coherence. As we see in

Tab. 3. Raad and Houman Labels Consistency Improvements: Coherence

Class	*Cohuci1*	*Cohuci2*	δ
H. Class 1	0.355	0.388	0.033
R. Class 3	0.395	0.420	0.025

Tab. 4. Houman Classification Results, Original vs. Refined Labels

Feature	SVM:Acc., F1	Reg:Acc., F1	DT:Acc., F1	NN:Acc., F1	RF:Acc., F1
WE	0.48, 0.31	0.28, 0.27	0.4, 0.41	0.48, 0.31	0.40, 0.35
WE_{DM}	0.32, 0.29	0.28, 0.27	0.20, 0.25	0.32, 0.29	0.32, 0.32
WEConcat	0.32, 0.29	0.36, 0.30	0.12, 0.14	0.36, 0.28	0.44, 0.36
WE'	0.65, 0.51	0.39, 0.40	0.39, 0.39	0.65, 0.51	0.39, 0.39
WEDM'	**0.70, 0.67**	0.61, 0.63	0.39, 0.43	0.65, 0.63	0.52, 0.49
WEConcat'	**0.70, 0.67**	0.65, 0.62	0.30, 0.31	0.65, 0.61	0.43, 0.46

Tab. 3, the exclusion of inconsistent instances improved coherence by an almost equal amount of 3 percentage points.

The coherence-change index could be applied in this manner to a variety of combinations between the two labelling sets to guide and to improve classification's performance through multi-participant supervised iterations and it was useful in our context of Hafez poetry classification.

For the automatic classification experiments, we used word embedding as features (Mikolov et al. 2011), which was the basis of our model (Doc2Vec) (Rehurek and Sojka 2010). Zhang and Lapata (2014) used word embedding in the poetry generation task and found it a powerful feature for capturing the semantic and context. To compare the impact of various features set and ML algorithms in each experiment with the initial and the refined training set of Houman labels. We used two Doc2Vec feature sets: Distributed Bag-of-Words (DBOW) and the Distributed Memory (DM), both separately and combined. Tab. 4 shows accuracy and F1 performance measures for different ML algorithms such as SMV, Regression, Decision-Tree, basic Neural Networks and Random Forest, abbreviated on the top row, respectively. The last 3 rows in the table are after excluding inconsistencies, and the first 3 rows are only the initial Houman's labels.

In Tab. 4, the *WE* feature stands for DBOW word embedding, W_{DM} for that of Distributed Memory and W_{concat} combined with the two feature sets (Le and Mikolov 2014). As we can see from the table, the SVM algorithm in conjunction with the concatenated word-embedding features of CBOW and DM, plus exclusion of inconsistencies, increased the accuracy of the automatic classification to 70% and the F1-score to 0.67.

By comparing the Houman labels with those of the contemporary Hafez scholar Raad, we not only improved the automatic classification of the Hafez ghazals, but were also able to find a new purpose for the experts' disagreements. We showed that by careful identification and exclusion of certain poems, we could drastically improve the classification accuracy. The three top rows in Tab. 4 are before the exclusion and the bottom three rows are after the exclusion of such poems from the corpus. We also proved that SVM not only showed this phenomenon but also outperformed some other machine learning algorithms (Hamidi, Razzazi and Ghaemmaghami 2009). In other words, we measured the deterioration in coherence, compared the effects of the inconsistent poems, and excluded the inconsistent instances if its improved coherence for both annotators equally. In Tab. 4, *WE* stand for before and WE' is after the inconsistent poems are excluded from training. Concatenated word-embedding features of CBOW and DM, plus exclusion of inconsistencies, lifted the accuracy of the automatic classification to 70% and the F1 score to 0.67. Inconsistency filtering lifted the accuracy of WE-SVM from 0.48 to 0.65 and F1-score from 0.31 to 0.51.

4. Discussion

We analysed the semantic properties of each class-label to shed some lights on which segments corresponded with hermeneutics of Hafez in the French literature. We showed that not only the two sets of labels were correlated, but their inconsistencies could guide to improve the accuracy of the predictions. Raad corrections on Houman helped the machine to better "understand" the semantics of the segments. For example, Hafez has three types of references to love in his poetry, according to Houman: Freudian, platonic, and mystic love, the former reflected in Armand Renaud's *Les Nuits persanes* (De Souza 2021). These types are contradictory, and therefore, cannot happen in the same time, but they exist throughout the evolutionary life of Hafez and appear throughout his poetry. The differences in annotations were mostly borderline and could both inform the interpretations of the segments and shed more light on the semantic properties and *explainability* of the machine learning predictions. Hafez never stayed in one type of love, according to Houman, but he even had the *knave's* instable attitude towards *love* itself consistent with Hugo's religious inquiries. Houman brings many supportive evidences from the ghazals where Hafez shows love towards righteousness or God and refers to human as a realization of righteousness. *Wine* also closely relates to the meaning of love; wine symbolizes love to come to life.

Hafez has references to *destiny* as cause and effect and sometimes as an unchangeable and predefined event. Raad and Houman map these philosophic changes to his maturity growth line. Similarly, Hafez has references to *dervish*, *Rend* or *knave* attributes to refer to freedom and sometimes to mean withdrawal and contentment. We have investigated how these concepts coincide regarding Houman vs. Raad classifications. Both scholars' classifications have common themes during the four stages of Hafez's life reflected in his poems. For example, class Youth was about *Lovers, Blood, Laughter, Soul* and *Wine, Harp, Angel*. Class two or before Mid-age was about *Dilemma, Guru, Hidden, Unreliable Cloak* and *Jewelry*. The Middle Age class was common about *Kandle, Sorrow, Looking, Ruin, Night, Triumph, Lovers, Eyes*. The class four or Senectitude was about *Love, Sadness, Dust, Desire, Universe, Wineglass, God, Moon* and *End* according to visualization we made using the tool from (Sievert and Shirley 2014). Hugo's references of Hafez correspond with prior to mid-age of Hafez's poems, in which he transcendent beyond religious contradictions and finds eloquence in human values. The hermeneutics of sensations of nature in farmlands and meadows are tractable in Gide's book, which are specifically inspired and reflected from the youthful segment of Hafez ghazals that are clear. Inherited from Gide, we can even find the extent of Hafez traces of coexistence of philosophical contradictions reflected in Sartre (1905–1980) views of poetry (Lang 2009), as an intimate self-reflection of values and meaning (Goux and DiPiero 1988). We mostly find the ontology of the first half of Hafez's poems affecting both the writing of Gide and Hugo, than the second half when Hafez becomes more introvert.

5. Conclusion

We collected new Raad's chronological labels, a contemporary scholarly and labelling for Hafez ghazals and compared them with the pre-existing one (Houman 1938) in terms of consistencies and semantic differences, overlaid semantic traces on the French literature. Although Raad put more emphasis on the political and social aspects of poems than Houman did, overall, the two scholars, although about 100 years apart, labelled the poems similarly. We showed that there was a 68 % inter-annotator agreement and almost 90 % correlation between the two annotators. We then proposed a classification refinement based on the inconsistencies between the two labelling systems. We showed that filtering label disagreements that entailed positive coherence fluctuations can guide the classification refinements. Using one segment of inconsistencies, we brought the accuracy up by about 20 %. We mapped traces of Hafez influence on French authors.

References

Barthes, R. (2001) "The death of the author". *Contributions in Philosophy* 83, 3–8. Westport: Greenwood Press.

De Souza, W. (2021) "The love that dare not be translated: Erasures of premodern sexuality in modern Persian mysticism". *Rethinking Iranian Nationalism and Modernity*, 67–86. Texas: University of Texas Press.

Fell, M. (2014) *Lyrics Classification*. Master Thesis. Saarland University.

Goux, J.J. and DiPiero, T. (1988) "Banking on signs". *Diacritics* 18(2), 15–25.

Hamidi, S., Razzazi, F. and Ghaemmaghami, M.P. (2009) "Automatic meter classification in Persian poetries using support vector machines". *IEEE International Symposium on Signal Processing and Information Technology (ISSPIT)*, Ajman, UAE, 14–17 December, 563–567. IEEE.

Herbelot, A. (2014) "The semantics of poetry: A distributional reading". *Digital Scholarship in the Humanities* 30(4), 516–531. https://doi.org/10.1093/llc/fqu035. (Accessed: 27 March 2022).

Hirjee, H. and Brown, D.G. (2010) "Using automated rhyme detection to characterize rhyming style in Rap music". *Empirical Musicology Review* 5(4), 121–145.

Hoffman, M., Bach, F.R. and Blei, D.M., (2010) "Online learning for latent dirichlet allocation". *Advances in Neural Information Processing Systems*, 856–864.

Houman, M. (1938) *Hafez*. ed. by Esmail Khoi. Tehran: Sepehr Tahuri.

Hubert, Lawrence J. (1978) "A general formula for the variance of Cohen's weighted Kappa". *Psychological Bulletin* 85(1), 183–184. https://psycnet.apa.org/doi/10.1037/0033-2909.85.1.183. (Accessed: 27 March 2022).

Kim, S., Kim, H., Weninger, T. and Han, J. (2010) "Authorship classification: A syntactic tree mining approach". *Proceedings of the ACM SIGKDD, Workshop on Useful Patterns*, Washington, DC, USA, 25 June, 65–73.

Lang, C. (2009) "Poetry, ontology, and autobiography in Gide and Sartre". *Life Writing* 6(1), 111–24.Oxfordshire: Taylor & Francis. https://doi.org/10.1080/14484520802550437. (Accessed: 7 March 2022).

Le, Q. and Mikolov, T. (2014) "Distributed representations of sentences and documents". *International Conference on Machine Learning*, Beijing, China, 21–26 June, 1188–1196.

Lustrek, M. (2007) "Overview of automatic genre identification". Jozef Stefan Institute, Department of Intelligent Systems, Slovenia.

Manning, C.D., Raghavan, P. and Schütze, H. (2009) *An Introduction to Information Retrieval*. Cambridge: Cambridge University Press.

Mayer, R., Neumayer, R. and Rauber, A. (2008) "Rhyme and style features for musical genre classification by song lyrics". *Proceedings of the 9th International Conference on Music Information Retrieval* (ISMIR08), Philadelphia, USA, 14–18 September Philadelphia: Drexel University.

McHugh, M.L. (2012) "Interrater reliability: The kappa statistic". *Biochemia Medica* 22(3), 276–282.

Mikolov, T., Deoras, A., Povey, D., Burget, L. and Cernocký, H.J. (2011) "Strategies for training large scale neural network language models". *Automatic Speech Recognition and Understanding (ASRU), 2011 IEEE Workshop on IEEE*, Waikoloa, Hawaii, USA, 11–15 December, 196–201.

Mimno, D., Wallach, H., Talley, E., Leenders, M. and McCallum, A. (2011) "Optimizing semantic coherence in topic models". *Conference on Empirical Methods in Natural Language Processing* (EMNLP), 262–272. Edinburgh.

Moussa, S. (2011) "Imaginary hybridities: Geographic, religioius and poetic crossovers in Victor Hugo's *Les Orientales*". In Guignery, V., Pesso-Miquel, C. and Specq, F. (eds), *Hybridity: forms and figures in literature and the visual arts*, 280–290. Newcastle upon Tyne: Cambridge Scholars Publishing.

Newman, D. et al. (2010) "Automatic evaluation of topic coherence". *Human Language Technologies: The 2010 Annual Conference of the North American Chapter of the Association for Computational Linguistics, Los Angeles, USA, 2–4 June*. ACL.

Rahgozar, A. and Inkpen, D. (2016a) "Poetry Chronological Classification: Hafez". In Khoury, R. and Drummond, C. (eds.) *Advances in Artificial Intelligence. Canadian Conference on Artificial Intelligence*, 31 May–3 June, Victoria, Canada, 131–136. New York: Springer.

Rahgozar, A. and Inkpen, D. (2016b) "Bilingual chronological classification of Hafez's poems". *Proceedings of the Fifth Workshop on Computational Linguistics for Literature*, San Diego, USA, 16 June, 54–62.

Rehurek, R. and Sojka, P. (2010) "Software framework for topic modelling with large corpora". *Proceedings of the LREC 2010 Workshop on New Challenges for NLP Frameworks*, Valetta, Malta, 22 May ELRA: University of Malta.

Renaud, A. (1870) *Les nuits persanes*. Paris: A. Lemerre.

Röder, M., Both, A. and Hinneburg, A. (2015). "Exploring the space of topic coherence measures". *Proceedings of the Eighth ACM International Conference on Web Search and Data Mining*, Shangai, China, 2–6 Gebruary, 399–408. ACM.

Scott, S. and Matwin, S. (1998) "Text classification using WordNet hypernyms". *Proceedings of the Coling ACL Workshop on Usage of WordNet in Natural Language Processing Systems*, 45–51.

Sievert, C. and Shirley, K. (2014) "LDAvis: A method for visualizing and interpreting topics". *Proceedings of the Workshop on Interactive Language Learning, Visualization, and Interfaces*, 27 June, Baltimore, USA, 63–70. Baltimore: Association for Computational Linguistics.

Simonton, D.K. (1990) "Lexical choices and aesthetic success: A computer content analysis of 154 Shakespeare sonnets". *Computers and the Humanities* 24(4), 251–264.

Tavakoli, H. (2018) "Les sources de Victor Hugo par rapport à la Perse". *Oriente Moderno* 98(3), 352–372.

Wiebe, J., Bruce, R. and O'Hara, T.P. (1999) "Development and use of a gold-standard data set for subjectivity classifications". *Proceedings of the 37th Annual Meeting of the Association for Computational Linguistics*, Maryland, USA, 20–26 June, 246–253.

Zhang, X. and Lapata, M. (2014) "Chinese poetry generation with recurrent neural networks". *Proceedings of the 2014 Conference on Empirical Methods in Natural Language Processing (EMNLP)*, Doha, Qatar, 25–29 October, 670–680.

Thierry Declerck

Chapter 14 On the Use of Knowledge Graphs for Representing Past Classification Schemes for Various Genres of Literature

Abstract: We describe work done in the field of folkloristics and consisting in creating multilingual ontologies based on well-established studies proposed by "classical" folklorists. This work is supporting the availability of a huge amount of digital and structured knowledge on folktales to digital humanists. The ontological encoding of past and current motif-indexation and classification systems for folktales was in the first step limited to English language data. This led us to focus on making those newly generated formal knowledge sources available in a few more languages, like German, Russian and Bulgarian. We stress the importance of achieving this multilingual extension of our ontologies at a larger scale, for example to support the automated analysis and classification of such narratives in a large variety of languages, as those are getting more and more accessible on the Web. This presentation is based on the results of a series of Bachelor/ Master theses and software projects conducted by students of the Computational Linguistics Department of the Saarland University.

Keywords: folktales, character detection, multilingual ontologies

1. Introduction

In the context of a series of Bachelor/ Master theses and software projects conducted by students of the Computational Linguistics Department of the Saarland University in the last decade, we could generate multilingual ontologies for supporting automated literary analysis in the field of Digital Humanities (DH). The ontologies are based on well-established studies proposed by "classical" folklorists, like Vladimir Propp, Stith Thompson, or the work by Jörg Uther, itself based on work by Anti Aarne and Stith Thompson. We present in the following sections our approach for transforming those classical studies into multilingual ontologies.

2. An augmented annotation scheme for fairy tales using Proppian content descriptors

A first work was dedicated to the creation of an annotation scheme that would support the encoding of fairy tales following the "Morphology of Folktales" by Vladimir Propp (Propp 1968). The annotation scheme was considering the 7 archetypes of characters occurring in (Russian) folktales, as well as the 31 narrative functions identified by Propp (but in the annex of his work, Propp is listing several sub-functions, which have also been considered for inclusion in the annotation scheme.). Besides the Proppian elements, the annotation scheme is including information on Part-of-Speech, morphology of the tokens to be analysed in fairy tales, as well as syntactic constituency and dependency. Time stamps and locations are also included in the scheme, which is supporting a sophisticated linking and referring infrastructure.

The annotation scheme, called APftML (Augmented Proppian Fairy Tale MarkUp Language), is available at http://www.coli.uni-saarland.de/~ascheidel/APftML.xsd and the Russian tale "The Magic Swan Geese" has been manually annotated with the help of the scheme.[1] The work is described in (Declerck et al. 2011) and (Scheidel et al. 2010). Fig. 1 displays the components of APftML.

1 The annotated tale is available at https://www.coli.uni-saarland.de/~ascheidel/APftML.xml.

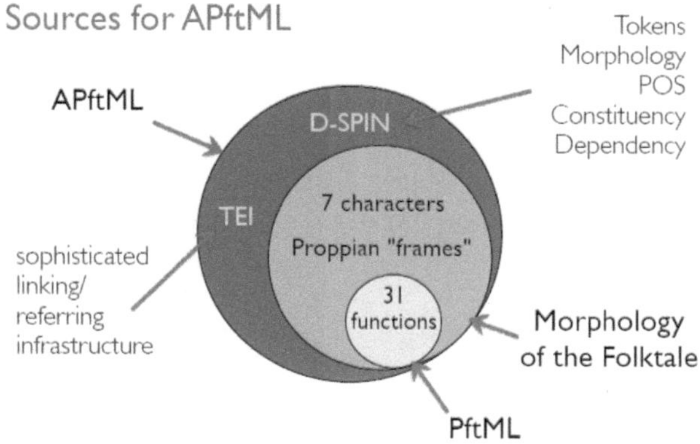

Fig. 1. Overview of the components of the APftML. Figure by Antonia Scheidel

3. Ontology-based iterative detection of characters and their recognition in folktales

The annotation scheme described just above was the departure point for describing multilingual ontologies, a first version of which was dedicated to the recognition of characters playing a role in fairy tales. For this, we mapped the annotation scheme described just above into an RDF-based ontology and added to the resulting ontology also information about family structures, as the parental relations play a central role in tales. This work allowed us to propose a persistent storage of referential elements of tales, which proved to be helpful in the context of co-reference resolution tasks. So that we also gained insights on the possible relations between Computational Linguistics and Ontologies for knowledge-based text analysis, also allowing for the definition of custom inference rules applied to ontology elements resulting from the text analysis and which can be added in an incremental fashion.

The ontology was created with the Protégé editor, and we used the Web Ontology Language OWL for modelling the domain. Characters (and other elements) in literary works can be uniquely stored (with an URI) and referred to from annotations within the text but also from other texts, also in a multilingual context ("Le Petit Chaperon Rouge", "Rotkäppchen", "Little Red Riding Hood", "Красная Шапочка"). This leads to an easy versioning of text and annotation, while changes in the (ontological) model are leading straight away to new annotations. And we also have the possibility to link to text external knowledge bases in the context of the Linked Data cloud. The work is described in more details in (Declerck et al. 2012) and (Koleva et al. 2012).

Fig. 2 shows the incremental population of the ontology resulting from the detection, recognition, and annotation of characters in folk tales.

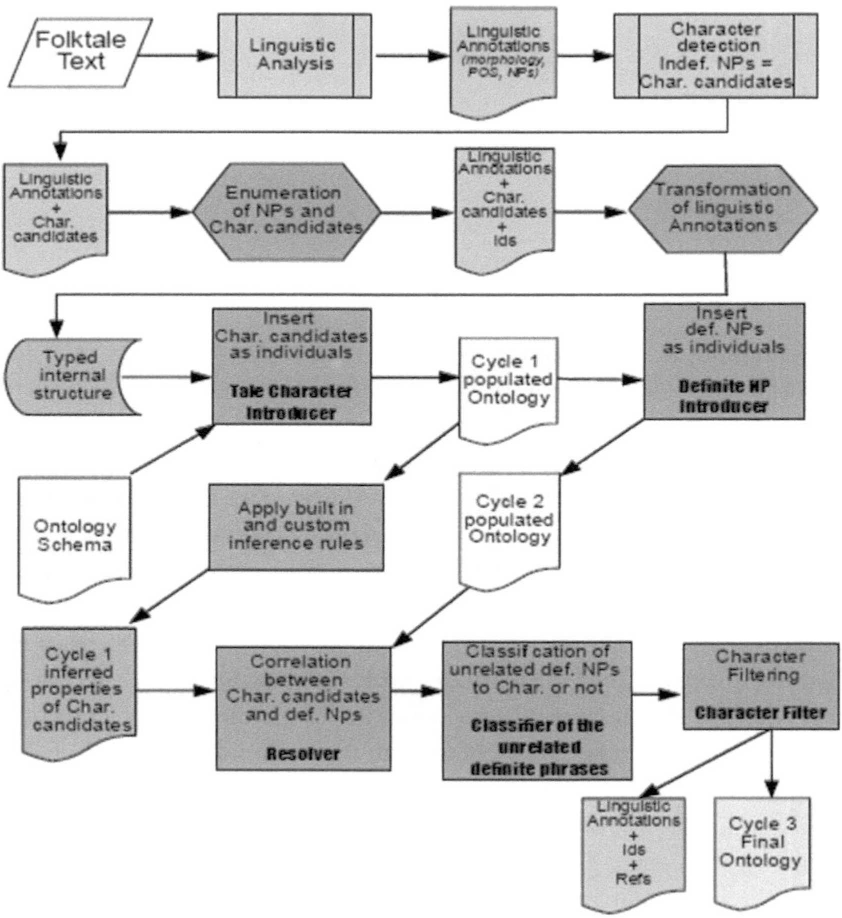

Fig. 2. Workflow of the ontology-based algorithm for the incremental detection, recognition, and annotation of characters in folk tales. Figure by Nikolina Koleva

4. Extending the annotation scheme and the ontology with sentiments, dialogue structures and voices for a TTS application

A next step consisted in extending the elements of the ontology with information on sentiments, dialogue structures and voices to be added for a Text-To-Speech application. The voices to be added were covering not only human voices, but also animals (the "frog" in in the tale "The Frog King"). And for the human voices, differences in ages must be accounted for. The sentiment analysis was performed automatically, for six different sentiments, based on existing relevant lexical resources. All those results were added automatically to the ontology, populating it with a fine-grained information on the characters of the tale and the actions they are involved in. The populated ontology was then used as the input to the Text-To-Speech system, which in a pre-processing step associated voices to the instances of the characters of the tale. An audio sample of the automatically generated "reading" of the "Frog Prince" is available at: https://bytebucket.org/ceisen/apftml2repo/raw/763c5eb533f09997e757ec61652310c742238384/example%20output/audio_output.mp3. More details on the architecture of the system are given in (Eisenreich et al. 2014). Fig. 3 shows the workflow that is leading to the ontology-based generation of speech "reading" the original text, taking into account emotions.

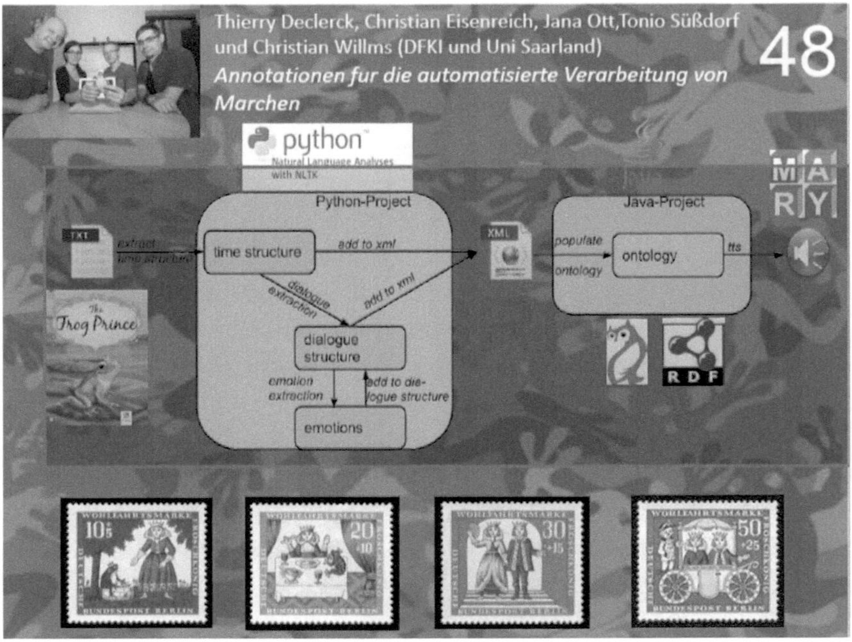

Fig. 3. The general architecture of the ontology-based generation of spoken tales

5. Porting "classical" indexing and classification schemes into an ontology

The next step of our work consisted in extending the "philological" coverage of our ontology to other "classical" works in the folklore literature. We dealt with two well-known classification/indexing systems used by folklorists:

3. TMI – Thompson-Motif-Index of Folk-Literature (Thompson 1955–58)
4. ATU – Aarne-Thompson-Uther classification of tale types (Uther 2004)

Both are available as printed sources, or as online resources in html or pdf format. The TMI resource is available at https://sites.ualberta.ca/~urban/Projects/English/Content/Motif_Quick_Index.htm, as an html document.

Elements of the ATU system are available at https://sites.ualberta.ca/~urban/Projects/English/Content/ATU_Tales.htm, together with several (multilingual) tales that have been annotated with the ATU indices. We had also partially access to the text of (Uther 2004) and could see that TMI elements are mentioned in the context of the summaries of tale types, thus establishing a link between the ATU and TMI systems.

Since the two systems are related to each other, our aims were to:

- organize them in one ontology with appropriate references,
- make the resulting ontology available online,
- implement a web interface for SPARQL querying, and
- implement an automatic classifier of texts based on statistical approach.

The integrated ATU/TMI ontology contains more than 60 000 classes and instances. The labels of the ontology were available only in English, but we are currently working on extending the language coverage, with German, Russian and Italian.

A cooperation was established with the "Digital Breadcrumbs of Brothers Grimm" project (https://www.etrap.eu/digital-breadcrumbs-of-brothers-grimm/) at the eTRAP Early Career Research Group (Computer Science Department / Digital Humanities) of the University of Göttingen, Germany. We could integrate from this project manual annotations of motifs applied to various versions of Snow White in 3 different languages (German, Russian and Italian), as instances of our ontology classes, with few adaptations of our model, especially concerning metadata associated with the annotated works. This was encouraging, as it was showing that the ontological approaches can accommodate the results of (manual or automatic) annotation of motifs detected in tales. This work is described in detail in Declerck et al. (2017a) and Declerck et al. (2017c).

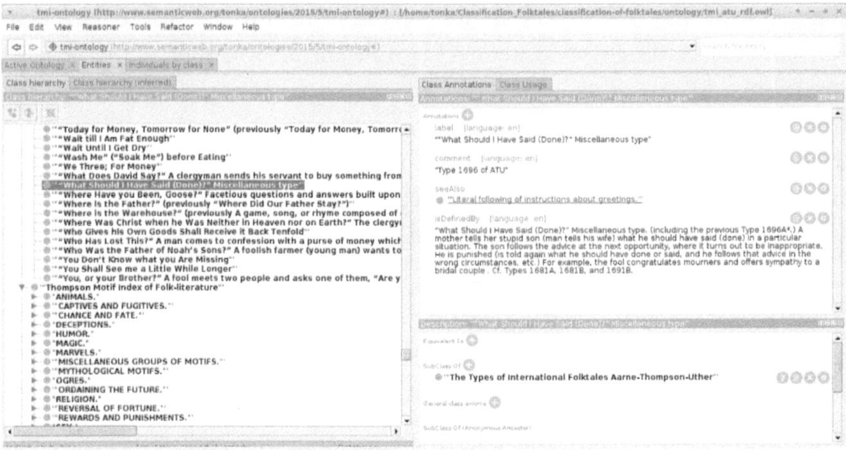

Fig. 4. Screen shot of a small portion of the integrated TMI-ATU ontology, using the Top Braid ontology editor. Work by Lisa Schäfer

6. A complete multilingual Propp ontology

Together with the multilingual extension of our Propp ontology, we introduce the notion of location in the ontology. As typical events tend to occur either inside or outside of a building (whereas we distinguish between various types of buildings), we added this information in our (ontologized) annotation scheme. The detection of locations is seen as a special case of named entity recognition, which we used until then only for the detection of characters.

We also reached a full ontology representation of the Proppian approach (including all the sub-functions), in 3 languages (English, German, Russian). And we added as instances of the ontology the annotations of three tales. The resulting knowledge base, for the Propp ontology, has 666 new Annotation Assertions (1178 in Total), 2875 new Object Property Assertions (3181 in Total), 346 new Data Property Assertions (346 in Total), 376 new Instances (613 in Total). Results of those 2 extensions are documented in (Declerck et al. 2017b and c) and (Lindemann et al. 2018).

Fig. 5 gives an overview of the updated Propp ontology, which now includes a class "Type" (linking to the ATU classification system) and other information, like "Location", for instance.

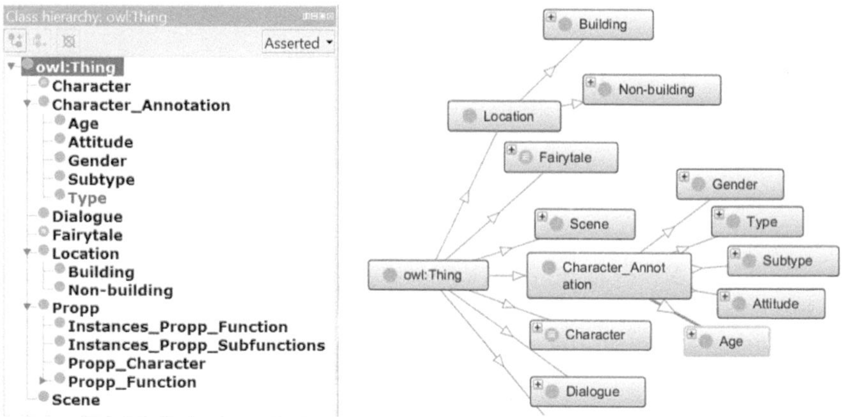

Fig. 5. The updated Propp ontology, with inclusion of the class "Type" (pointing to the ATU classification system)

7. Current and future work

One aspect of our current (and ambitious) work consists in linking the Propp ontology with the ATU/TMI one, at the both the class level and the instance level. The aim is to establish relations that could help in unifying the different approaches designed by the scholars.

A second topic of our work consist in extending our ontologizing work to other literature genre, with a first attempt dealing with drama. We started for this with the "36 Dramatic Situations" (Polti, Georges. The Thirty-Six Dramatic Situations, original in French). We are expecting a possible overlap between Propp and Polti. And some motifs that are recurrent in tales could be also present in drama.

Interlinking all those approaches, where appropriate, would lead towards a semantic digital repository of "theories" for the analysis and annotations of literary texts.

Acknowledgements

I would like to thank all the students who were involved in the works presented here: Antonia Scheidel, Nikolina Koleva, Lisa Schäfer, Anastasija Aman, Martin Banzer, Dominik Macháček, Natalia Skachkova, Christian Eisenreich, Jana Ott, Tonio Süßdorf, Christian Willms.

References

Declerck, T., Scheidel, A. Lendvai, P. (2011) "Proppian Content Descriptors in an Integrated Annotation Schema for Fairy Tales". In Sporleder, C., van den Bosch, A. and Zervanou, K. (eds.) *Language Technology for Cultural Heritage. Selected Papers from the LaTeCH Workshop Series, Theory and Applications of Natural Language Processing*, 155–169. Heidelberg: Springer.

Declerck, T., Koleva, N. and Krieger, H.-U. (2012) "Ontology-Based Incremental Annotation of Characters in Folktales". *Proceedings of the 6th Workshop on Language Technology for Cultural Heritage, Social Sciences, and Humanities (LaTeCH 2012)*, 30–35. Avignon, France, ACL, Association for Computational Linguistics (ACL), 209 N. Eighth Street Stroudsburg, PA 18360. USA, 4/2012.

Declerck, T. and Kostová, A. and Schäfer, L. (2017a) "Towards a Linked Data Access to Folktales Classified by Thompson's Motifs and Aarne-Thompson-Uther's Types". *Proceedings of Digital Humanities*. Montréal, QC, Canada, ADHO, 8/2017.

Declerck, T. and Schäfer, L. (2017b) "Porting past Classification Schemes for Narratives to a Linked Data Framework". In *Proceedings of DATeCH2017*, Göttingen, Germany, 1–2 June. Göttingen: ACM.

Declerck, T., Aman, A., Banzer, M., Macháček, D., Schäfer, L. and Skachkova, N. (2017c). "Multilingual Ontologies for the Representation and Processing of Folktales". In Dinu, A., Osenova, P. and Vertan, C. (eds.): *Proceedings of the First Workshop on Language Technology for Digital Humanities in Central and (South-)Eastern Europe*, 20–24, Varna, Bulgaria, INCOMA Ltd, Shoume, 9/2017.

Eisenreich, C., Ott, J., Süßdorf, T. and Willms, C. and Declerck, T. (2014) "From Tale to Speech: Ontology-based Emotion and Dialogue Annotation of Fairy Tales with a TTS Output". *Proceedings of ISWC 2014*, Riva del Garda, Italy, Springer, 10/2014.

Koleva, N., Declerck, T. and Krieger, H.-U. (2012). "An Ontology-Based Iterative Text Processing Strategy for Detecting and Recognizing Characters in Folktales". In Meister, J.C. (ed.): *Digital Humanities 2012 Conference Abstracts*, 467–470, Hamburg, Germany, Hamburg University Press, 7/2012.

Lindemann, M., Grünewald, S. and Declerck, T. (2018) "Annotation and Classification of Locations in Folktales". In Frank, A.U., Ivanovic, C., Mambrini, F., Passarotti, M. and Sporleder, C. (eds.): *Proceedings of the Second Workshop on Corpus-Based Research in the Humanities*, Vienna, Austria, Gerastree Proceedings, GTP 1., Academy Corpora of the Austrian Academy of Science, Sonnenfelsgasse 19, 1010 Wien, Austria, Vienna, 1/2018.

Propp, V. (1968) *Morphology of the Folktale*. Translated by Scott, L.. 2nd ed. Austin: University of Texas Press.

Scheidel, A. and Declerck, T. (2010) "APftML – Augmented Proppian Fairy Tale Markup Language". In Darányi, S. and Lendvai, P. (eds.): *First International AMICUS Workshop on Automated Motif Discovery in Cultural Heritage and Scientific Communication Texts*. Szeged University, 10/2010.

Thompson, S. (1955–1958) *Motif-Index of Folk-Literature: A Classification of Narrative Elements in Folktales, Ballads, Myths, Fables, Medieval Romances, Exempla, Fabliaux, Jest-Books, and Local Legends*. Revised and enlarged edition. Bloomington: Indiana University Press.

Uther, H.-J. (2004) "The Types of International Folktales: A Classification and Bibliography. Based on the system of Antti Aarne and Stith Thompson". *FF Communications*, 284–286. Helsinki: Suomalainen Tiedeakatem.

Notes on Contributors

Haifa Alharthi is an Assistant Professor at Saudi Electronic University. She received her PhD from the University of Ottawa, School of Electrical Engineering and Computer Science. Her research interests focus on Natural Language Processing.

Ovidiu Babeş defended his PhD in philosophy in 2022 at the University of Bucharest on the topic of René Descartes' scientific activity. His research focuses on the history of science and philosophy of the 17th century.

Valentin Bottez is an Associate Professor at the Faculty of History of the University of Bucharest, where he heads the "Dinu Theodorescu" Laboratory of Archaeology. He is a specialist in Classical Archaeology and Roman History and heads the archaeological mission of the University of Bucharestat Istros/Histria (Constanţa County) and at the Beidaud Archaeological Microzone (Tulcea County, Romania). He has largely published on issues concerning provincial archaeology and Roman religion.

Ana-Maria Bucur is a PhD student at the Interdisciplinary School of Doctoral Studies, University of Bucharest. Her research interests are in applications of Natural Language Processing. Her research covers a variety of interdisciplinary topics, ranging from approaches to mental illness detection and human well-being to corpus-based analyses of academic writing.

Ioana Bujor is a PhD candidate at the University of Bucharest, where she is working on a translation of Baruch Spinoza's Compendium of Hebrew Grammar. Her primary research interests include early modern philosophy and Biblical exegesis.

Mădălina Chitez is a Senior Researcher in Applied Corpus Linguistics at the West University of Timisoara, Romania. She holds a PhD in Corpus Linguistics from Albert-Ludwig University of Freiburg, Germany and worked as a researcher at the University of Zurich and Zurich University of Applied Sciences, in Switzerland, for eight years. She also participated in research exchange programs at the University of Oxford, Coventry University (UK) and Siena University (Italy). She is the Founder and

President of CODHUS (Centre for Corpus Related Digital Approaches to Humanities) where research projects, language technology applications and trainings are conducted in interdisciplinary areas that centre round the use of digital methods in the humanities. She has published in numerous international journals and collective volumes. She is the author of the monograph "Learner Corpus Profiles: The case of Romanian Learner English" (Peter Lang 2014) and co-editor of three volumes on academic writing and corpus linguistics. Her areas of interest and expertise are: applied corpus linguistics, digital humanities, academic writing, contrastive linguistics, computer-assisted language learning, language teaching and higher education policy making.

Miguel Cavadas defended his Bachelor dissertation in 2019 at the University of Santiago de Compostela under the title of "Automatic authorship attribution techniques applied to the theater of Tirso de Molina", which granted him an End-of-degree Extraordinary Award. In order to continue his literary research, he got a La Caixa Fellowship to pursue graduate studies in the United States of America, where he lives since 2020.

Davide Colla is a PhD Student in Computer Science at the University of Turin. His PhD is focused on Natural Language Processing, in particular on Lexical Semantics. His research concerns Word Sense Disambiguation, Lexical Resources, Knowledge Representation, Language Modeling, Word/Sense Embeddings. Since the beginning of his PhD, Davide is involved in the PRiSMHA (Providing Rich Semantic Metadata for Historical Archives) project.

Thierry Declerck is a Senior Consultant at the German Research Center for Artificial Intelligence (DFKI GmbH) since 1996, working in the field of multilingual language technologies. Thierry has acquired a larger number of projects in various fields, like multimedia semantics, information extraction, sentiment analysis, multilingual knowledge systems, etc. He is currently responsible for the DFKI contribution to the "Prêt-à-LLOD" project on "Ready-to-use Multilingual Linked Language Data for Knowledge Services across Sectors" (https://pret-a-llod.github.io/). Thierry also contributes for the Austrian Center for Digital Humanities to the ELEXIS project (https://elex.is/), especially investigating the role of Linked Data for the representation and generation of lexical data. Additionally, Thierry is the Scientific Communication Manager of the COST Action CA18209 – European network for Web-centred linguistic data science ("NexusLinguarum", https://nexuslinguarum.eu/). One of his interests lies in the Semantic Web based representation of literary classification schemes.

Andreea Dincă is a doctoral researcher at the West University of Timişoara, where she is currently pursuing a PhD in applied corpus linguistics. Her research concerns phraseology in Romanian Learner English writing in an academic setting. Her main research interests are applied corpus linguistics, Learner Corpus Research, phraseology and academic writing.

Anca Dinu is an Assistant Professor at University of Bucharest, Faculty Foreign Languages and Literatures and director of The Digital Humanities Research Centre, University of Bucharest. Her main research interests are Digital Humanities, Natural Language Processing, formal and distributional semantics, corpus linguistics, experimental linguistics, etc. She obtained her Ph.D in 2011, under the supervision of Professor Solomon Marcus. She authored the book "A computational perspective on natural language semantics", co-edited three conference volumes and she has written alone or with collaborators over 40 peer-reviewed articles. She has been a member of 16 national and international projects. She initiated and currently coordinates the Digital Humanities master programme at University of Bucharest, for which she has received "University of Bucharest prize for the most innovative programme" award in 2019.

Liviu Dinu is Professor at University of Bucharest, Faculty of Mathematics and Computer Science, Computer Science Department, and director of Human Language Technologies Research Center (nlp.unibuc.ro). His main research interests are Computational Linguistics and Natural Language Processing, with a particular focus on languages similarity, computational approaches of historical linguistics, authorship identification and computational stylometry, topic analysis and text categorization, corpus analyses, etc. Solomon Marcus was his PhD supervisor (obtained in 2003), and in 2014 he defended his habilitation thesis entitled "Similarity and Decision Problems in Computational Linguistics". In 2007 he received "Grigore

C. Moisil" Prize, awarded by the Romanian Academy (for 2005), and in 2005 "In Hoc Signo Vinces Prize" (Magna Cum Laude), for research and publications awarded by the National Research Council for Higher Education. He published 2 books, 5 chapters in books, and more than 130 peer-reviewed scientific papers. He has initiated and managed a number of 12 national and international R&D projects and was involved in other 14 RD projects. He has also initiated a master program in Natural Language Processing at University of Bucharest, starting with 2020.

Mihnea Dobre is teaching and doing research in the history of philosophy and science at the University of Bucharest. He is the author of "Cosmologia carteziană" [Cartesian Cosmology] (2021), "Descartes and Early French Cartesianism: between metaphysics and physics" (2017), and co-editor of: "Cartesian Empiricisms" (2013). Dobre's principal interests are the relations between philosophy, religion and science in the early modern period and how new forms of scholarship, such as digital humanities, can inform research practice on these topics.

Dan Ioan Dobre is a Political Sciences graduate part of the Centre of Behavioural Studies.

Oana-Adriana Duță teaches Spanish linguistics and translation at the University of Craiova, Romania. She holds a PhD from the University of Bucharest and has published three Spanish language coursebooks and over 60 articles in scientific journals. She has performed extensive research on foreign language teaching in 6 international projects focusing on education and has co-edited 4 volumes, such as, inter alia, "Sustainable and Solidary Education. Reflections and Practices" (Peter Lang 2017). She holds a PhD in Economics and a postgraduate diploma in terminology from the Pompeu Fabra University of Barcelona. Her research interests include contrastive linguistics, cognitive semantics and translation.

Annamaria Goy is a Researcher at the Computer Science Department of the Università degli Studi di Torino (Italy), where she works in the area of web-based systems and semantic technologies. She obtained her Ph.D in Cognitive Science at the same university, with studies in the area of lexical semantics. She currently carries on her research and development activity applying knowledge representation, ontology modelling and human computer interaction approaches mainly to the Cultural Heritage and Digital Humanities areas. She teaches Web Technologies and Web Programming classes.

Diana Inkpen is a Professor at the University of Ottawa, in the School of Electrical Engineering and Computer Science. She obtained her Ph.D. from the University of Toronto, Department of Computer Science. She has a M.Sc. and B.Eng. degree in Computer Science and Engineering from the Technical University of Cluj-Napoca, Romania. Her research is in applications of Natural Language Processing and Text Mining. She organized seven international workshops and she was a program co-chair for the 25th Canadian Conference on Artificial Intelligence (AI 2012, Toronto, ON, May 2012) conference. She is the editor-in-chief of the Computational Intelligence journal and the associate editor for the Natural Language Engineering journal. She published a book on Natural Language Processing for Social Media (Morgan and Claypool Publishers, Synthesis Lectures on Human Language Technologies, the third edition appeared in 2020), 9 book chapters, more than 30 journal articles, and more than 100 conference papers. She received many research grants, from which the majority include intensive industrial collaborations.

Eugen Istodor is a lecturer at the Communication Science Department, University of Bucharest. He teaches courses on Media Communication, Social Media, Humour, and Creative Writing.

Marco Leontino is a research fellow in Computer Science at the University of Turin, Department of Computer Science. His main interests are related to Artificial Intelligence in general, focusing particularly in Natural Language Processing, Lexical Semantics, Knowledge Representation and Cognitive Science. Since his graduation summa cum laude in 2018, he is involved in the PRiSMHA (Providing Rich Semantic Metadata for Historical Archives) project.

Alexandra Lițu is currently a lecturer in Ancient Greek history at the University of Bucharest. She holds a degree in Classics and a PhD in History awarded by the same university. She is currently taking part in archaeological excavations in the Greek colony of Istros (Romania). Her main areas of interest are Greek material culture and epigraphy in the

Black Sea area, Greek religion, material culture and the body in literary texts. She has published among others on issues pertaining to material culture and epigraphy in the Black Sea area, Greek religion, and material culture in Plato.

Andreea-Codrina Moldovan is a PhD student in Computer Science at ISDS. Her activity is centered on computational linguistics and social issues.

Valentina Mureşan is a senior lecturer at the West University of Timişoara, Romania. Her PhD centred on the analysis of oral classroom discourse, while her research interests, published papers and her involvement in post-doctoral research have focused on various aspects of linguistics, language teaching pedagogy, conversational analysis and translation studies.

Elena-Daniela Nicolescu is a graduate of the Digital Humanities Master's programme, University of Bucharest.

Pablo Gamallo Otero is an Associate Professor at the University of Santiago de Compostela (Galiza/Spain) and member of the Centro Singular de Investigación en Tecnoloxías da Información (CiTIUS). His main scientific interest is Natural Language Processing and Information Extraction. He is author of more than 70 articles in journals, many of them indexed in WoS or Scopus, such as Computational Linguistics, Corpus Linguistics and Linguistic Theory, Language Resources and Evaluation, Natural Language Engineering, or International Journal of Corpus Linguistics. He has been the Main Investigator of 8 R&D projects (two of them from the European Commission) and 9 transfer contracts/agreements with companies and organizations, all of them within the field of natural language processing.

Cecilia Mihaela Popescu is a Full Professor in Applied Romance Linguistics, General Linguistics, and Pragmatics at the University of Craiova, Romania. She received her PhD in 2006, in the field of Philology (Romance Linguistics subdomain), under the supervision of Prof. Maria Iliescu. Her research activity is structured around four major topics: (a) studies on Latin linguistics issues, (b) the semantic-functional behavior of certain verbal compartments in Romance languages viewed in synchronicity, diachrony, but also in contrast, (c) lexical borrowings from French to Romanian, (d) discursive markers in Romance languages. In

2013, she published her postdoctoral thesis entitled "The Future and the Conditional in Romance Languages. A Morphosyntactic and Semantic Approach from a Diachronic Perspective". She also published papers in prestigious scientific journals, as well as other international peer-reviewed volumes. From 2016 up to 2022, she was selected member in the Board of the International Society of Romance Linguistics (Société de Linguistique Romane).

Arya Rahgozar is a Part-time Professor and a Postdoctoral Fellow at the School of Electrical Engineering and Computer Science, University of Ottawa. He received his Ph.D. in DTI from the University of Ottawa, specializing in Natural Language Processing, specifically in multilingual semantic text classification and clustering. Arya obtained his Masters from the University of Waterloo in Management Sciences, specialized in Process Modelling with Temporal Event Predictions. Arya has over 15 years of industrial experience as an analytics manager, team leader and Principal Data Scientist in banking, credit risk, marketing, healthcare, insurance and retail. Arya has worked both for the Canadian private sector and the government.

Mehran Rahgozar is a digital humanities scholar who has developed bilingual research tools that includes Hafez and Ferdowsi corpora in Persian and English with proper word tokenization and features such as compound lexical and lemmatized search, dynamic Persian and English dictionaries, text to voice and accessibility for the blind. Mehran was among the few earliest English teachers in the 60s at Shokuh institute in Tehran. He was also among the pioneers of software engineering in the country who carried out both technical and executive roles since the 60s. For example, he implemented the first national university entrance exam and its automatic scoring system, introduced and managed CDC mainframes in Tehran's Sharif University and took executive IT roles in the Atomic Energy Organization of Iran. In more recent years he played an advisory role in the implement of digital retrieval and information extraction systems with the government agencies such as with the ministry of culture and the National Library of Iran.

Cristina Re is a graduate in Communication, ICT and Media at the University of Turin. Cristina is involved in the PRiSMHA (Providing Rich Semantic Metadata for Historical Archives) project and she defended her Bachelor's dissertation in 2021 under the title of "The OCR system as an effective tool to ensure accessibility to textual content of historical documents: the PRiSMHA project and the Fondazione Istituto piemontese Antonio Gramsci in Torino".

Roxana Rogobete is a Teaching Assistant at the Department of Romanian Studies, where she teaches Literary theory, Ethics, Romanian literature and New approaches in literary studies. Her PhD in comparative literature focused on German-language migrant literature written in the postwar period. She has been involved as a postdoctoral researcher in projects such as ROGER and DACRE and her interests include Romanian literature, digital humanities, new methods in literary studies, academic writing.

Andrea Sgarro is with the Dept. of Mathematics and Geosciences, University of Trieste, Italy. He got a chair in Cybernetics in 1990. He is interested in the foundational and mathematical aspects of theoretical computer science; his research interests are information theory, cryptography, fuzzy logic and computational linguistics. He is quite active in scientific communication: his two books "Codici segreti", Mondadori, translated into several European languages, and "Crittografia", Muzzio, have introduced for the first time the new cryptography to an Italian-speaking audience. In his free time, he studies, reads and speaks languages (he lectured in five different ones) and plays the baroque transverse flute.

Tommaso Spinelli is a scholar of ancient Greece and Rome working primarily on Latin language and literature, the interactions of ancient texts with material culture, and the digital humanities. After graduating in Classics at the University of Rome "La Sapienza" he completed a PhD in Classics at the University of St Andrews and a PostDoc at the Salesian University of Rome. Currently, he is an Honorary Research Fellow at the University of Manchester, a Researcher at the Pontificium Institutum Altioris Latinitatis, and a teacher of Italian and Latin at the International Education Institute of the University of St Andrews.

Claudius-Marian Teodorescu is a scientific researcher with the "A. Philippide" Institute of Romanian Philology of the Romanian Academy. He is also a PhD candidate of the Interdisciplinary School of Doctoral Studies, University "Transilvania" of Brașov, Romania. He worked for six years as scientific researcher with the Cluster of Excelence "Asia and Europe" of the University of Heidelberg, Germany. He is interested in and currently works for developing software products for computer-assisted linguistic research.

www.ingramcontent.com/pod-product-compliance
Ingram Content Group UK Ltd.
Pitfield, Milton Keynes, MK11 3LW, UK
UKHW041825031026
15587UKWH00002B/566

9 783631 811474